Somos Latinas

Somos Latinas

Voices of Wisconsin Latina Activists

Andrea-Teresa Arenas

Eloisa Gómez

WISCONSIN HISTORICAL SOCIETY PRESS

Published by the Wisconsin Historical Society Press
Publishers since 1855

The Wisconsin Historical Society helps people connect to the past by collecting, preserving, and sharing stories. Founded in 1846, the Society is one of the nation's finest historical institutions.
Join the Wisconsin Historical Society: wisconsinhistory.org/membership

Publication of this book was made possible in part by a gift from the D. C. Everest fellowship fund.

Front cover image: © 2017 Favianna Rodriguez, Favianna.com
Poem "Yo Soy Eva" on page 260: © 2012, Latina Poetry Group, Centro Hispano, Madison, WI

Printed in the United States of America
Cover design by Wendy Holdman
Typesetting by Wendy Holdman
22 21 20 19 18   1 2 3 4 5

Library of Congress Cataloging-in-Publication Data
Names: Arenas, Andrea-Teresa, 1951– author. | Gómez, Eloisa, 1955– author.
Title: Somos Latinas : Voices of Wisconsin Latina Activists / Andrea-Teresa Arenas & Eloisa Gómez.
Description: Madison, WI : The Wisconsin Historical Society Press, [2018] | Includes bibliographical references and index. |
Identifiers: LCCN 2017042880 (print) | LCCN 2018006203 (e-book) |
   ISBN 9780870208607 (e-book) | ISBN 9780870208591 (pbk. : alk. paper)
Subjects: LCSH: Hispanic American women—Political activity—Wisconsin. | Hispanic American women—Wisconsin—Interviews. | Women political activists—Wisconsin—Interviews. | Wisconsin—Politics and government—21st century.
Classification: LCC F590.S75 (e-book) | LCC F590.S75 A74 2018 (print) |
   DDC 305.4868/073—dc23
LC record available at https://lccn.loc.gov/2017042880

Contents

PART I: THEIR ACTIVISM, THEIR STORIES

PART II: EXPLORING KEY THEMES

Foreword

Welcome and enter the realm of Latina community building as told by older Latina activists from Wisconsin—voices largely hidden until now.

In reading this book, I had a chance to reflect on my own path of activism.

The influences of my own entry into the organizing world came early in my life through two key role models, my parents and my *cultura* (culture). My mother, a woman of much compassion, was nontraditional in her own right. She was a businesswoman and active in responding to community needs. I was aware of her contributions and learned that I could do this, too. My father spent much of his life fighting for union rights in New Mexico and California. I learned that unions could uplift the lives of people.

From my Mexican American culture, I learned the quiet, daily selflessness of family and community members that helps to build and sustain communities. Family and community were intertwined in creating a quality of life in which everyone thrived.

These childhood experiences led me to my own *llamada* (calling). As a teacher in Stockton, California, I became more dissatisfied with the plight of migrant children and their families. Too many children were poor, malnourished, and disenfranchised in our local community, and I knew this was happening in all parts of California. When I learned of a successful community organizing effort by Community Service Organization (CSO) in Los Angeles, I felt it was time to take action.

I met Fred Ross, lead CSO organizer in California, in 1955. I started as a volunteer community organizer and this led to being hired by CSO. As inexperienced as I was, I began to take on leadership responsibilities even though I did not feel ready for those roles.

It was during these early years that I met César Chávez, who also worked for CSO. César, his wife, Helen, and I moved on to start the National Farmworkers Union in 1962, which eventually became United Farm Workers.

Over the next fifty years, my work with César and the United Farm

Workers was my life: organizing farmworkers and union boycotts, becoming a lead organizer, then a national organizer, and so much more. You would not know that I was once a shy and quiet child. It amazes me to think about what I have done with my life over the years.

Through these efforts, gains were made because of committed organizers. Through community, we achieved the right of farmworkers to organize, foremost; we also obtained health benefits, improved sanitary and housing conditions, and secured better wages for farmworkers, and we won the legal right to organize for collective bargaining rights.

As a woman in a nontraditional role, I've had my share of challenges. I've had to take many risks as an activist. I've been physically threatened, even injured. Attempts have been made to terrorize me, and I have experienced verbal intimidation countless times. This has only fortified me to continue my work on behalf of oppressed and disadvantaged people. I am an unabashed feminist. Whether our Latinas view themselves as feminists or not, we need to support the empowerment of all girls and women. Societies thrive when all are uplifted equally.

What I learned from my many years of organizing, you will find as key takeaways in this book:

- Uphold the dignity of the poor and other disenfranchised people. There is no role in feeling sorry for others.

- Take responsibility for what needs to change. If not you, who?

- Remind yourself and others that you have power in your person and that you maximize this power by working together.

- When you experience uncertainty or are fearful in your organizing work, remember that knowledge is a strong motivational force.

- Do not be discouraged. Persevere!

- Find time to renew yourself. Prayer and meditation have been a large part of my life. Prayer has been a force for renewal and hope for me, so find what helps to renew you and gives you hope.

- Being an activist should be a lifetime commitment.

- Break new boundaries. You have to move outside your comfort zone; risks can lead to growth.

After I left the United Farm Workers in 2002, I founded the Dolores Huerta Foundation, a nonprofit organization located in California. The organization trains grassroots activists to be effective in changing and improving their communities. They come from and work in low-income communities. They engage in advocacy around public education; community health; immigration reform; voter education, registration, and policy; and quality of life issues like LGBTQ equality and reproductive rights for women.

I recall meeting with Latino community members in Arizona in 1972 about a law that we needed to change. Their response to me was, "This is Arizona, not California; no se puede (no you can't)." My immediate response was, "¡Sí, se puede! (Yes, you can!)" This rallying cry, adopted by President Obama in his first presidential campaign, continues to remind us that change can happen. *It is always possible.*

We continue to need committed women and men of all colors and economic classes to be engaged in change. As a society, we must include the voices, intelligence, and intuition of our girls and women. We need our women out in the world creating change along with our men to eliminate injustice.

Let's continue to organize for social and economic transformation! *¡Sí, se puede!*

—Dolores Huerta

The authors both volunteered for *La Guardia* in the early 1980s. SOMOS LATINAS PROJECT ORAL HISTORIES AND COLLECTED PAPERS

PREFACE

The Somos Latinas Digital History Project

This book is coauthored by two Milwaukee-born Chicanas[1]—Dr. Andrea-Teresa "Tess" Arenas and Eloisa Gómez—who have been active in the Latinx[2] communities of Wisconsin for over thirty-five years. We met for the first time in the early 1980s in the office of *La Guardia*, the bilingual community newspaper on Fifth Street and National Avenue in Milwaukee. Tess was the new, novice editor of the paper, a job she'd landed through an internship at Alverno College, when Eloisa stopped by and offered to help. It was the start of a *"comadre-ship"* (a close friendship between women) that has spanned decades and continues to this day. After a long stretch of living and working in different cities, we reconnected through the Somos Latinas Digital History Project.

THE PROJECT HISTORY

In 2012, Tess was the director of the Office of Service Learning and Community Based Research in the College of Letters and Science, and instructor in the Chican@ and Latin@ Studies (CLS) Program,[3] at the University

---

[1]The term *Chicana* is often used to refer to Mexican American women born or raised in the United States, while the broader term *Latina* is used to refer to any woman of Latin American heritage living in the US. The term *Chicana* became popular in the 1960s; it conveys cultural pride, while also making reference to the group's struggle against racial/ethnic oppression in the US.

[2]The Oxford Dictionary defines Latinx as "a person of Latin American origin or descent (used as a gender-neutral or non-binary alternative to Latino or Latina)." In this book, the authors have chosen to use the term *Latinas* to refer to groups of Latin American women, *Latinos* to refer to groups of Latin American men, and *Latinx* to refer to groups of mixed-gender Latin Americans. The term *Latinx* is pronounced La-teen-ex. https://en.oxforddictionaries.com/definition/Latinx.

[3]Much like the x in Latinx, the @ symbol in Chican@ and Latin@ is meant to indicate both genders. The UW program's website notes, "The @ ending ("a" at the center of "o") offers a simultaneous presentation of both the feminine and masculine word endings of Chicana, Chicano, Latina, and Latino and allows the reader/speaker to choose the form she or he prefers." https://pubs.wisc.edu/ug/ls_chicla.htm.

of Wisconsin–Madison. That spring, Linda Garcia Merchant—technical director of the Chicana Por Mi Raza (CPMR) Digital History Project, which captures and archives Chicana activists' voices from across the nation— approached Tess with an idea. She asked Tess to consider starting the first state-focused project to document Chicana/Latina activists in Wisconsin, and offered her expertise if Tess chose to pursue the project. Tess loved the idea and embedded the community-based research project, which was later called the Somos Latinas Digital History Project, into her CLS courses. In the project's first two years, Merchant was a constant source of guid- ance, support, and wisdom, and she made frequent self-funded trips from Chicago to Madison to lecture and train students. Maria Cotera, director of CPMR, also served as an invaluable resource. Additional information about CPMR can be found in this book's acknowledgments.

PHASE I: VIDEO INTERVIEWS AND THE WISCONSIN HISTORICAL SOCIETY

Tess's newly established Somos Latinas Digital History Project would even- tually have two phases. In Phase I, which took place between 2012 and 2015, UW–Madison students in Tess's community-based research courses were trained in qualitative research methodology and design, data analysis, videography, editing, archival selection, interviewing, and transcribing. They traveled to various parts of Wisconsin to record video interviews of Latina activists, mostly age fifty or older. During their road trips in a UW van, the students became acquainted with one another, exchanged music, and frequently fell into fits of laughter, but they also engaged in serious discussions deconstructing and reflecting on their interview experiences.

The students' efforts led to a total of forty-six women's stories being recorded. The students also collected, sorted, digitized, and archived ma- terials donated by the interviewees. The interview footage was used to pro- duce short (approximately hour-long) films about each Somos woman. Forty-one of these films, along with other archival materials donated by the interviewees, ultimately became the Somos Latinas Project Oral His- tories and Collected Papers at the Wisconsin Historical Society. The CLS undergraduate students did UW–Madison proud. *¡Buen trabajo!* (Good job!)

Many students enrolled in multiple CLS courses in order to continue working on the project between 2012 and 2015. The entire endeavor, including this book, would not exist if not for the continued support and efforts of these CLS students. Their names are listed in the acknowledgments.

This project had no official name until the assistant director of the CLS Program, Petra Guerra, called Tess in 2012 and asked, "What's the status of Somos Latinas [We, Latina Women]?" At that moment, the project was officially christened.

Somos Latinas Advisory Committee

Phase I was also made possible by the Somos Latinas Advisory Committee (SLAC). This volunteer group formed in the summer of 2012 and included some of the original members of the Latina Task Force that existed in the mid-1980s in Milwaukee and Madison: Dr. Yolanda Garza, Emerita Assistant Dean of Students at UW–Madison; Barbara Medina, compliance manager at La Casa de Esperanza; and this book's coauthor, Eloisa Gómez, community volunteer and director of the Milwaukee County UW–Extension Office.

The SLAC *mujeres* (women) helped shape the criteria used to identify Latina activists for interviews, identified some of the women to be interviewed, developed areas of inquiry for the interviews, searched for financial support, and held two wonderful fund-raising events in Madison and Milwaukee. Furthermore, the SLAC assisted in problem-solving and served as a critically important sounding board throughout the project.

To guide the collection of archival materials and share historical resources, Jonathan Nelson of the Wisconsin Historical Society was invited onto the committee. Karen Herrera, a teacher in the Madison Public Schools, joined the SLAC in 2015 to guide the development of K–12 curricula about the Somos women, which is in progress at the time of this book's publication.

Identification of the Somos Women

Tess made the decision to focus on older Latina activists—she knew that some were already in their eighties, and her greatest concern was losing their rich stories. With this in mind, she sought Latina activists fifty years of age and older for the project. In some geographic regions where she was unable to identify Latinas older than fifty but was aware of younger Latinas who met other community engagement criteria, she decided to include them. Out of the forty-six women interviewed for the Somos Latinas Digital History Project, forty-three were older than fifty at the time of their interviews. Tess undertook the following strategies to identify Latina activists for Phase I:

- Making telephone calls and sending emails to members of municipal committees focusing on Latinx issues or concerns, like Hispanic councils and Latinx literacy committees

- Sending letters of inquiry to the Multicultural & Disadvantaged Coordinators in the UW System and asking for nominees

- Searching the Internet for nonprofit agencies serving Latinx communities across Wisconsin, and following up with telephone inquiries

- Making telephone inquiries to various United Migrant Opportunity Services offices

- Reviewing local newspapers for articles relating to the Latinx community

- Posting on Craigslist in Appleton, Oshkosh, Green Bay, Beaver Dam, and Burlington

- Faxing letters of inquiry to all Catholic churches offering Spanish Masses in Wisconsin

- Asking for referrals from Somos interviewees

- Posting on the Somos Latinas History Project's Facebook page

When Tess retired from UW–Madison in 2015, the identification of Latina activists to be interviewed came to an end, though it was understood that many more women's voices could have been captured. Some women who were identified could not fit interviews into their busy schedules, others retired or moved out of state, and some experienced health issues that prevented an interview. Tess also sought proportional representation of Latina activists throughout the state; many more women from Milwaukee and Madison could have been identified. The forty-six women who were interviewed in Phase I certainly represent only a fraction of the Latina activists in Wisconsin.

PHASE II: AUDIO INTERVIEWS AND THE BOOK

Upon completion of Phase I, with forty-six Latina activists in Wisconsin successfully interviewed, Tess and the CLS students had plenty of work to do to organize the information gathered from the interviewees. The Wisconsin Historical Society had already agreed to create the Somos Latinas Project Oral Histories and Collected Papers, which would house the recordings and archival materials in Madison. We felt that a book was an important next step to strengthen the public's knowledge of Latina contributions in the state.

This book is based on two key components: shortened transcriptions of the oral histories from the video and audio interviews, and the Somos women's responses to a set of common questions. We recognize that, as a primary source, oral history is not intended to present a final, verified, or objective narrative, or a comprehensive history of events. These spoken accounts reflect the opinions of their narrators, and as such, they are subjective.

In these interviews, we used a Human Subjects Protection–approved set of common questions, which can be accessed in the Somos Latinas Project Oral Histories and Collected Papers at the Wisconsin Historical Society. The narratives in this book are the result of a hybrid approach combining oral history and in-depth research interviews. We also submitted our shortened transcripts of the interviews to the Somos women for their review.

To make the book manageable in size, we selected twenty-five of the original forty-six women to include in Phase II. In 2015 and 2016, we engaged these women in several rounds of telephone interviews to gain further insights and to ensure accuracy. Each initial interview was followed by a second, and occasionally even more contacts. Key themes that emerged from these interviews are explored in Part II.

For the purposes of this book, portions of the Somos women's transcripts have been edited for grammar, syntax, and clarity, with their permission. Whenever possible, dates, events, and names have been checked for accuracy. With the exception of the introductory material and some analysis at the beginning of each section in Part II, this book consists entirely of the thoughts and recollections of the twenty-five Somos women.

Why We Wrote This Book

This book begins to fill in the gaps in local histories where Latina activists are missing, and it explores their community-building strategies. It creates a platform of knowledge for current and future generations to build upon. We want all people, but particularly our Latina women and girls, to gain confidence in their own community-building skills, and to find strength in the earlier efforts of other Latinas.

We believe the voices of the twenty-five Somos women featured in this book, and the forty-six interviewed in Phase I, provide ample evidence that Latina activists have a long history of community engagement in Wisconsin. Their stories confirm that Latina activism, though influenced by the Chicano movement and the Anglo women's movement, did not develop as an offshoot of either. While the 1960s and 1970s were a time of important civil rights and gender equality efforts for many racial and ethnic groups in the United States, these decades represent just a small portion of the time that Latina community activism has existed. As Martha P. Cotera states in *Chicana Feminist*, it has existed since "year one."[4]

To provide further acknowledgment of the long-standing legacy of Latina activism, we knew we needed more than just our convictions. To use a phrase from Maylei Blackwell's book, *¡Chicana Power!*, we wanted to "retrofit memories," or historically re-insert Latinas into local history narratives to more accurately reflect their contributions.[5] The Latina activists in this book have shared "standpoint" moments, when they recognized

---

[4] Martha P. Cotera, *Chicana Feminist* (Austin, TX: Information Systems Development, 1977), 22.

[5] Maylei Blackwell, *¡Chicana Power!: Contested Histories of Feminism in the Chicano Movement* (Austin: University of Texas Press, 2011), 2.

gender (and other forms of) oppression and made a conscious decision to fight for justice as a result.[6] Over years, the Somos women invested their energy into work on issues concerning civil rights, immigration, migrant workers, bilingual education, ethnic and gender discrimination, domestic violence, higher education access, union organizing, and so much more. Many continue their efforts to this day.

We have always respected our fellow activists, but we have been truly invigorated by the Somos women's countless acts of sacrifice to improve the lives of Latinx people in Wisconsin. We hope that this book, along with the work of other Latina authors—such as Theresa Delgadillo's *Latina Lives in Milwaukee*[7]—will add to the canon so that we can "retrofit" history and place Latina activists in their rightful place in the continuing narrative of Latinx history.

---

[6] Standpoint feminist theory asserts that marginalized groups, given their unique experiences of oppression, can recognize and identify issues, concerns, and realities of the oppressed better than non-marginalized groups. When a woman recognizes her oppression and begins to take action, it is considered a standpoint moment. Sandra Harding, ed., *The Feminist Standpoint Theory Reader: Intellectual and Political Controversies* (New York: Routledge, 2003).

[7] Theresa Delgadillo, *Latina Lives in Milwaukee* (Champaign: University of Illinois Press, 2015).

Dedication

In the early 1980s, Latina activists in Milwaukee began forming exciting coalitions, ad hoc groups, and political engagement organizations. One such formation became the Latina Task Force (LTF), an activist women's collective. The LTF was founded by more than a dozen women—many of us in our twenties and thirties—from various Latinx cultures, and mostly from Southeastern Wisconsin. The LTF *mujeres* (women) had a collective sense of ownership over their roles in improving conditions in the Latinx community in Milwaukee and elsewhere. We also agreed that Latina needs were not receiving enough attention from nonprofit agencies, municipalities, and state government. While engaging with other Latinas, we felt strong, confident, and determined to create change.

Aurora Weier, then in her mid-forties, served as a role model to many of the LTF women. She founded and directed a successful nonprofit, El Centro de Enriquecimiento (The Enrichment Center), that served Milwaukee's northeast side (a largely Puerto Rican community), while also balancing responsibilities as a wife and mother. At that time, Aurora was one of a small handful of Latinas who had been the director of a Latinx-serving agency in Wisconsin, along with Irene Santos (in Kenosha) and Anita Herrera (in Racine).

Many of the original LTF members, like so many other baby boomers across the United States, can remember where they were when they learned of the assassination of President John F. Kennedy. For many Wisconsin Latina activists, the murder of Aurora Weier on November 4, 1985, was a similarly shocking moment in time. Aurora was shot and killed as she walked toward her agency's building with her young son. Latinx activists were aware that the perpetrator viewed Aurora's leadership role in Milwaukee's Riverwest neighborhood with hostility due to her accomplishments, but her murder was incomprehensible to us. Latinx activists' reactions ranged from shock to rage; for Latina activists, this also included fear. As Latinas, we had to ask ourselves, was this the price we could pay for our activism?

Members of the Latina Task Force in the early 1980s. Bottom row, left to right: Yolanda Garza, Patricia Villarreal, and Blanca Malpartida. Top row, left to right: Ramona Sosa, Alma Gonzalez, and Gloria Vasquez. SOMOS LATINAS PROJECT ORAL HISTORIES AND COLLECTED PAPERS

Today, we stand on the shoulders of those Latinas who came before us, who challenged systems and created social and political change in their time. Oral history endeavors tend to focus on the living, and we regret that we missed the opportunity to interview and learn from some of our "fore-*madres*" (foremothers) who paved the way for us as role models in the Latinx community *sin fronteras*(without borders).

Therefore, this book is dedicated to the memory of Aurora Weier and the many *compañeras* (colleagues) who inspired us but are no longer with us:

- Marla Anderson, civil rights and higher education advocate, Milwaukee;

- Clementina Castro, early childhood education advocate, Milwaukee;

- Olivia Garcia, community volunteer, Waukesha;

- Irma Guerra, immigrant and civil rights activist, Milwaukee;

- Aileen Lopez, former director of La Casa de Esperanza, Waukesha;

- Mary Ann McNulty, honorary Chicana, Milwaukee;

- Genevieve Medina, founding member of United Migrant Opportunity Services, Milwaukee;

- Maria Ortega, community activist, Milwaukee;

- Juanita Renteria, former director of La Guadalupana Center, Milwaukee;

- Mercedes Rivas, bilingual education advocate, Milwaukee;

- Maria San Miguel, community activist, Waukesha;

- Hilda Thomas, founder of Centro Hispano, Madison;

- and the many other Wisconsin Latina activists who should also be listed here.

INTRODUCTION

Latina Activists in Wisconsin

In 2014, the Latinx population in Wisconsin, estimated to be 370,000, became the state's largest minority group at 6.34 percent. Women made up slightly less than half of this population (176,000). Latinx people in Wisconsin with US citizenship totaled 294,000, and 76,000 were noncitizens. (The term "noncitizen" does not imply that these residents were undocumented immigrants; this category includes those here on visas and permanent residents of the United States.)[1]

According to the Pew Research Center's 2014 data, the median age of Latinx people in Wisconsin (twenty-four) was much younger than that of Anglos (forty-two). Young people between the ages of five and seventeen made up the largest subset of Wisconsin's Latinx population (105,000). The second-largest subset of the Latinx population in the state was people between the ages of eighteen and twenty nine (72,000).[2]

Also, Wisconsin's Latinx population is projected to grow significantly in the coming decades. According to demographic data analysis conducted in 2014, the Latinx population in Wisconsin is "projected to grow at a rate of 25 percent per decade and eventually make up 14 percent of the state's total population by 2060."[3]

However, there is a deep disparity between the economic status of Latinx people in Wisconsin and that of Anglos. In 2014, the average annual income of Anglos was $31,400, that of African Americans was $21,000, and that of Latinx people was $20,000.[4]

---

[1] Pew Research Center, Demographic Profile of Hispanics in Wisconsin. www.pewhispanic.org/states/state/wi/.

[2] Ibid.

[3] Adam Rodewald, "Changing Face: Minorities to Triple in Coming Decades," USA Today Network-Wisconsin, October 22, 2014. https://www.usatoday.com/story/news/local/2014/10/22/changing-faces-minorities-triple-coming-decades/17689341/.

[4] Pew Research Center.

Gaps exist in education, as well. In 2015, 77.5 percent of Wisconsin's Latinx students graduated from high school in four years, which is close to the national average for Latinx students (77.8 percent). The statewide rate for Wisconsin, however, was 88.4 percent. In Milwaukee's public high schools, which have larger numbers of Latinx students than other schools in the state, only 58.7 percent of all Latinx students graduated within four years.[5]

Sixteen of the twenty-five Latina women featured in this book identify as Mexican American, Chicana, or Mexican-born, which is consistent with the state average: 70 percent of Wisconsin's Latinx people trace their roots to Mexico.[6] Four of the Somos women are of Puerto Rican descent; of this group, three were born on the island and one is Nuyorican (born on the mainland in New York and of Puerto Rican heritage). Four of the Somos women were born in Latin American countries—El Salvador, Cuba, Peru, and Colombia—and later made Wisconsin their home. Finally, one interviewee is a first-generation Wisconsinite whose parents emigrated from Spain.

Unsurprisingly, given the important role of Latinx people in Wisconsin agriculture, four Somos women were migrant workers as children, and two are descendants of migrant workers. All twenty-five women are bilingual in Spanish and English to varying degrees, and many grew up speaking Spanish as their primary language.

As many of the Somos women's stories demonstrate, Latinx people are not newcomers to the state. Latinx populations migrated to Wisconsin in sizable numbers in the early 1920s. Yet historical records, documentation, and analysis of Wisconsin's Latinx people, including their contributions and achievements, are limited in scope and depth. The experiences and contributions of Latinas in these communities are even less well known.

From the early 1900s to the 1940s, as Mexican immigrant families settled in US cities and formed communities across the country, many Mexican immigrant women became part of *las sociedades mutualistas*, or

---

[5] Erin Richards, "Wisconsin Posts Largest White-Black Graduation Gap," *Milwaukee Journal Sentinel*, October 17, 2016. http://www.jsonline.com/story/news/education/2016/10/17/wisconsin-posts-largest-white-black-graduation-gap/92306710/.
[6] Pew Research Center.

mutual aid societies. These early societies raised funds to support struggling families in their communities. Many of these women were also active
in their churches, environments that provided some of the few sanctioned
leadership roles for Latinas of faith at that time. During the US labor short-
age of World War II, many Latinas left their homes and took jobs that had
previously been reserved for men. Factories and other industries were
eager to hire women—until the men returned home.

Books such as *The Tejano Diaspora: Mexican Americanism and Ethnic
Politics in Texas and Wisconsin,*[7] *La Causa: Civil Rights, Social Justice and the
Struggle for Equality in the Midwest,*[8] *Struggle for Justice: The Migrant Farm
Worker Labor Movement in Wisconsin,*[9] and *Mexicans in Wisconsin*[10] provide
insight into the most documented activist period for Latinx people in Wis-
consin: the civil rights era of the 1960s and 1970s. Through these histories,
the general public can learn a great deal about the struggles and actions of
Latinx people in civil rights and migrant labor rights movements.

As a result of our experiences working both individually and together
on community issues, we were fortunate to observe the leadership efforts
of older Latina activists in Wisconsin who served as our role models and
inspired us with their determination, as well as the personal sacrifices
they made to improve conditions for Wisconsin's Latinx communities
and beyond. As we reflected on the efforts of these elders, we searched
through publications and archival sources to see if their tremendous
contributions had been documented, but unfortunately very little evidence or analysis exists. Too many Latinas have passed away without our
truly understanding or commemorating their legacy of service. We hope
that both the Somos Latinas Project Oral Histories and Collected Papers
and this book will contribute to this important, largely undocumented
history.

---

[7] Marc S. Rodriguez, *The Tejano Diaspora: Mexican Americanism and Ethnic Politics in Texas
and Wisconsin* (Chapel Hill: University of North Carolina Press, 2011).

[8] Gil Cardenas, *La Causa: Civil Rights, Social Justice and the Struggle for Equality in the Midwest* (Houston: Arte Público Press, 2004).

[9] David Giffey, *Struggle for Justice: The Migrant Farm Worker Labor Movement in Wisconsin*
(Milwaukee: Wisconsin Labor History Society, 1998).

[10] Sergio González, *Mexicans in Wisconsin* (Madison: Wisconsin Historical Society Press,
2017).

Latina Community Activism

Community or grassroots activism seeks change from the ground up; it is a historical cornerstone of our democracy. According to social scientists, community activism is a natural extension of women's historically limited leadership roles. In her article "Women's Leadership, Social Capital, and Social Change," social scientist Nancy A. Naples writes,

> Any researcher or activist who has spent substantial time in low-income and working-class communities cannot help but notice the significant role women play in fighting to improve access to quality education, health care, and housing and to increase security and economic well-being for their families and neighbors. Women community activists also contribute countless hours of unpaid labor to campaigns to enhance the physical and environmental quality of their communities. . . . Their approach to community development and leadership often involves collective and empowering strategies that encourage other women and other residents frequently left out of decision-making roles in formal voluntary associations and political parties to increase their political participation.[11]

Particularly in the South, the Southwest, and other regional hubs with large Latinx populations such as New York and Chicago, historical research has uncovered Latina community activism. Books such as *500 Years of Chicana Women's History*[12] and *Puerto Rican Women*[13] reveal a range of Latina-led activist movements to improve community conditions (though no Wisconsin Latinas are included in the first book).

---

[11] Nancy A. Naples, "Women's Leadership, Social Capital, and Social Change," in *Activist Scholar: Selected Works of Marilyn Gittell,* edited by Ross Gittell and Kathe Newman (Los Angeles: SAGE Publications, Inc., 2011), 265–266.

[12] Elizabeth Sutherland Martínez, *500 Years of Chicana Women's History/500 Años De Historia de las Chicanas* (New Brunswick, NJ: Rutgers University Press, 2008).

[13] Carmen Delgado Votaw, *Puerto Rican Women/Mujeres Puertorriqueñas* (Washington, DC: National Conference of Puerto Rican Women, 1995).

Defining Community Activism

Without providing a strict definition, we would like to offer some parameters for thinking about the term *community activism* as we use it in this book.

First, there are both similarities and distinctions between community activism and community organizing. Both terms are used to describe people mobilizing to create change. Formal community organizing often involves training and relies on an existing infrastructure and a set of rules. We often think of various civil rights movements as examples of community organizing, or of Saul Alinsky and the Industrial Areas Foundation (IAF), which was established in the 1940s and continues to this day. The IAF efforts started in Chicago and expanded nationwide. Many other community organizing models and trainings exist today, such as the Midwest Academy and the Gamaliel Foundation.

Few of the women in this book participated in formalized community organizing training. While several women learned specific skills from unions and organizations like the Socialist Worker's Party, the majority of these activists learned by doing. A number started by working in or volunteering with organizations led by Latinos or white women; subsequently, many felt disenfranchised and either went out on their own or collaborated with others who were more welcoming to Latina leadership. Additionally, from the Phase II interviews we learned that several Somos women did not identify as community activists, and many did not have a specific definition for their contributions.

Academic researchers Susan Stall and Randy Stoecker describe women-centered activism as having "an emphasis on community building, collectivism, caring, mutual respect, and self-transformation."[14] They write: "The Alinsky model begins with 'community organizing'—the public sphere battles between the haves and have-nots. The women-centered model begins with 'organizing community'—building expanded private sphere relationships and empowering individuals through those

---

[14] Susan Stall and Randy Stoecker, "Community Organizing or Organizing Community? Gender and the Crafts of Empowerment." Paper presented at the American Sociological Association Annual Meetings, 1994.

relationships."[15] Our understanding of community activism as it applies to the Somos women can be found under the umbrella of this women-centered model.

In a dialogue we conducted with seven of the Somos women in 2013, most of the women verbalized that community activism cannot be categorized solely as "taking it to the streets," or in-your-face protesting. If readers expect all of the women in this book to be highly visible, outspoken, and confrontational activists, they will be disappointed. However, if readers want to gain an understanding of how each Somos woman used her time, energy, and skills to advocate for others, respond to community issues, and collaborate to create change, then there is much to learn from these stories. Can their efforts be categorized as community activism? As coauthors, we respond with a resounding *grito* (shout) of yes!

---

[15] Ibid.

PART I

THEIR ACTIVISM, THEIR STORIES

Dolores Huerta once stated, "Every moment is an organizing opportunity, every person a potential activist, every minute a chance to change the world." Part I of this book contains descriptions of the extensive community work accomplished by twenty-five Somos Latinas activists. In response to questions posed to them, the women provided context for their activism, including childhood experiences, socioeconomic conditions, and significant events that shaped their consciousness over the years. They often encountered institutional barriers, were faced with intra-ethnic conflicts, confronted stereotypes of Latinx people, and struggled to define their own cultural and gender identities in US society. By listening to their stories, we can better understand how their community activism was achieved through relationship-building with individuals, institutions, and communities.

You will note that at the start of each woman's narrative, we provide background information that relates to their activism, including two key questions: "Do you consider yourself an activist?" and "How do you define community activism?" By taking this approach, we allowed the women to define themselves within the context of community activism. As a conclusion to these interviews, we requested that each woman share any community recognition she received over the years. Some responded and others did not.

At the time of the Phase II interviews, the majority of these women ranged in age between their early sixties and late seventies. Over half of them are now in retirement, and those with fewer health restrictions have found opportunities to stay involved in community issues. At the time of this book's publication, we know of several who continue to show up for marches, advocate for Latinx rights, and seek collaborations for community change.

NEDDA AVILA

Nedda Arroyo was born on February 19, 1939, in Puerto Rico. Nedda went from working as a crossing guard to being elected Precinct Committee Person in East Chicago, Indiana, to becoming a case manager at the Milwaukee Women's Center, where she expanded programs for women who live with domestic violence as well as men and women suffering from alcohol and other drug abuse. She also served on the boards of La Causa and United Migrant Opportunity Services for more than twenty years.

Ethnic identity: Puertorriqueña [Puerto Rican].

Do you consider yourself an activist? Yes, I do. I didn't even know I was an activist until someone told me that I was raising a lot of hell. I just saw myself as someone helping people; that's all I cared about.

How do you define community activism? Knowing and responding to the needs of the Latino community.

Areas of activism: Women and families in domestic violence situations and other areas.

Location of activism: East Chicago, Indiana; Milwaukee.

Years of activism: Since 1982 in Milwaukee and for about twenty-five years prior in East Chicago, Indiana.

EARLY YEARS OF ACTIVISM

I was living in East Chicago, Indiana, when I married at sixteen years of age in 1955. After I had my kids, I started working in 1959 or 1960 as a substitute crossing guard. I was getting involved in things that only men did. My then-husband [now ex-husband] was involved in politics, and I would go to the meetings and listen to them, but I couldn't say anything because women weren't supposed to do that. One time, however, when I was at a meeting where the mayor was, I said, "Hey, wait a minute, Mr. Mayor, sir!

You say that you would do anything for the Latinos right now because you are running for office? Could I have a job?" And he looked at me and said, "Well, what do you know how to do?" I said, "I could be a secretary," even though I was just filling in as a crossing guard. Then one day this gentleman came by at the corner where I worked. He looked like a Kennedy-kind of person and he said, "Are you Nedda Almeda?" (my married name back then), and I said to him, "I don't talk to strangers and why do you want to know who I am?" He said, "I want you to go to an interview for a job at the City Hall for the Building Department," and I go, "Oh my lord." So I went and took a typing test. I was soon hired as a clerk for the Building Department. My husband was very angry because I was not supposed to be working, but that's how I started and I worked there for twenty-some years.

I went up in the ladder and got involved with politics; that's when they called me something else besides activist, but I am not going to say it here. At that time, only Puerto Rican men in East Chicago were involved with city elections and getting out the Puerto Rican vote. I was the Precinct Committee Person (PCP), who supports the alderperson. I ran and was elected about five times for a three- to four-year term from about the late 1960s to the mid-1970s. A district precinct was an area of about ten to fifteen blocks, and combined precincts made up the alderman district. So there were five or six Precinct Committee Persons for every aldermanic district, and there were about six or seven aldermanic districts. The PCPs would meet with the alderman once a month to make sure that we were doing what we were supposed to do. It was not a paid job.

So our thing was make sure that everyone was registered to vote. PCPs had to make sure that we knew if there were teens that were going to be eighteen and make sure they'd get registered. We got them absentee ballots, made sure that the alleys and streets were clean, that teens were getting jobs at fifteen. What else? Oh! We had to open up the polls early in the morning. We had to hire people to stand outside so many feet from the area where people voted to pass out campaign literature. We went door-to-door and passed out literature, and we were making sure people were voting for our candidate.

There were only a few other Latinas who were Puerto Rican and Mexican that were PCPs from other areas of East Chicago. There must have been five or six of us in the whole city of East Chicago. A Precinct Committee

Person had to go to houses and talk to people. You know, it's funny because now that I think about it, it was difficult because a lot of the [people in our precinct were] Anglos—Polish and German people and other Europeans. You had to convince them we weren't monsters. They didn't know what a Puerto Rican looked like except for when they said, "You don't look Puerto Rican." And I said, "What does a Puerto Rican look like? Do we have a third eye or something?" I said, "I'm an American, I was born an American. You know that can happen?" So you had to convince the people that you would be able to be a good representation of the whole community, not only of the Spanish community, but that's what they thought. We also had to let the mayor know that there were Latinos here and that he was to help all people.

I worked in the Building, Plumbing, and Electrical Department for the city at the same time I was a Precinct Committee Person. My other community activism in East Chicago included helping the union when the steel mills went on strike. My girlfriend and I would march with them. Also, because we worked for the city, we were supposed to make time to volunteer at different banquets, at different things, like when presidents or governors came. We were supposed to be there as hostesses and help out. They didn't have to tell us; we already knew it. I met a couple of presidents and governors that way. Before I left Indiana, I was the Acting Bus Transit Director.

I moved to Milwaukee in 1982 because my girlfriend in Indiana got married and moved to Brookfield. When I divorced, I came to visit her and I met somebody, got married, and moved here. My girlfriend took me around and I filled out applications. Three months later, I heard of an opening at the Sixteenth Street Community Health Center. So then I found out that they worked with the Latinos and the Hmong, and I said, "Here is where I am going." When I applied, the only job they had open was a file clerk position. So, mind you, when I left Indiana I was the Acting Bus Transit Director. I started all over again as a file clerk at the clinic. I didn't know anything about medicine, I didn't know anything about clinics, but I started working there and that got me involved with the Latino community.

I went from clerk to the supervisor of the front area. At the same time, there was a need for the Sixteenth Street clinic and the director to get out more into the Latino community, so I made myself a position of PR-PR: Puerto Rican Public Relations. When I moved [to Milwaukee], I still had politics in my blood. It was totally different politics, but it was the same thing: women were supposed to be quiet, women were not supposed to say anything. So I said, "Yes we do. We have a right. God gave us a mouth." So I took the clinic director to community meetings and introduced him to Latinos involved in the community, or, if he couldn't go, I would go for him.

Work in Counseling and Support Services

I worked [at the Sixteenth Street Community Health Center] for ten years, and from the health center I became aware of issues facing women and began getting more involved in the area of domestic violence against women, as well as drug and alcohol abuse. Very little support was available to help our Latino population with the drugs and alcohol and domestic violence. At that time, few people were helping them. So I said, "Wait a minute," and began searching for opportunities to advocate for these kinds of services. In 1992, I read about an opening at the Milwaukee Women's Center, an agency that provided referrals and support for battered women and alcohol and other drug abuse (AODA) individual and group counseling services. I applied for the job as a case manager and counselor of clients with AODA issues. I first began in this role working with African American women because Latinas were not going to the center or to domestic violence shelters because they didn't know what it would entail.

In the 1990s, I got involved with the Governor's Council on Minority Affairs for a year or two and tried to get some services for the Latinas, but I left when I felt they weren't doing enough. I gradually started bringing Latinas into the Milwaukee Women's Center's shelter to talk about their domestic violence experiences. My role was to help them realize that it was okay for them to leave these kinds of situations and to seek help. I also started working with more Latinos on AODA issues. At the time, they had United Community Center's (UCC) New Beginnings Counseling Program for Latinos with AODA problems, but the women were not going there because they saw it as mostly for the men. UCC finally opened up a residential program for the women. Before then, I was taking the women to other places and I would be the interpreter. I was interpreter for anything they needed. I was doing more and more case management, so the Milwaukee

Women's Center saw the need and they applied for a grant to allow me to work with the Latino families and the other case manager would work with African American women or families, and the beautiful part about this was that my counterpart was one of my ex-clients.

ADVOCACY FOR WOMEN AND THE S.O.S. MUJER GROUP

I continued to advocate for more services for Latinas who suffered from domestic violence wherever I went. I kept asking why we were not teaching Latinas that it was okay to leave the home when they experience violence. So a small group of women started meeting in Milwaukee and Madison quarterly for about a year to discuss what was needed. This was in the late 1980s. Leonor Rosas, Irma Guerra, and Gladis Benavides were part of our group. David Duran, who worked for state government, helped us at times, too. We even had a name for it. It was S.O.S. Mujer [Woman], like help. Half of us wanted our own shelter because Latinas didn't go to a shelter where they didn't speak our language. Others argued the point that there were already two shelters in Milwaukee. So the thinking became: maybe we just need a place to teach the women, like how to prepare for leaving the home. We didn't get too far, as our group moved apart due to job and other life changes.

I kept searching for ways to offer workshops. I went to the Hispanic Chamber of Commerce. I had asked Maria Monreal-Cameron, the executive director, if I could present at a Hispanic Chamber luncheon for women and talk about the domestic violence. She supported the idea one hundred percent! Socorro Gonzales and other women were instrumental in supporting a workshop at the Chamber luncheon, so there were several meetings to plan it.

Ben Ortega, who used to work for the Milwaukee Women's Center and who was the first male who worked in domestic violence counseling, and I worked together on this workshop and we presented the man's view and woman's view. The following year we presented again, but this time I took a Latino therapist that spoke about how Latinas don't go for mental health therapy because they think that people are going to categorize them as *locas* [crazy] and they knew they weren't. I took one of my clients so she could talk about her experience being battered. So this workshop created a lot of attention. This helped spark interest in getting services for our women. In the early 2000s, a consortium of Latino agency directors began to meet on this matter at the encouragement of Maria Monreal-Cameron; they were La Causa, UMOS [United Migrant Opportunity Services], Spanish Center, and Hispanic Chamber of Commerce. They started exploring how funding could be identified or who could add this program to their agency.

Starting the Latina Resource Center

Lupe Martinez, director of UMOS, invited me to attend these meetings since I was on the UMOS board. He went to two or three of these meetings. Finally, he said, "You know what? We'll take it over." So UMOS set up an office and agreed to fund a staff person for the first year, but said that whoever has that job has to go and write grants, has to go out there into the neighborhoods and find out what's going on and what is needed. And that was nine, ten years ago. And that's how the Latina Resource Center (LRC) started. I was involved from the beginning to make sure that the LRC became something. Each year the LRC has a Bride's Walk. [In 2015,] it's going to be the ninth one. Women dress in white gowns and we walk on the street all the way to UMOS, which is about one and a half miles away. We chant to let the onlookers and the media know that domestic violence needs to stop, and about available services. One year we had twenty to twenty-five men join us on the walk. Right now, I'm trying to make sure that it's financially stable. The program is also growing and we actually need more room.

Long-Term Service on Boards

I also serve on the board of directors of two different organizations. One is La Causa. I've been on the La Causa board for at least twenty-two years and am on their executive committee. La Causa has a day care center and social services, and now they have started a crisis nursery. They bought a little house to be a respite center for moms that have to go to the hospital, that have a doctor's appointment, or that needed time out; they can leave their children, from birth to twelve years old, for twenty-four to seventy-two hours. Once they bring the baby or the child there, [the staff members at the nursery] take care of them and they then try to get help for the mom. It's the only one in Wisconsin.

Before La Causa, I joined the board of UMOS; I've been on this board for the past twenty-five years. I have seen the services they provide to migrant workers. I learned about the way the migrant workers travel from state to state, like from Texas and Florida [to Wisconsin] and back, and the conditions that they lived and worked in. I saw UMOS build homes for them, and [UMOS] can help a person if their car breaks down. I said, "This is just a wonderful, wonderful agency to be in." UMOS has a passion to provide ser-

Nedda Avila in a bridal gown at the Latina Resource Center's 2012 Bride's Walk. NEDDA AVILA

vices to migrants, and I said, "If I am going to join something, it's going to be for something worthwhile." That was twenty-five years ago. I don't think anybody else has been on the board that long, and you're voted in by the members.

The reason I knew about La Causa was because at that time, UMOS used to own the building where La Causa was, on Eighth and Greenfield. I would see all these little kids come when I used to go to meetings. I would see these little children and the moms, and one day I saw David Espinoza, the agency director, in front of the day care. And because he knew every child and mother by name, I said, "My gosh! I would love to belong to this organization because they're doing so well with the kids and with many that are bilingual." So when they had an opening, I joined on board and that's when I got interested in all of the other things that they do.

OTHER VOLUNTEER AND ADVOCACY ROLES

Starting around 2005, I served on the Puerto Rican Foundation Board for about six years. I was board chair in 2010–2012. The board had a mission to provide high school graduates with a $2,000 scholarship toward their college education. We gave out three per year. We had many fund-raisers for these scholarships. Another of my volunteer projects is the Latino Non-profit Leadership Program, run by Dr. Enrique Figueroa from the University of Wisconsin–Milwaukee. I've been a mentor since it started. I mentor people who are in the program because they want to be leaders within the community. The program teaches them skills, and they give volunteers a mentor. I have had a mentee since the program started. At first there were not many Latinas in professional roles here. But, like I said, now to see all these professional women, Latino women—I mean, it just makes my heart proud. The seeds that we have planted are flowering. Different ideas, different perspectives, different ways of doing things. Nevertheless, they're doing it, and I could say for myself that I'm very proud of what has come of the Latino professional women nowadays.

LIFE TODAY

I'm also trying to find funds for support services for elderly Latinas. Some are being abused by their children or having their checks taken from them. I've done workshops for the elderly at Spanish Center, and also at UCC. Both are doing a fantastic job, but more services are needed for them. We need to let them know that it's okay if you've been married forty-five or fifty-five years and your husband, or wife, is still mistreating you verbally or physically that you should say something about it and get help.

Today I'm enjoying my life in a different way. I don't have any family here in Milwaukee, but I have the most wonderful friends and they are my family, too. I am now retired, but I'm still involved. My husband tells me, "I thought you were retired!" I say, "Yeah, I'm retired from the Milwaukee Women's Center, not the community."

In 2016, I received an award from the long-standing Latino bilingual community newspaper *El Conquistador*. I was one of ten women who received recognition for our years of service to Milwaukee's Latino community.

Do Not Give Up Hope

You took me, a young girl I was, suffering as a
battered child, again to suffer as a teen bride
and mother to be.

Married life, what a joke, was I a wife, a servant,
or your child!

You beat me, ridiculed me, put my self-esteem to
the ground. But in the back of my mind I knew that
someday I would get out.

Mother of two children at the age of nineteen, self-
taught by books my son brought home to me, with
support of my daughter, I read, learned, listened,
worked and met wonderful people that gave me the
incentive to grow.

Twenty-three years later, I finally did get out.
With a master's degree from the College of Experience
and a PhD in the University of Hard Knocks, I
learned to survive the blows.

Today a professional woman, self-taught by my own,
I thank the Lord for the courage and strength to make
it to the top, to carry on and empower my sisters
to survive in life and their tolls.

Do not give up. Your time will also come, when
you get tired of being a victim and spread out
your wings, you too will learn how to fly and you
too will get out.

—Nedda (Lopez) Avila

LUPITA BÉJAR VERBETEN

*Born Maria Guadalupe Béjar Fuentes on August 18, 1945, in San
Luis Potosí, Mexico, Lupita moved to Milwaukee in 1965. She was
a line worker at an American Motors auto plant for thirty years
and an active union member. On weekends, she spent much of her
personal time as a singer/activist and promoter of Latin American
culture, playing the guitar and using music and costumes to call attention to injustices. She considers herself "una cantante del pueblo,"
a singer of the people.*

Ethnic identity: I'm from Mexico, so call me Mexican.

Do you consider yourself an activist? Yes.

How do you define community activism? A community activist is a person who has a deep concern for people, and about the unity of the community and being together as a group.

Areas of activism: Immigration, union activism, worker rights, and cultural education through music.

Location of activism: Mexico and Milwaukee.

Years of activism: Since childhood.

EARLY INFLUENTIAL EXPERIENCES

My parents were both from Mexico and I was the fourteenth of sixteen
children. My mother was only thirty-four years old when she died of cancer in 1951. My father moved to the United States afterward because he
had to sell our house to pay for the hospital expenses for my mother. He
came in search of work so that he could send money to Mexico for us to
live, but it was never enough and life was difficult; we did our best to take
care of one another. I was five and a half at the time, and I even helped to
take care of my younger sister.

I was musically inclined all my life. My father used to tell a joke to his friends that when I was born, instead of saying "waah," my first words were "do re mi fa so la ti do!" I was not even two years old when my brother Chuy took me out to the town square. I was still in diapers and everything. And he would go, "Go and sing to that guy." So I went up to him and said, "If I sing for you, will you give me a nickel?" And he said, "Yeah, of course," and I start singing, "La la la la la la la la." My brother would take the money and spend it. I never got any of that money.

When I was a little bit older, I heard somebody playing the guitar. I looked at the mariachi playing the guitar and said, "Ooh." So I went home and I got an empty shoebox, then I used rubber bands of different thicknesses to make different tones. And I would sing with it. It made a *dong dong dong dong* sound. Whenever I had the chance to, I would play my cousin's guitar. I would say, "Pepe, I will come and wash your car if you let me play your guitar." He said, "Okay, okay," and then he taught me a little bit. I began to learn by listening and watching. Then my father gave me an old guitar, and I started practicing. I don't read music, but if I liked a song, I would listen to it long enough until I could play it. It didn't matter how difficult the song was.

EARLY POLITICAL INVOLVEMENT

My family in Mexico was very politically involved. They were members of the Partido Acción Nacional [National Action Party]. We were similar to the Democrats here in the United States. The other party, the Pristas [members of the Partido Revolucionario Institucional, known as PRI], were marching in front of the house in Mexico. We were little kids, and we threw stones at them from a roof. How terrible! But we thought we were doing something good. And so when I came here to the States, [political involvement] was nothing new to me, except that I felt the freedom to do it. When I was seventeen years old, we used to have elections in my hometown, and we were putting up our propaganda on the corners. We didn't have a lot of money, so we would make sure they were in the right places so people would see it. So the Pristas got others to put their propaganda on top of ours, which is a federal offense, but they could do it because they had the power. I was so angry about this that I went and I tore them off. I had a whole bunch of their propaganda, so the police came and arrested me and took me and put me in jail. So my brother came over and said, "She's only seventeen; she doesn't know what she's doing." So they let me go free, but I knew right there that I wasn't going to have a good life in Mexico.

And later, when I was nineteen, I was going to law school because I wanted to be a lawyer, and one of the teachers told me, "With your ideas, you're not going to make it here, Lupita. Your father lives in the States. Go and live in the States where you are able to speak up without the danger of being arrested or being badly hurt." Because people would "disappear" for being against the government. So that's what I did. I told my father I wanted to come to the States. So it was just heaven for me and my ideas. Here, I was able to express myself through music. I didn't write music, but I would change the words to a song I knew to what I wanted to say. So this is what I did, and the guitar was a perfect instrument for me to do what I felt was my moral obligation to society. I sing mostly folkloric songs. I am *una cantante del pueblo*, a singer of the people. I like all kinds of music, especially music that has a message.

BECOMING A PART OF THE MILWAUKEE COMMUNITY

I came to Milwaukee on November 20, 1965. The following day, I was invited to sing at the Folk Fair, an annual citywide event sponsored by the International Institute; it was held at the old arena downtown in Milwaukee. Thousands of people were there. So here I come from a little town and in front of all these people. I got nervous, of course. From then on, I was performing for the International Institute at different gatherings. So it became part of my schedule to perform Friday, Saturday, and Sunday, here and there. Wherever they called me, I went, no matter who the group was. No matter if they were Catholics, Masons, or Baptists, that didn't stop me from going and doing performances in the community.

I would represent the institute at all kinds of gatherings. I did a lot for them because I kind of felt obliged. My father needed a letter of recommendation from an institution to be able to bring me to the States, so he went to the International Institute and they gave him the letter. I felt like I owed them a lot, and the only way I could do it was through the talent that I have. I sang at their events for years, and I later added clowning to my performances. I went to schools and festivals and represented them, so they gave me an award for my contributions to the community.

ACTIVISM IN MILWAUKEE

Within a short time after I came to Milwaukee, there were open housing marches in Milwaukee in the late 1960s because black people were discriminated against in renting on the South Side where I lived. When I was asked by Father Pete to bring my guitar and join a group from my church, Our Lady of Guadalupe, to march with Father James Groppi, I said, "Sure!" It was my cup of tea. I was also asked to perform for the many local United Farm Workers' grape and lettuce boycotts and *huelgas* [strikes] under César Chávez's leadership. People who knew of me just called me and asked me if I would like to perform, and I said yes. At one of the United Farm Workers' boycott events, I had to get up in front of the public and stand up and tell them to cooperate with César Chávez. He was asking just for drinking water, better housing, and better pay for the migrant workers. They weren't asking the impossible. I knew by stepping up or standing up that some people were going to be angry because of the issues I supported. When I first came, I would sing for everybody. Once I started singing protest music and going to marches, some of the people I knew completely rejected me. I was asked, "What are you doing with these marches?" I knew I was taking a position that had consequences. One of the songs that I loved to sing was "Huelga en General" [General Strike]. I sang it during César Chávez's hunger strike, and it's a beautiful song.

Lupita Béjar Verbeten with a Citizen of the Year Award from the Lawyers' Wives of Greater Milwaukee in 1977. SOMOS LATINAS PROJECT ORAL HISTORIES AND COLLECTED PAPERS

About 1990, Milwaukee Area Technical College (MATC), which managed the local public television station in Milwaukee [Milwaukee Public Television], decided to cut locally produced Latino programs, including my friend Yolanda Ayubi's program. I think it was from having less funds. I told my friend, "Oh, that's so unfair because I love these shows. I watched them all the time; they're very educational." So Yolanda and I decided to protest their decision at an event hosted by the station. They didn't allow us to give out leaflets that we created, so we left and returned dressed up as clowns. The staff kept looking at us like, "What the heck is this?" as we walked inside without a problem. So we caught them by surprise. We immediately started giving out the leaflets about the program cuts and the need to have them restored. We made the people aware of the problem, so that was good. They did kick us out in the end, though. So, yes, when you want to do something, it doesn't matter how many obstacles, you will find a way to do it.

In 1991, I became involved again with MATC because Yolanda Ayubi, who worked for the station, was going to be let go, and I said, "Well, that's not fair; let's go and protest." So I took vacation time and was able to join Yolanda and another person. We marched from MATC to City Hall, and it received publicity in the local news. There was really no response, so we went to meet with officials from the Department of Education in Washington, DC, and also talked to our federal representatives. Other people became involved, and this made a difference. MATC offered my friend the job back, but she said no. She decided to move to Chicago, and I don't blame her, because she felt it would be too much of a negative environment at the school.

When I was called to support a protest, like the community/unions' protest against the Firstar Bank in 2000, I used an existing song, but I changed the words a little bit.

The outdoor protests against the bank were held on Mitchell Street, at one of their branch offices, and the other at their downtown headquarters. Esperanza Unida, a nonprofit agency advocating for injured workers' rights, invited me to sing. The agency, several unions, and community people were calling attention to a state law that allowed banks to be in the first position to take remaining assets of a bankrupt company, even before the employees, who were still owed wages and other benefits. The coalition wanted to change the law, so that employees of a bankrupt company, in this case, US Leather, would be the first to receive what was owed them from a company's remaining assets.

Hice un carácter para los Firstar Bank eventos. En las fotos, me visto todo de blanco; tengo una bandana roja y pintura de tres lágrimas de sangre saliendo de mi ojo derecho. Entonces yo era la "Fantasma de Hambre." Y así fui a cantar afuera de las oficinas de Firstar Bank. [For these Firstar Bank events, I created a character. In the photos, you see me all in white; I have a red headband and three tears of blood painted below my right eye. I became the "Phantom of Hunger." That's how I looked when I sang outside the Firstar Bank offices.]

At the end of my songs, I gave a little speech. With the microphone in hand, I told the crowd that if these executives were looking at us from the top of their offices, that here's my message to them: "Look at me again. I'm the Phantom of Hunger and Despair. Christmas and New Year's will come to you with plenty of food, drinks, and laughter, but I will be in your memory, reminding you of the poor workers who have nothing to celebrate because their wages were taken from them and they have no job. Workers of Wisconsin, join us in our cry and take a stand now. Act now."

Lupita Béjar Verbeten dressed as the Phantom of Hunger at a Firstar Bank protest in 2000. ELOISA GÓMEZ

Then I sang, "My Lord, what a morning. My Lord, what a morning. My Lord, what a morning when the stars begin to fall." I felt it was too unjust not to deliver a big message. I believe people notice when people stand up for themselves, and I felt the moral obligation to help out.

Overall, I support employees because I know that a person's race can be a reason why he or she is not hired, or is fired for any little thing. This is injustice, and I just cannot tolerate it; that's why I believe in the unions. I worked for Chrysler [American Motors] full-time and I was a part of my union, so I was protected. My strength and my talent have been in the service of the labor movement. I will always protect the union, and I will always protect the employees.

The Power of Music

When music is put to words, the message is intensified. When we didn't have radios or TVs, we had the troubadours. They'd go from one town to the other telling stories of what was happening in the little town, and they put music to it. So they brought the news, but they would sing it because people pay attention more to music than to words. There's something about music—it's the essence of a soul when you are able to communicate to somebody your feelings, like love. You are able to communicate a lot better. I find it that way.

I sing in Spanish and sometimes I find it very difficult, especially when I go to the public school system and sing to English-speaking kids. I'm singing in another language so I really have to make the extra effort to play music that would touch them. I really put my guts on the line singing for the kids in another language. I really don't know how I would feel if I was in Mexico and I had an American come and sing songs. I was never exposed to that, but I suppose it would be kind of strange, you know. I tell the kids that they heard someone sing in another language. Other countries have music, too, and they have feelings and express themselves through music.

I'm glad, also proud, of the many years that I could bring music to the different Hispanic groups in Milwaukee. I would represent Mexico at our annual Folk Fair and other community events throughout the year. I was also asked to represent Puerto Rico at their festivities. Other requests came from Cuban groups, too. By doing this I think I helped support and be a bridge among cultures. In 2012, I was recognized by the International Institute and received the Expressive Cultural Heritage Ambassador Award. I feel very honored to have received it.

I retired in early 2000, and right now I'm not as active in the schools or in the community as I once was because I have difficulty walking due to an auto accident. However, I still volunteer at a nearby hospice, Ruth Hospice House. I offer prayers and presence to those Spanish-speaking patients. I visit the hospice as I am able.

GLADIS BENAVIDES

Gladis Hayder Patricia Benavides Aranzaens was born on February 27, 1946, in Lima, Peru. Gladis came to Wisconsin in the 1960s after meeting the man who would become her husband. In 2000, she became the director of Wisconsin's Office of Civil Rights Compliance. She utilized formal and informal networks to reach out to and serve migrants and other populations who believed they experienced discrimination. She now teaches cross-cultural communications and conflict resolution and is a volunteer in Latino and African American communities in many cities.

Ethnic identity: Peruvian, Latina.

Do you consider yourself an activist? Yes. Every position I have held was advocacy related. I am personally committed to advocate for fairness.

How do you define community activism? Consistent, relevant, and honest commitment and work in and with the community and the agencies (government, health, and social services) that serve them.

Areas of activism: Education, civil rights enforcement, and community outreach.

Location of activism: Racine, Milwaukee, northern Wisconsin cities, Madison, and others.

Years of activism: From the 1960s.

LIFE IN WISCONSIN

I came here from Peru in the 1960s to meet with my cousin, who taught at Beloit College. He was going to give me some ideas as to where I should continue my studies. I met my husband, and within a month we decided that he should go to Peru and ask for my hand in marriage. Afterward, we moved to Beloit, Wisconsin. We had three children, and later we divorced. I moved to Madison and got a job with the nonprofit agency Community

Action Commission as an administrative assistant who resettled migrant families to find work and housing.

At the time I started my divorce, I moved to Milwaukee with my children and we lived in subsidized housing in the 1970s. That was another experience. In this housing unit, I became close friends with four black women. We shared everything. We shared cooking for the kids and figured out who had the most food. And then, when we went for interviews, we actually looked at everybody's clothing to see what looked the nicest. It was a sisterhood of sorts, and it was a wonderful experience.

My next job was with Reverend [James C.] Wright, who was the director of the Equal Opportunities Commission in Madison; he was my mentor. My position was to investigate discriminatory situations, both in the public sector and also with businesses in Madison. It was a wonderful experience to utilize laws that actually protected people from discrimination, whether they were here as citizens or not. And so I learned a lot. Reverend Wright was such an incredible human being. I learned much from how he viewed the different communities and our responsibility to them, like fairness and equity. We had available to us the federal laws, the city's Equal Opportunity Commission, and other resources.

After I left my position with Reverend Wright, I got a job with state government, where I stayed for thirty years. I started as an affirmative action officer, and I ended my career being the director of the Office of Civil Rights of the State of Wisconsin. Our division monitored compliance with civil rights laws both internally and externally. We determined compliance based on federal regulations. And it wasn't something where you walk around saying, "We are going to shut you down," or whatever. It was about getting people to understand that it wasn't just about being nice, it was about being fair, whether it was employment or services. To me, the joy was that we had the tools to educate people, but if they chose not to comply, to not treat people fairly, we had the tools to make them understand that the federal funds go with compliance.

CIVIL RIGHTS AND SISTERHOOD

I met Irma Guerra, a Chicana activist who passed away years ago, in the early 1980s while we were both working for state government. We were

Gladis Benavides receives an award in the 1980s. SOMOS LATINAS PROJECT ORAL HISTORIES
AND COLLECTED PAPERS

in the same department, the Department of Health and Family Services,
but in different capacities. Irma's position was in the Division of Community Services and designated to provide services and information to
the Latino community. My position was at a departmental level. That's
where we really kind of combined our commitment and our knowledge.
We understood that it took being inside the system and outside the system
to identify and address unfair treatment.

Irma Guerra was an incredible person who many people in the community will tell you about. One of her contributions included creating
the CIA, the Chicano Inter Agency. It had, like, five people in it. What
she would do was she would file a discrimination complaint with my office when she felt there was a likely legitimate problem, particularly in
the fields or in smaller cities where migrant people lived and worked. It
was difficult for people like migrant workers to be able to come and file a
complaint, so she did it on their behalf. The CIA would send a letter to my
office saying, "We have received a complaint with a county or a provider
agency and your office is required to investigate it." I would go to my boss
and say, "I received this formal complaint letter; I have to go and investi-

gate it." There were no violations of any kind, at any time, but we used our offices aggressively to pursue and stop discrimination against people.

We really felt that one of our primary responsibilities was to be translators between the community and the system, and also to strategize to get the benefits for our communities that they deserved. I tell people, cultural competence is a performance issue; it's not a sensitivity issue. It is how you treat the people you work with and how you serve the people you serve. The results were that we were able to address discrimination. I believe that if we have the knowledge, we have the responsibility to go into the community and let them know their rights and responsibilities. So there was a real sense of trust in that we could, in the context of our positions, influence the system and get the knowledge to the community [that needed it], as to how to access service, how to complain, how to connect with other organizations or people that could be of help.

Irma and I were able to have an ongoing relationship, in and out of our regular positions. She and I became the best of friends, and became even closer when my son and her son died in a car accident together. Though Irma has passed on, I'm still in contact with the rest of her family.

The Latina Strike Force

In the late 1980s or early 1990s, a group of eight to ten Latinas who worked for different organizations began meeting. We did not give it this name, but I refer to it as the Latina Strike Force. We started with lunches at Latino restaurants on Milwaukee's South Side. We agreed that it was good for us to share what was going on in our own agencies with the community and we advised each other on how to handle difficult workplace situations. Our group was diverse. There were women like Elisa Romero, who is Puerto Rican, and there were Latinas that came from Mexico and other Latin American countries.

One of our group decisions was about a vacant position in Milwaukee County, and it was kind of an understanding who was supposed to get the job, and it was not a woman. We felt that there was a particular woman who was incredibly competent and capable for it. We decided to target seven or eight male leaders in the community and assigned one or two women to go and meet with them and advocate for the woman. In most cases, [the men] might have been uncomfortable, but we mentioned to them that we wanted to approach them in a respectful way, not because they were the power guys, but because we wanted them to understand that it was important to have valid representation from our communities that included women. We let them know that women were competent and capable of some of these jobs. So nobody threw us out, but at the same time I think there was some tension around our effort.

I called our group the Latina Strike Force because one of the Puerto Rican leaders who worked at a community agency at the time said, "You guys are like a strike force." And it was said with a smile! And so we didn't take it too seriously. We didn't take it like, "Oh, it was really mean and nasty, and look at these women!" So in a sense, when somebody called us a strike force, we all smiled because it meant, "Hey! Then we're hitting something!" You know? Some people thought that we were acting as white women, which was very interesting! As women, we were more aggressive and not the kind that were supposed to be the softest-spoken, wonderful Latinas who love, respect, and care about [our men], and ones that stay home and have kids. We translated what we saw culturally with [how we understood white women's sense of self]. This was an interesting conversation because then we were labeling white women as aggressive and direct.

Being an Entrepreneur

I retired from state government in 2000. I started a business called Benavides Enterprises, Inc. I do exclusively cross-cultural communications for nonprofits or any organization receiving federal funds, state funds, etc. The training is about cultural competency based on the target population they serve, and cross-cultural communications within a team to create a workforce that's respectful and can understand each other's cultures—that kind of thing. I also have been Skyping internationally, which has been really interesting, with companies that are buying companies in Europe or other places and need to build their cultural competencies to work with that culture. It is never boring.

Once in a while, I get invited on a radio program and talk a little bit about civil rights and organizations' responsibilities toward these laws. One time I was on *La Movida*, a radio station, and I was talking about people's rights and saying whether you have papers or not, you have certain rights under federal law. I got this call from a woman. A supervisor had tried to rape her by bringing her really early to work; her husband, son, and brother worked at the same place. They were very scared. The husband had to look at this man, who was a supervisor, every day. They didn't know they had rights. I offered to meet with her and she came over to my place with her husband and her kids, a big family, and we talked about it. I was so furious and said she should go to the police; it doesn't matter what her status was. I told her that I'd go with her to the police and would translate for her. We did that. I also encouraged her to go to the Equal Rights Commission and file a complaint because she had gone to the owner and told him what happened. By the way, the manager who tried to rape her was a Mexicano. The owner brought him from Chicago, and so I said, "You can file a complaint with the state," which she agreed to do. They found the company in violation of the law. Unfortunately, the owner shipped the guy back somewhere and he was never picked up. But, you know, those are the situations that anger me to no end because of the abuse. And this didn't happen twenty years ago.

Gladis Benavides with students after her Somos Latinas interview in 2014. TESS ARENAS

I try to volunteer as much as possible in terms of working with the small agencies in the Latino community, or for nonprofits that don't have the funds to do training. People call me and say, "Señora, I'm having this kind of problem, what do I do?" I give them priority to explain how to access the system or how to deliver services, and that's basically the volunteering I am doing these days.

In 2015, Centro Hispano of Madison honored me with the Latino of the Year Award. I volunteered for many years with the agency, and it included working with young people. The Latino Chamber of Commerce [of Dane County] also gave me an award. Both recognized me for my community involvement and advocacy work on behalf of the Latino community.

I'm enjoying time with my grandchildren. I talk to them in Spanish and share cultural knowledge and their heritage, rooted in Peru.

Marie Black

Marie Antoinette Olveda was born on April 1, 1946, in Coahuila,
Mexico. She came to Racine, Wisconsin, at the age of eight, in 1955.
As an adult, she owned several businesses, served on numerous boards
of directors, and was on the Racine Police and Fire Commission from
2002 to 2012.

Ethnic identity: Mexican.

Do you consider yourself an activist? I do, but not in the sense of public protesting. My activism involved promoting Hispanic businesses and quality education for Hispanic students.

How do you define community activism? I think a community activist is somebody who becomes involved in the community, someone who cares and is concerned about the quality of life in the community where they reside.

Areas of activism: Education, culture, history, connections between Latinos and non-Latinos.

Location of activism: Racine, Kenosha, and Milwaukee.

Years of activism: Since the early 1990s.

Early Years in Racine

My parents moved to Racine, Wisconsin, in the mid-1950s to assist my aunt, Consuelo Arocha Segovia, to operate the [city's] first Mexican grocery store and bakery. My mother and Consuelo were twins, and they were hardworking businesswomen. The store was called Casa Segovia, and they later opened a store in Milwaukee called La Perla. I also had aunts in Mexico who owned their own businesses. In the 1950s, this was not the norm for women to own businesses, especially in Mexico.

My aunt sold fresh tortillas and fresh baked goods, even chorizo that we made, and other store products. I have fond memories of working there as a teenager. I would help my mom make chorizo and stuff it in the casings. With the corn tortillas, I would count out twelve and wrap them as they came off the conveyor, and then, the following day, my dad would load up the van and we would go to an area on the outskirts of Racine, which was considered a Mexican village. We sold the food right from the truck. The bakery was eventually sold to a Mexican business owner in the 1970s.

The store was actually in a non-Hispanic neighborhood. And so I just kind of got thrown into the neighborhood, and I said, "Okay! Sink or swim!" It's one or the other. So I went out and I made friends even though I didn't speak the language. And this was like early June, probably. And I learned some English from the kids in the neighborhood, so somehow we communicated, played together, and had a good time. You know, I never really considered myself different than anybody else. My parents always taught me that we're no different than anybody else and nobody's better than another. So I never really had any problems with that. There might have been someone making a face here or there, but nothing that made an impact on me or made me ashamed of who I was.

I mostly remember that all of the neighborhood kids would come over because they loved to get the fresh Mexican pastries, and so that was our introduction to them. At that time, there weren't any Tostitos or anything like that, and my mom always would make us a batch of tortilla chips and we would all sit outside and eat them. By the time I got to school, I did have some difficulty with the language. In those days they didn't have bilingual teachers, but I worked hard and caught on.

SERVICE ON AREA BOARDS OF DIRECTORS

I started my activism with non-Hispanic organizations. That's how I became more involved. The first board that I was asked to be on was the Girl Scouts board of directors in 1991. It was through the Johnson Wax Company that I was recommended. They wanted Hispanic representation on the board, so I was asked and that was the beginning of my involvement. After that, several other boards started asking me to be on their boards because they also wanted Hispanic representation, and so I kind of became the person to go to. After a while, I said, "Wait a minute, now I need to do this for the Hispanic community." I saw a need for unity as one of the main things that needed to be addressed in the Hispanic community. I felt a need to give back to my culture and my heritage.

BECOMING A BUSINESS OWNER AND WORKING IN RACINE

In my career, I've worked for large corporations, until my husband and I bought our first business, beginning in 1990. Our first business was a Scandinavian furniture and gift store [in Door County]; my husband was Danish. We returned to Racine and owned a full-service camera store that included film processing and a portrait studio. In the 1990s, there was no Hispanic business association [in Racine]. The closest kind of association was the Por La Gente [By the People] Association. It was largely a male organization, a nonprofit sports recreation program. They gave out scholarships, and it's a very good organization.

In 1991, I joined the West Racine Business Professionals Association (WRBPA), which was an entirely Caucasian organization until I joined because that's who all the business owners were. My husband was invited to join the association because our camera/portrait studio business was located in West Racine. He didn't want to participate, and so I went. There were one or two other businesswomen who were members, but I was the only woman on the board. Little by little, I got to learn about the way that the organization worked, and then I was elected president and served for two terms. I knew that the Hispanic community needed an association just like this one, and that's when I started the Hispanic Business and Professionals Association (HBPA) in the early 1990s. I hoped that the Hispanic businesses in town would promote and advocate for the Hispanic community.

From what I had learned in the WRBPA, I called some Hispanic business owners and professionals who I knew and asked if they would be interested in meeting to see if we could start such an organization for Hispanics. The group liked the idea, and we went ahead and formed the association. There was an educator, a police officer, another business owner, and a lawyer. There were about five of us. The HBPA started around 1992. It wasn't hard or difficult; we all felt that we should do it. I didn't want to be president of the association. I wanted the freedom to be a little more active because sometimes when you're president you have to go by certain guidelines, and I thought that somebody else should do it. By not being president, I could introduce more ideas. I could say, "Why don't we do this? Why don't we do that?"

We started with monthly business meetings. We called it "Business After Five" and we would invite not only Hispanics, but non-Hispanics. We had guest speakers who had different business knowledge, and we had good turnouts. We offered seminars, and some were conducted in Spanish on how to file and pay taxes, and other business-related items that some people weren't doing. In 2005, HBPA also brought the Mexican Fiesta event to the Racine Civic Centre, which is next to Lake Michigan. Our group raised money from this event so that we could issue scholarships to students and promote Hispanic businesses. HBPA is still in existence. It had over one hundred business and professional members when I left in 2006 because that's when my husband and I were starting to travel; he wanted me to slow down a little bit, and so I did.

OTHER VOLUNTEER SERVICE

I volunteered with other organizations over these years [while active with HBPA]. Around 1995, a group of ladies from the Ms. Latina Racine Scholarship Corporation invited me to be one of their judges of the scholarship selection process. It's a Latina organization, and they give out college scholarships to graduating high school students. There wasn't a beauty pageant involved. When I saw what a great job they were doing and the positive impact that they were making, I asked if I could be on the board and they accepted the offer. I was on the board for about five years. The organization is going strong. They have one or two males on the board, I think, but at the time when I was there, it was all female.

I decided to start a newspaper business in 2002. It was called the *Hispanic Chronicle*. It was always full of positive stories about Hispanics in the community. I never ran anything negative—no murders or killings. I wanted to highlight the positive image of our culture and our people in the community. I did all the interviews, wrote all the stories, and I went out and got advertising. I didn't do the layout, that's the only thing that I didn't do. My son helped with photography and graphic designing, then my husband and I would deliver it. We delivered in Milwaukee, also, for a time. It was a lot of work, but I enjoyed it. And I got to know a lot of people that I never would have had the opportunity to know. There were a lot of nice and wonderful people in the Hispanic community that owned businesses. We ran the newspaper until 2007.

[Also] in 2002, I was appointed by the mayor of Racine to the Police and Fire Commission. I served on the commission for ten years. This was a great honor. For one thing, it was a wonderful way for me to serve the community, because we hired and fired police officers and also the police and fire chiefs. So it's a very important role in the community. I was very proud of the work that we did.

Life Today

Today I reside in Las Vegas, Nevada. My husband, Bruce, and I moved there in 2013. We were not there long before Bruce passed away. It's nice that my son and daughter-in-law live there. I joined a Republican women's organization, and we meet once a week; they are very nice women. So that gives me something to do. And I'm involved in volunteering at a hospital twice a week. I'm at the front desk giving directions to people to find patient rooms and other assistance.

I've met some very, very nice ladies, and we've formed a little breakfast club. The other thing that I hope to be doing is to volunteer for Hispanics for School Choice. The organization started in Milwaukee to support school choice programs. Nevada is now going to be giving vouchers. So the president of the Hispanics for School Choice called me recently and asked if I would help them get information out here in this area, so I have been working on that. I feel that I'll be able to contribute something. Education is important to me; without it, we'll fail.

Marie Black, 2014. ELOISA GÓMEZ

Finally, my biggest project is writing a book on the first Hispanic people who came to Racine County. It will highlight our Hispanic pioneers, our first families. I spoke with the UW–Parkside chancellor and we may be able to find students who will assist in this effort. I think that we have the responsibility of letting our young generations know our past. Once we better know our history and culture, we can be proud of it. It will encourage them and give them hope and let them know that they can accomplish many things, too!

Patricia Castañeda Tucker

Patricia Castañeda was born in Racine, Wisconsin, in 1958. She is an artist/educator. After her first year as an undergraduate at UW–Madison, she left for San Francisco and joined a socialist political organization in the late 1970s and remained active with it for four years. She believes education can be transformational and has recently dedicated her talents toward this goal.

Ethnic identity: I identify myself as an Internationalist/Chicana.

Do you consider yourself an activist? Not really, because it is more about doing the right thing at every moment, or at least trying to do that.

How do you define community activism? Anyone who lives in a community and takes an active part in looking out for the others in that community.

Areas of activism: Soliciting for candidates running under the Workers League Socialist Party ticket, and reporting and writing for the youth newspaper of the organization. Mobilizing youth in urban areas around the struggle for education, jobs, and social justice.

Location of activism: San Francisco; Detroit; Washington, DC; Europe.

Years of activism: 1979–1983 and when I became an artist/educator.

EARLY INFLUENTIAL EXPERIENCES

My maternal grandparents were originally from Mexico. They moved to Racine, Wisconsin, in the 1920s, where my mother was born. My father came to Wisconsin from Texas in the 1940s. My parents were married in Racine, and I was born in 1958. I graduated from high school in 1976. In high school, there were a lot of things going on, like the Vietnam War. I was in the tenth grade when President Nixon resigned before being impeached because of the Watergate scandal. As a young person at the time, the whole Vietnam War, the civil rights movement, prior to that, all of those things influenced a lot of us because we experienced it, saw it on the news and in our neighborhoods. It also politicized how we saw ourselves. I mean, at the time I always knew I was Mexican American. I always felt proud of that, and that had a lot to do with my father because his family [members] were migrant workers, and they came up to Wisconsin in the 1940s. He stayed with his father because they got jobs in the foundry, and they later moved their family up here [to Racine]. So he had a different experience. My father and mother were always involved whenever the elections came around. I remember my father was involved in the Racine LULAC [League of United Latin American Citizens] organization. He was also involved with the Spanish Center of Racine. He was always involved with the Mexican American community politics.

I didn't hear of the word Chicano until much later. I had my own sort of reeducation. I would have to say I was a junior or senior in high school when I started to find out more about it. Of course, Wisconsin wasn't the epicenter of the Chicano civil rights movement, although there were a lot of things going on in Chicago. It wasn't until about 1979 or 1980, when I moved out on my own to California, that I learned more about the movement.

After high school, I went to UW–Madison for a year. I took mostly art classes, and I took a Latin American history class. It was okay, but very generic. From this Latin American history class, the indigenous groups we learned about were only the Mayans, the Incas, and the Aztecs. Of course, we know today there were so many different peoples, before the Spaniards came, that originated from this part of the world. To see if I could get more information, I wrote a letter to my maternal grandmother and asked if she knew any of our own indigenous history from Mexico. Her response changed my life because she said, "Oh, no, we aren't Aztec, we're Tarascan." And then she just proceeded to tell me in this letter about who our people were. They were very creative artisans, and they have their own language. I was just blown away. I had no idea. My mother didn't even know! So that's actually when I started to really investigate. It wasn't so much about being a Chicana. It was more about a sense of self and awareness of identity. Where do I come from? What is this all about? I started investigating the history of indigenous people. I found out that Tarascans were first called Purépechas. They were called the Tarascans by the Spaniards because Tarasca means "son-in-law." And of course many of our names got changed, transferred to the Spanish language, because that's who conquered us. So, I mean, that's really when I became more cognizant of my own identity. A year and a half later, I moved out to California and became more interested in my family's genealogy.

Right before I left Racine to go to California, I met some women that were a part of a labor movement. I went to some meetings with them. I remember one of the women was a Latina woman. It was like a labor movement organization; I can't remember what they call themselves. They had set up this meeting with members of the Racine/Kenosha chapter of NOW, which is the National Organization of Women. Back then I called it NOWW—National Organization of White Women—because that's what it was, pretty much. I remember we went to that session, and I didn't feel very welcomed or comfortable. I felt like the NOW people had their own agenda, and they were just sort of listening to us like, "Oh yeah, that's very interesting, and maybe we can do something." I didn't get the sense of community from them, like they were willing to be open to build a coalition. I felt no incentive to do more.

FINDING A SOCIALIST CALLING

I moved to the Bay Area in 1979. I had some friends in California and my main interest was to study art, so I took classes at a community college. I've always been an artist, so I wasn't thinking about moving there for politics and public art. But while I was out there, I started getting involved with a socialist organization called the Workers League, which was a Trotskyist movement. They had a youth group called the Young Socialists. I met some people there who were Marxist. They had a newspaper, and I started looking into that and really agreed with a lot of their statements. Their main campaign was to organize a third political party, which was centered on the working class, and it was grounded in socialist politics to establish socialism in the United States, which was, like, pretty revolutionary because, of course, we live in a two-party system. So I was like, "Yeah, third party." I had very little knowledge about previous labor history, and that's when I really started to read on my own independently.

I was about twenty when I moved to the Bay Area. I lived in the Mission

District, which is primarily Latino. We had a youth newspaper. We sold the papers, set up meetings, organized a basketball team, and we held tournaments against the kids in the other districts, which were primarily African American. It was always a lot of fun, but it was always based on talking about the politics of the day, what was going on, the conditions for the youth in that area. I also recruited on the campus of the San Francisco Community College.

In the 1979–1980 school year, there was a San Francisco School District teachers' strike. I remember going into a Mission high school; at the time I was pretty young and looked it, so I just walked into the school and no one said anything to me. I knew a couple of students who went there. They were kind of upset because they were going to school and had scabs as teachers. They were just, like, not learning during the strike. I was like, "Well, you know you can support your teachers." They asked, "How are we going to do that?" I suggested that if they got the students to walk out of the school, based on wanting your teachers back, that would show support. There were about three students that said, "Yeah," so I helped them. They made up some leaflets and they passed them out and announced a walk-out time. It was kind of surprising; they actually solicited other students during the school day. I can't remember what time it was, I think maybe it was around one o'clock or something, all the kids came out. It was really great! It was kind of cool, you know. But stuff like that was always a struggle because people don't just pick up on the ideas of socialism and say, "Oh yeah, that's great!" It's a struggle to organize, especially among young people, who think, "Why do I want to get involved in that?"

WORK ON BEHALF OF THE WORKERS LEAGUE

In 1981, I really got involved in the Workers League. I moved to Detroit, an epicenter for the league. There were a lot of things going on in the early 1980s in Detroit; a lot of factories were closing and neighborhoods were completely devastated. I had a job in a printing factory. It was a printing shop that printed both our political newspapers as well as nonpolitical materials. When I wasn't there, I was organizing: going to demonstrations, going to union meetings, selling the newspapers at grocery stores and in front of factories when people were going to work, setting up and organizing in different communities and neighborhoods to build the political party. I was also pretty heavily involved with the youth meetings and activities. All in all, I wanted to help build a third political party that was socialist. I did that for three and a half years, mostly in Detroit.

During these years, I had a conflict with not being able to recruit people because they were religious or had a certain sexual orientation. Some of the lead members of the organization were homophobic. I just thought that was strange. It's totally not conducive to what I believed in and how I saw the ideas of socialism and Marxism. I felt we needed to provide for an open, inclusive dialogue. The party didn't seem to believe in this, so I moved on.

While I was in Detroit, I was invited to go to Europe to participate in the Karl Marx march, which was commemorating one hundred years since the death of Karl Marx. This was in 1983. I went with two other people from the United States; we were invited as guests. The Karl Marx march was organized by the International Youth Committee of the Fourth International, which is a socialist movement. We marched from Trier in Germany, which is where Karl Marx was born, to London, where he died and is buried. We marched from Trier to Saarbrucken, Germany; we took the train from Saarland up to northern Germany to Bonn; we marched from Bonn to Cologne, to Belgium, to the northern part of France; and we took the ferry across to England, where we spent the last week marching through the different boroughs in England. We marched from town to town. There were advance teams, and I was on one advance team in Germany. We went to the trade unions, and we went to the political organizations. In Europe, they have socialist parties and they have the labor parties. So they have multiple political parties that are actually part of the government. We approached them in supporting us, and we'd get them to either set up a place to stay, provide food, or meals or other needs. We would pick people up as we marched from town to town. There were people, especially young people, who would come and march with us. I remember in Brussels, Belgium, there was a big labor demonstration because there was also a labor strike, and we marched along with them. I believed even more that it was possible to have socialism.

The Karl Marx march was followed by a big international conference in England. It was a six-week experience in total. Over 125 youth were there, mostly between ages fifteen and twenty-three. There were people from Australia, New Zealand, and Spain, not just Britain, Ireland, Scotland, Germany, and France. The experience was an inspiration for me. This experience helped me maintain an internationalist perspective. I know and understand that it's impossible to have socialism in one country alone. It has never happened or succeeded. You have pockets, and you have countries that are struggling for that and trying to maintain autonomy like in South America—Venezuela and Ecuador, for example. All these other countries that are paying off their debts, wanting to become more sovereign and independent, which is a really good thing. And in many ways, they are following socialist ideals. Yet it has to expand internationally in order to really succeed. Having this experience was good for me as a person, and it gave me hope.

ART EDUCATION AND HUMANITY

After I left Detroit, I came back to Wisconsin in 1983 and started working at the Racine Spanish Center. I married in 1985, and I returned to school at UW–Parkside and decided to become an art teacher. I really believe that teaching is the key, that education is the key to set your mind free. When we started having children, we thought very deeply about what they were going to face when they hit school. My husband is an educator as well, so that's partially where that energy began to become an effective educator. I felt I couldn't just teach about art; teachers need to bring society into the classroom and help students explore issues, along with responsibilities.

In 1993, our family moved to Madison because my husband got a job there and he was finishing a PhD. I had not finished school, so I enrolled at UW–Madison and I continued my artwork. I went on to get my master's degree [in art], which I completed in 1999. That year I took a visiting professor position at UW–Parkside. I then taught Chicano art history at UW–Madison Chicano Studies in 2001–2002. I took a part-time position at La Follette High School for five years and stayed in the Madison School District until 2008. A few years later, I returned to UW–Madison's Chican@ and Latin@ Studies Program as an instructor.

I love teaching and offering a challenging curriculum to my students. I'm always thinking about what readings will challenge them intellectually. The courses I'm teaching always deal with difference, justice, humanity, identity, race, and class. I'm not just going to pass on a textbook just to get them through my course. I'm always thinking about if I am giving them enough information to think critically. It's all about that: to think critically for yourself.

I contributed my art to two murals that are on the campus of UW–Madison. They promote the images of our multicultural experiences.

Patricia Castañeda Tucker, 2015. PATRICIA CASTAÑEDA TUCKER

MARIA DOLORES CRUZ

Maria Dolores Perez was born on August 10, 1939, in Humboldt, Kansas. She and her first husband, Salomon Flores, volunteered with the League of United Latin American Citizens and many other organizations. This affiliation eventually brought them to Milwaukee in 1977, where Maria immersed herself in Latino community issues. She was possibly the first Latina to run for the state legislature in Milwaukee, in 1982.

Ethnic identity: Chicana. Chicana is a person of Mexican descent that has been politicized, who knows and understands history, and, in my case, the language as well.

Do you consider yourself an activist? Yes, from my teenage years to the present, I have taken it as my duty and privilege to serve, in whatever way I can, my family, friends, and others in order for them to experience a better quality of life.

How do you define community activism? My definition of community activism is being directly involved in activities as a participant or advocate in order to enhance the quality of life for the present and for the generations to come. The way I carried out my community activism was to identify a problem, try to do something about it, take a stand.

Areas of activism: Education access, civil rights, civic organizations such as LULAC and LAUCR, electoral politics, writing history and memoirs, prison ministry.

Location of activism: Humboldt, Kansas; Kansas City, Missouri; Joliet and Chicago, Illinois; Columbus, Ohio; Montgomery County, Maryland; Washington, DC; and Milwaukee, Wisconsin.

Years of activism: From 1958 to the present.

Early Influential Experiences

I was born in Humboldt, Kansas, in a cement block house in the section of town where other Mexican immigrant families lived, many of whom worked for the Monarch Cement Company. In those days, kids were born at home. I was an only child but had a lot of *primos* [cousins] and a large extended family. My father was a laborer; he worked for the Monarch Cement Company. My mother was a homemaker and worked from time to time cleaning offices and at an egg processing plant, and took care of children. She was really active in her community. During World War II, when practically every house on our street had one to three servicemen in the war, my mother, even though she was not Catholic, organized weekly rosary sessions at our house or at another woman's. She would read her Bible while the women said the rosary.

In my little town, I witnessed overt racism. The town was only an hour away from Topeka, Kansas, where *Brown v. Board of Education* took place. The KKK had a presence in nearby towns. Our home was near the Oklahoma border, where signs read "Whites only." The first time I experienced open race discrimination, I was about four years old. This was in the early 1940s. I went with two aunts and an uncle to the theater in Nebraska. After we entered, we didn't know where to sit, and we must have sat in the "whites only" section. We were told to sit somewhere else or leave, so we left. I remember my aunt holding me and saying in Spanish, "Ya no llores, aguantate" [Don't cry, put up with it]. That's one of the first lessons I learned.

Two other early memories I have occurred in the early 1950s. Mexicans had to sit in the back of buses. Black and Mexican people could not sit in the front of the bus. Another time, when I was about twelve or thirteen, I had gone to a church conference in Topeka, Kansas, with my parents. Five or six of my friends decided to go to a nearby restaurant to eat. We sat down, but no one came to take our orders until the owner came over and told us the restaurant did not serve Mexicans. While we were conditioned to know our place in our small town of Humboldt, I did not expect this same treatment in the larger city of Topeka. I didn't cry, but it was the beginning of a rage within.

My mother died when she was only forty-six. As a result, I grew up really fast. I was fifteen years old. My grandfather would also have an impact on my life. He was the one that instilled in me an interest in Mexican history and culture, and he began to politicize me of the reality of el Mexicano [the Mexican], Mexico, and los Mexicanos [Mexicans] migrating to the States.

I was a kid myself when my mother would say, "Little Juanito or little Maria is having a difficult time reading or at school; go help her out." I was about in the third grade, and I was already teaching someone how to read or write. Later on, I learned how to play the piano, and then there was always someone who wanted to learn, too, so I would teach the basic piano skills. Over those early years, I taught Sunday school as well. As I grew older, I realized that I liked teaching, so I became a teacher in 1964.

I met and married Salomon Flores in 1958, and we moved to Kansas City, Missouri. Since Salomon was a Korean War veteran, he joined two national Latino organizations—the GI Forum and LULAC [League of United Latin American Citizens] and went to many of their meetings. I was a tagalong at that time, so I didn't really know what it was all about, but I came to find out that LULAC was an excellent service organization. We moved to various states as my husband's career developed and remained involved with LULAC over those years.

When we were living in Chicago in 1975–1976, my husband was working for a university at the time and continued his interest in Mexican American empowerment. One day he said to me, "We need to go to this Chicano rally." I was reluctant to go, but we went anyway. People came from Illinois, Michigan, Wisconsin, and all over. It was a big rally. The meeting was in a church and they had different groups talking and giving out information, and so I went to this one group. There were these two gentlemen talking, and they were making sense, political sense. One of them was Narciso Alemán, and the other was Ernesto Chacón. They were from Wisconsin's La Raza Unida Party[1] and LAUCR [Latin American Union for Civil Rights]. I thought, "Wow, this is an interesting group; I guess I will just sit here and listen." They were talking about community involvement,

---

[1] La Raza Unida Party was a political party formed in Texas in the 1970s and 1980s; there were chapters in various parts of the United States.

intervention, and direct action—all these neat words that sparked my interest. I thought that sounded pretty good. What I didn't know was that these two gentlemen and other Chicanos were instrumental in recruiting my husband to come to UW–Milwaukee as a tenured professor; it's also how I found out about LAUCR.

We moved to Milwaukee when my husband started his position in 1977. I took a position at Milwaukee Area Technical College (MATC) and worked there for twenty-plus years. On my first day in Milwaukee, I ran into Oscar Cervera, who also worked for MATC and was a board member of LAUCR. He asked me about helping out at LAUCR as a volunteer. I said, "Sure, lead me to it." And so he said, "How about Mexican Fiesta?" And, of course, that was interesting to me because I was aware of Mexican fiestas ever since I was a little girl in Kansas. My parents, and especially my grandfather, had been very active in Mexican fiesta activities. This was a major undertaking, however. The event was held on the Summerfest grounds next to Lake Michigan. Ethnic groups held their outdoor cultural events over an entire weekend. These ethnic events attracted people from all over the Midwest, if they were successful. You've never seen so many people, the volunteers, working like little ants to put on this big show. I was involved in helping Oscar put together the program. At that point, we only had two main stages. We brought together local musical groups and some from Texas. This took months of planning, and we pretty much lived there for that weekend.

But the most important experience that I had with LAUCR was with their educational program for Latino children from 1978 to 1980. Chacón, as his friends called him, was absolutely right about education for our kids. The program consisted of a group of tutors who were high school kids, and they worked with elementary school students on their daily homework assignments. My job was to coordinate these activities and to accompany the tutors when they visited the homes. Well, those were some of the most poignant moments of my experiences working with LAUCR, because, as adults, as board members, we were working directly with families. We were adults helping youth as they were helping children. Those were interesting times for me, and I am still friends with some of the tutors to this day.

I also became active in LULAC. Our chapter was 9900 and we put on Fiesta Navideña [Christmas Party], which started in 1980–1981 and went for another four to five years. For this event and Mexican Fiesta, we felt a need to create the Hispanic Scholarship Fund because we thought if we were to get involved in fund-raisers and big events like Fiesta Navideña, there should be a purpose, rather than just having a good time. So the Hispanic Scholarship Fund was formed, but in so doing, we were able to recruit many people from the community. We joined forces to put on these events.

Running for the State Legislature

A new senate district had just been created on Milwaukee's South Side in 1982, due to population shifts based on the 1980 US Census data that led to statewide redistricting. This new senate district covered much of the South Side, where the majority of the Latinos lived. No one from our community had ever run for the state senate. A group of us got together and agreed that a Latino should run for the new seat. Once we made that point, they all turned to me and said, "It ought to be you." I was stunned. The only time I had ever done something like that was when I was president of my high school back in Humboldt, Kansas. What did I know about running for office? However, I think they wanted someone without political baggage. I think they thought a Latina with educational credentials would more likely win this race. I was aware that Erlinda Morales had run for alderwoman or county supervisor on the South Side, but did not win. It did not take me long to decide to do it. These were people I trusted and respected. I knew it was a campaign about furthering our empowerment as a community.

We already were aware that there were a lot of things not happening in the district. For example, businesses and industries were starting to move out of Wisconsin at that time. I knew that because I was holding the position of counselor and administrator at MATC. We were aware that businesses, for which we were training our students for jobs, were moving out. At first the businesses were going to Texas and the South because it was less expensive. We now know that some businesses aren't even in the United States anymore. We looked around our community; people were barely getting out of high school. So job training and graduating from a two- and four-year college were very important. There was a line in my campaign brochure that says something like this: "We want to create an environment to support businesses, schools, training institutions, and the community that they serve." So it was jobs, training, and education.

Because I was an inexperienced candidate, I relied heavily on the staff that surrounded me and basically it was three people. They were Rigoberto Hernández, my campaign manager; Salvador Sánchez; and Cindy Neuman, who kept the books. These two men were Tejanos who had worked through the migrant stream. They were *veteranos* [veterans] of past political campaigns, specifically with La Raza Unida Party. Those were rough-and-tumble politics, and these were the people that surrounded and guided me. My opponent was John Norquist, who later became the mayor of Milwaukee. He held a seat in the state assembly, so that meant that he already had his campaign set up. He already had money and his father was well known on the South Side. Everyone knew the Norquist name, but who knew me?

That didn't hold us back, and so a group of individuals came together across the Chicano community, men and women that had been in other campaigns. The thing that was interesting about coming together was that there was no voting bloc history for Hispanos [Hispanics]. Yes, people were voting, but people weren't taking it as seriously as they should have when Dante Navarro and Narciso Alemán ran for office earlier. Narciso lost by a small amount of votes. So the idea was to coalesce the Latino vote, and we believed we did that. I don't have the numbers, but I want to say that our campaign took about a third of the vote. That wasn't bad for a new kid on the block. But it wasn't just a new kid on the block, it was a new group of kids on the block.

After the campaign, I continued with my advocacy and volunteer work in numerous ways. I continued to raise my three children and remarried a special man, Juan Cruz. I retired in 2003.

BIRTHING A PROJECT FROM PAIN AND SORROW

After Juan died in 2006, I was devastated. He was in hospice and I took care of him for ten months. I sold my little house and I put my things in storage and I went to live with my daughter for a few months. Then I went back home to Humboldt, Kansas. I had to go back to that little town where I was born. I got an apartment, and I walked those streets again. I went to my high school. I visited old friends and family. I took long walks on the river walk. I went to all the cemeteries where friends and families are buried. While there, I heard a story, which people believed to be true, and it affected me profoundly. Because of the railroads, many Mexican men and women came to live in Humboldt, Kansas, in the early 1900s. The railroads were the opening to come up north after the Mexican Revolution of 1910. And the United States railroads contracted with the Mexican government for workers, some of whom brought their families. Most of them lived in boxcars at the beginning. By 1918, this little town in Kansas already had Mexican families living there. I talked to the priest, who let me check the baptismal records and the marriage certificates, and I verified this fact.

The flu of 1918 killed a lot of people all over the world, and it didn't miss the Mexican workers. A woman that lived in one of those boxcars, Doña Maria Ramirez, was my next-door neighbor. I grew up knowing her and her family. Her first husband was one of those workers. She and some of her daughters came down with the flu. When she got better, she asked for her husband. Her two little girls said that he had been taken away, but they did not know where. The girls said that others put him on a flatcar owned by the railroad. Years later, the two girls tried to figure out where he was buried or where he went. So when I heard that story, I believed that there must be some record, so I went to the archives of the local library and looked through their microfiche. I found obituaries of African American, Native American, and white people's names and articles referencing deaths for that year, but no Mexicanos were listed; so where did their bodies go? I started asking around. One of my cousins worked for Monarch Cement Company. She knew someone who worked there. Based on what she heard, she thought that they probably buried men in the cement quarry. I was pretty stunned by that possibility. A cement quarry is huge! It's a big pit. Every time I go across the quarry, I wonder if Doña Maria's husband is there and how many more of the Mexicanos are possibly buried there.

I felt something has to be done to honor the Mexicanos who lived in this little town in those early years. I interviewed many people and took a lot of notes, I went to the cemeteries and took pictures. It helped me realize what needed to be done. *Se me prendió el foco* [The light went on]. If there is anything that Mexicans have, it's pictures. I thought a pictorial exhibit of as many of the Mexican families as we could identify from

Humboldt, Kansas, should be done. About fifteen families responded. We rented a church hall. We put up booths and tables. They brought their pictures. Everybody had an American flag to honor their men and women in the service. I contacted and spoke with the head of the Monarch Cement Company and said, "I want to share with you the purpose of the pictorial exhibit: to honor the Mexican men and women who lived in this little town and worked in the Monarch Cement plant." I also wanted to call attention to the economic impact of the Mexican families on this little town. I believe that the pictorial exhibit had an impact on the families and the town. The exhibit went on for two days. My daughter, two cousins, and I covered the costs. This event is the culmination of my life as a Chicana activist.

LIFE TODAY

Recently, I have concentrated on my writing. I have written a memoir called *Life under the Shadow of a Smoke Stack*. It's my story as a child and adolescent living in Humboldt, Kansas, when Jim Crow laws were still in effect. I hope someday to have this book published.

I'm also doing a lot of outreach work through Facebook with my friends and family. I try to post on Facebook entries that have a political tinge and/or a historical aspect. So, you see, I am still teaching. Recently, there has been much more overt racism, in particular, during President Obama's election. It has always been there, but really came out during the Obama presidential campaign. It was so hateful that I began to read more about American history. Right now, I am reading the first volume of Sandburg's book on the Civil War, to learn how racism evolved and manifested in this country.

Maria Dolores Cruz, 2017. MARIA DOLORES CRUZ

DAISY CUBIAS

Daisy Cubias was born on May 21, 1944, in San Lorenzo, El Salvador. The repressive political regimes in El Salvador impacted Daisy's life at a very personal level and motivated her to help the people of Nicaragua when her efforts to help the citizens of El Salvador failed. She became an advocate of bilingual education and has advocated nationally for school choice. In addition, Daisy is a poet.

Ethnic identity: Hispanic; Salvadoreña.

Do you consider your efforts to be community activism? I do not like to call my work "community activism." I like to call it advancing human rights (AHR) to make this world a better place to live.

How do you define community activism? Working on issues related to human rights—and doing whatever you can to solve problems affecting people.

Areas of AHR: Education, politics, human rights, women's issues.

Location of AHR: Milwaukee, Nicaragua, El Salvador.

Years of AHR: Since the 1980s.

EARLY YEARS IN EL SALVADOR

I was raised by my mother and grandparents. My grandfather was a farmer. He was very strong and intelligent. He was raised in a small village and the people around the city of San Lorenzo elected him mayor. He didn't even live in that city. My mother was a seamstress; she made dresses and gowns for people. She was a stay-at-home mom.

I was never very poor. We had land, and we had a place to sleep. It was really nice, but I didn't get to live in the town for a long time. I moved to the city with my aunt. My grandfather had horses and cows. I had a friend who lived in a little hut—a *rancho*. I used to go play with her. One day when I was six years old, when I went there, the little hut was gone. I asked my grandfather what happened to it, and he explained to me that the man who owned the land decided that he didn't want people living there and flattened the whole place. I asked why, and he said because the land didn't belong to the people; they were peasants and they would be going from town to town to make a living, and picking people's vegetables or fruit to eat.

That hit me because I never had that experience. I always had food on my table and a place to sleep, and those people didn't. I asked him why, and he became concerned that I was asking so many questions. He told me that in our country, a person could not speak freely and that maybe one day, I could go to another country and do that. From then on, everything I saw, I wrote it down—especially if it impressed me or didn't make sense. It was hard to understand why it was like that.

LIFE IN THE UNITED STATES

I lived in New York between 1965 and 1970. I went to New York University to learn English. There I met a guy from Austria who said, "Are you from El Salvador? Then you know about the *Matanzas* [killings]." I looked at him like, "What?" He added, "The government killed the indigenous people. If your mother was born in 1922, she must have told you about all this." Well, I didn't know this. My country had denied us our history. So he took me to the library, and I started reading. There were so many things I didn't know about my own country; I couldn't believe it. For example, it was in the constitution of El Salvador that if a woman married a black person, they would immediately lose their citizenship and be thrown out of the country because the mixing of races was illegal. That's how racist we were as a country. I realized then why my grandfather didn't want me to write things down and make it public. He just wanted to keep it in a box. After learning all this, I refused to go back to El Salvador.

I married in 1968 and had my son in 1970. That year, we came to Milwaukee to see some friends and we decided to stay. At first we lived in the suburb of Pewaukee. I worked for an A&P store as a cashier between 1970 and 1975. Then I left my husband, and I moved to Florida for three months but came back to obtain a divorce.

In 1980, I learned that my brother and sister were killed in El Salvador. I found out through my mother that their children were still alive. My brother had three children—Jennifer, Leonel, and Francisco—and my sister's son was Edwin; he was only two at the time. According to the law, they couldn't automatically come because they had to be an immediate family member, like a parent, brother, or sister. I went all over trying to figure out how to legally bring them to this country. I went to Congressman [Clement J.] Zablocki. I explained my situation to him. A reporter from the *US News & World Report* happened to be there and covered the story. In private, Zablocki said, "Well, between you and me, if you can bring the children to this country, even if it's illegally, then you can file for political status." I thought that was okay. I talked to my mother and I asked her to get round-trip tickets to Mexico City or the government wouldn't let citizens leave the country. I met them there, and then I brought them to Milwaukee. That was 1981.

The day after we arrived in Milwaukee, I took all the paperwork with me to the Immigration and Naturalization Services office to file a special permit for them to stay here. They are safe and married now with children. Leonel is a staff sergeant for the US Army. He helps doctors in the field and the victims. He helps all over the world. They all have two children. My other nephew, Edwin, lived with me and later returned to El Salvador. He's an English as a Second Language teacher. He is married and has three children.

Working for State Government

In the mid-1980s, my good friend, Irma Guerra, and I worked for Wisconsin state government. There was a special law in 1968 that anyone who came before that time could apply for citizenship or legal status. Many people didn't know about this law or maybe didn't understand it. My job was to go all over the state of Wisconsin, to Black River Falls, Kenosha, Racine, Green Bay, and other places where migrant workers lived and/or worked. I would ask the farm owners to let me talk to workers and explain the law to determine if they were eligible to apply for legal status. I went to every camp I could find to explain the law and help people to file an application. Some of the owners did not want me to speak to [their workers] because then the people would become residents and [the owners] would have to pay the minimum wage. I was glad that I had the law behind me to help eligible migrant workers.

There was a man over sixty-one years old who was a legal resident because he had the papers, but did not know what it said. He came through the Bracero program. He used to find ways to cross the border back and forth, which was always dangerous. I told him he could now take a plane. He was surprised by this news; he didn't know. I think the owners wanted him to stay as he was. He gave me a hug because he was so grateful. For twenty years, he crossed the border into Mexico to see his family. Imagine the distance to and from Black River Falls, the northern part of Wisconsin.

Humanitarian Efforts in Central America

We had an organization in Milwaukee known as the Ecumenical Refugee Council (ERC). I was involved from 1983 to 1990. I visited [Nicaragua and Honduras] as a member of the council and as a humanitarian. We started working with the refugees living in Nicaragua. Over the ten years, we brought over $10 million worth of needed supplies. We went to Honduras and Nicaragua, but we were not allowed to go to El Salvador. A group of people got together and we worked with the Committee in Solidarity with the People of El Salvador, an organization from Washington. We worked in the sanctuary movement and got the Salvadorans sanctuary here in Milwaukee. People of all religions helped. We had a big ceremony bringing them.

At that time, my good friend Dr. Thomas Schlenker was one of the people who worked with Children's Hospital. He established a children's aid program for Nicaragua. He got all the hospitals in the Milwaukee area to donate leftovers, like certain surgery tools they throw away, like scissors. And so he asked them to not throw them away and to keep them in a container. By the end of the week, we would go and pick everything up. We got samples from drugstores and doctors. We got everything we could find, including sheets and blankets. That's how we started. We traveled to the countries in delegations to make sure the donations were going to the right places and to see which hospitals and orphanages needed more help.

One night, I really had to think about what we were going to do with those children who didn't have parents. I said to my friend Sally Pettit, the founder of the ERC, "Let's ask Americans to donate $10 a month to sponsor a child, and that money we'll send there and buy food for the kids." We did that. At one point, we were getting $2,000 a month for the orphanages.

Then we started Cooperativas [Cooperatives]. We put everything we could think of in the containers—clothes, materials, sewing machines, and thread. We did that for ten years. At one point, we took a delegation of eighteen people, including representatives from Channel 6 TV and the *Milwaukee Journal*. We were there to prove that the country was better off with the Sandinista government than President Somoza's dictatorship in taking care of their citizens.

Getting medical aid to Nicaragua was not easy. I became involved with the politicians because we couldn't send anything through the embargo. I found out that John Norquist, who was the state senator representing a part of the South Side, was going to Nicaragua as part of a delegation sometime in the 1980s. Someone told me I should ask him to take medicines there because they could bring anything they wanted. I met with him, and he said that he was going to ask everyone he was going with to take ten pounds. A week later, he called me and said everyone wanted to help and agreed to take up to twenty-five pounds of medicine in their bags. It was fantastic for him to do that, and that's how I started to know him. We continued to send medical supplies to Nicaragua. One time, we were sending X-ray machines to El Salvador that they needed. The government blew up the whole shipment in the warehouse. So it didn't get there even though the equipment was needed. The government didn't want us to help. In Nicaragua, however, we distributed tons of medicine. We did a good job in that country.

COAUTHORED BOOKS AND PUBLISHED POETRY

From the humanitarian efforts, I met the poet Ernesto Cardenal and other writers from Nicaragua. I started writing political poetry and became friends with them. The civil wars in Central America were hard for me. I don't believe in psychologists, but I believe in poetry. When you have pain or are happy, you write poetry. That's my therapy. People from Jobs with Peace, a local labor-community activist group, asked me if we could put together a book and have all the funds go to Nicaragua. I told them it was a fantastic idea. They proofread the poems that were contributed, and they did all the marketing. All the money went to the Central American Project. The book became a part of the curriculum in Michigan. The university used it for a class for a few years.

I was asked to speak at many colleges in Milwaukee for the work I was a part of. One time, I went to UW–Whitewater and met Fran Leeper Buss, who was a writer and had been an instructor there. She was trying to understand the war in Central America and asked me if I could write something about El Salvador. She said she didn't speak Spanish and was going to interview Spanish-speaking people and needed a translator. I agreed to assist her. We went all over Wisconsin and Chicago to interview people. That's how the book *Journey of the Sparrow* started. It was originally an 800-page book. It showed more of what happened than any history book. Nobody wanted to publish it at first. We were advised to trim it down and change the audience for the book. With those changes, the book was published in 1991 and it targeted children. The funny thing about it is that it was translated into Spanish, German, and other languages. It was adapted into curricula for school districts in Boston, Oakland, and Washington, and adapted for the stage in Chicago. It was successful because people wanted to know what was going on.

My poetry is also a part of the anthology series *I Didn't Know There Were Latinos in Wisconsin*, which came out in 1989, 1999, and 2014. Oscar Mireles, a fellow poet, and I were reading our poetry in some city. Someone said they didn't think there were Latinos in Wisconsin because it's so cold. Oscar said that was a good name for a book, and that's how we got the name. He and I sat down and figured out who would participate in the book. He edited the second book, and the third one came out in 2014.

Public Speaking against the US Trade Embargo in Nicaragua

At one time, when [Nicaragua's civil war of the 1970s] was going on and I spoke at Marquette University, one of the students said I was a communist. I never got upset, and I asked him to define communist. He was looking around, and I asked if it was a disease or something. The professor also asked him to define it, but he sat down because I don't think he was sure of what it really meant or what my efforts were about. The University of Alaska–Fairbanks invited me to their university for a week. It was interesting because they had read most of my books. In the evenings, we had a reading. The students always asked me what I thought of different things.

The war was over and they could reflect on what had happened. I went to four different campuses and we did poetry readings, followed by discussions. I went everywhere they asked me to go.

Becoming an Antiviolence Advocate for Women

As Latinas, we are discriminated against and suppressed by many people. First by our parents, when we marry, by society, and then by world religions. No matter how you look at it, women are always told where to go, what to do, and how to act. Only men can do whatever they want, and that's considered okay. We women have to be careful of our reputations and have to be careful of what we do and how we act and dress. We are always blamed, even if it is not our fault.

I was the first Latina [in Milwaukee] to come out and talk about violence against women. We had a group called Women Against Rape, and then we had another group called the Women's Task Force on Battered Women. We gave information to people related to violence and rape. I was going on the radio and talking against violence. My husband was a very violent man, and that's why I divorced him. I found Latina women, especially, didn't speak against violence because it's such a private matter, but I came out and spoke against it.

Becoming an Education Advocate

I became an education advocate in 1982 because of my son Daniel's experience at school. By three years old, he started to read; however, by the sixth grade, he was having a hard time in the public school he attended. The teacher called me and said he might have to go to special education. I thought she was telling me this because I couldn't speak English very well and he was a Latino, so I asked what he was being taught and also asked for a psychology examination. I thought he was likely further ahead of the curriculum. The teacher said the exam cost money. That's how I started fighting for education in Milwaukee—because of my son.

A couple weeks later, after meetings with elected officials and the school board members, he received the examination. The teacher called me in, and she was speechless. She told me that he was at an eighth grade reading level and his communication level was at twelfth grade, his math/science was all above average. According to his IQ, he was considered a gifted child. I went to the principal and I said I wanted everyone, whoever was in special education, to be tested. They said they couldn't do a thing. A couple weeks later, we found twenty-five kids who were talented—all of them were Latinos, mind you. I knew the power of politics and newspapers by then. One of my friends, Jim Moody, was a state representative from Milwaukee and later became a congressman. I told him what was going on, and I also went to the school board. I explained the situation to my girlfriend who worked for a newspaper. Her article on this appeared in the press right after. The school didn't seem to know what to do. I told them that we're going to start the first gifted program for Latinos.

We didn't have any money. I took from my home what I could and got much else donated—books, microscopes, etc. With this, we started the first Gifted & Talented Program for Latinos in the Milwaukee Public Schools. It's still there; it's at Allen-Field public school. After that, a second article came out saying the program existed but didn't have any money for materials. The school board came under fire and found a way to put some money there. It was a big success for the kids.

Then in 1990, I had the great opportunity to start a program for parents in Milwaukee Public Schools. The Greater Milwaukee Education Trust helped provide funds to involve the parents. It was one year of training. We started with two schools and ended with eighteen. So, to begin with, we started one in the Hispanic community and another in the African American community. The program received additional national foundation support and became very successful.

At the parents' center, I recruited parents to work there. In one month, at South Division High School, we had 2,500 hours of parent involvement. By the third year, we were teaching English as a second language, flower arrangement, and cooking to parents; and for teachers, we had Spanish for education. In the third year, some of the helpers were paid. It was something for the parents to be proud of. I brought in the resources of the welfare system, called W2. I worked with parents to come to schools and help the teachers. It didn't involve a curriculum, but other kinds of help. We had lunches with ethnic food. The teachers had lunches with the parents. I set up a way for the parents to talk to the teachers. There were parent-teacher conferences in the evenings on Saturdays. The teacher's union was upset about it. Then I got the schools to do orientation day the week before school started; staff gave tours and everyone was happy. The Edna McDowell Foundation, which gave us program funds, was happy with the results. They wrote a book about it. After ten years, the program closed.

In 2000, I went to work for [Milwaukee] Mayor John Norquist. He was a school choice advocate. I went to many cities with him talking about school choice, which started in Milwaukee. I later became active with Hispanics for School Choice, when this group started in 2010 or 2011, because they saw that most Latino families didn't take advantage of the school choice program. Many parents who would qualify for school choice didn't apply. Our goal was to inform parents about the great opportunities for their children. That's why we started it. We wanted it to work everywhere. The opportunities you see by going to a school of your choice are incredible.

From 2004 to 2011, I continued to work in the mayor's office as a senior staff assistant to Mayor Tom Barrett.

LIFE TODAY

I am now retired, though I serve on several advisory committees that include the United Community Center's Latino Arts Board and the Bruce-Guadalupe [Charter School Advisory] Board. I also serve on the advisory board of the Hmong American Peace Academy.

I received various awards over the years. They include the Virginia Hart Governor's Award in 1988 for my humanitarian work in Nicaragua, and recognition for my poetry from the Milwaukee Public Theatre and Woodland Pattern Book Center. Last, but not least, I continue to write poetry.

Daisy Cubias, 2014. ELOISA GÓMEZ

CARMEN DE LA PAZ

*Born Carmen Lydia Sayan on May 7, 1941, in San Juan, Puerto Rico,
Carmen moved to Waukesha in 1967. She has worked for the nonprofit
agency La Casa de Esperanza since 1971 and has been a strong education and community advocate in a variety of volunteer roles.*

Ethnic identity: Puerto Rican.

Do you consider yourself an activist? If activism means to use your influence to help a group of underserved people to become active in their
search for their rights and well-being, then, yes, I'm an activist.

How do you define community activism? Community activism is just
that—the voice of the community activating for change. Organizing the
community to activate, to shed light, put a voice and face behind the
rights and needs. Activism, if done respectfully and appropriately, can
and should reach beyond the activist. Activism educates those affected
and not affected by the issue at hand. Activism initiates change by giving
voice to and shedding light on a real need in *our* community and *our* life.
I feel a community activist holds a long-term commitment to better their
community and the people who live in it. Activism is not a one-time deal
or event. A true activist sees it as a life commitment to their community.

Areas of activism: Education, Hispanic families in need of housing and
jobs.

Location of activism: Waukesha and Milwaukee, Wisconsin; northern
Illinois.

Years of activism: Since 1971.

EARLY YEARS IN PUERTO RICO

I was very lucky. I had a very beautiful childhood. I was the only girl with
five brothers, and four were older than me. As the only girl at home, I had

special treatment, but at the same time I had to function at the same level as my brothers and their friends. I was a tomboy and a leader. I climbed trees and fences. It was fun, but I had to figure out how to survive and, in the process, learn to be a leader. In the 1940s, girls, they were not allowed to ride bicycles, roller-skate, fight, or wear pants. But being in a boys' group, I wore pants, learned to ride a bicycle. I was a good roller-skater, played *beisbol* [baseball]. And I used to fight. I boxed with my brothers and their friends. I was about ten years old. My father had us use professional boxing gloves, so they were big and heavy. He had a friend who was a boxing coach in Puerto Rico, and every time he had leftovers that were not good, he gave them to my father.

We also had to lift weights. At that time, we didn't have any fancy weights. My father used two big cans with cement and a big bar in the middle. So the rule at home was, when I fought, I was not supposed to cry. I remember that my father put a bandana around my head and that I had to fight with other boys, and I was not allowed to cry. If my father saw that I was losing, then my older brother would jump in. I did good! I really had good punches. I think my father did this because he wanted me to be able to survive in society. Maybe he didn't want his daughter to maybe be abused by a man. And he wanted to make sure that I was able to defend myself, and he also considered it very important for me to go to college. I think he prepared me for life.

My activism started in Puerto Rico. My father was very involved in politics; *era bien politico* [he was very political]. I remember being the only girl at the meetings held on the streets when a candidate was running for a position, like for governor or the senate. A stage was set up for the candidate to speak to the crowds. I was five, six, seven years old and I had to go with my mom and my father to these meetings. So I was raised in this political environment. When I was fifteen or sixteen years old, I worked as a volunteer on *los comites* [the committees] of a political party. Each party had their own office and it was run by volunteers. I used to register people to vote. So that's why I consider myself a very strong person, too.

My father was a supervisor *en una compania de barcos en Puerto Rico* [for a Puerto Rican shipping company] that brought loads of food and much else, and he was involved with the union. He used to go to a lot of meetings away from home for days to organize people, and so maybe I got my organizational skills from him.

LIFE IN WAUKESHA

The reason I came to Waukesha was because after my husband returned from Vietnam, he came to Waukesha to visit his father and decided this was where we would live. Our daughter and I joined him here. The Hispanic community back then was very small; there were not many Puerto Ricans in Waukesha. The majority were Mexicans and they were not well educated. They were very hard workers who came to work in the many foundries in Waukesha. There were only a very few African Americans living in Waukesha then.

When I came to Waukesha, we moved into an apartment. I remember that the manager of a four-unit apartment told us that the other three neighbors, when they were told that he was renting to a Puerto Rican family, were against it. They told the manager that if he rented to us, they would move. My daughter was only a year and a half at that time. I remember one of the families that lived right across from our door didn't allow their kids to talk to or play with my daughter. We lived in those apartments only two years because, right after, my husband was able to buy a house. But, listen to this! When we moved, I remember one of the tenants, who was a teacher in the public schools, came to our house and said that we were the best neighbors they ever had.

When we moved to our new house, we were the only Hispanics in the area. The wife of our next-door neighbor was from Germany. None of them liked us! Their oldest boy used to come and knock on my windows in the basement, or would ring our doorbell. They were very mean to us. But you know my husband said, "You know what? We have to show them what kind of a people we are. Don't worry, honey!" He used to call me "honey." After a few years, I can tell you, those neighbors loved us. They cleaned the snow for us, and they were very helpful. They became the best neighbors we ever had.

Beginning a Career at La Casa de Esperanza

When I started to work at La Casa de Esperanza in 1971, my husband was not too happy—and I only worked two hours a day at that time. The nickname for the preschool program was Escuelita [Little School][1]. It was only three or four days a week in the mornings. I came with an education degree from Puerto Rico. My English at that time was not that good, so I started as a teacher's aide and worked with Hispanic families. I made home visits to let the families know how important it was for the children to attend the preschool, so that they could function at the same level as other children when they started kindergarten. At that time, we only had twenty-four kids. Today we have over two hundred kids!

La Casa de Esperanza was in a very small house on Ryan Street [in Waukesha]. Josephine Chacon was a part-time secretary; she only worked about one day a week. Escuelita had only twenty-four children enrolled and there were no services for our families. There were no bilingual teachers, bilingual programs, medical services in Spanish for our families, Spanish Mass at church, nothing! At the library, they didn't have any books in Spanish. Around 1975–1976, I was asked to work with the librarian to establish a Spanish section in the library. I did this because I took the Escuelita children there and I wanted them to read, so I helped them to order books for the children. This created a nice variety of Spanish-language and bilingual books.

I used to take the people to vote. I would stand outside by the door with that person, and from the outside, I'd point to the voting space where they would have to go. I would tell them, "You see that little cubicle over there that has a little curtain? That's where you go to vote. And they're going to have a pencil and give you a ballot that looks like this." And I was the one who helped to translate the ballot from English to Spanish.

Waukesha is still very conservative, but it is a very good city to live in. Looking back, I can see how I started getting fully involved in the community. Remember, I came from Puerto Rico, and there the women didn't do

---

[1] Its formal name was La Escuela Preparatoria [Preschool].

these kinds of things; the woman was to stay at home! When I started getting on so many boards in the community, my husband saw this as a threat
to our family. One day he came home and he told me, "You choose: the
community or the family." I knew that the best way to continue my community work would be to have him get involved with me. He was always
a good religious person; he was very Catholic, *very* Catholic. We had to
drive from Waukesha to Milwaukee because we didn't have a Spanish Mass
in Waukesha, so we went every Sunday to St. Francis Church, on Fourth
and Brown on Milwaukee's North Side. It was through the church that I
got him involved. He became a member of El Santo Nombre de Jesús [the
Holy Name Society] and I became a member of the ladies' auxiliary. That's
how I started pulling him in. Then after that, he was in charge of Adult
Christian Formation, and I was in charge of Christian Formation for the
children. Next, we began to work with married couples as lay ministers.

In Waukesha, I remember at that time, St. Joseph's Church was in the
process of opening St. Joseph's Clinic for Hispanic families. I convinced
him to become a board member of the clinic. I think he saw how important it was and how needed his help was. After that, nobody stopped him.
When I became a member of the Kiwanis Club, he joined me for all fund-
raising activities. Every time we have any event here at La Casa, we work
together, hand-in-hand.

We became leaders with the program Encuentras Matrimoniales [Mar-
riage Encounters] in Wisconsin at a state level. We worked with hundreds
of couples who came to our retreat. We went to Indiana, Iowa, Chicago,
Florida, and Texas to train couples to become leaders in their community through the church. And today I have people that come to me and
say, "Don't you remember me? We went to your house to prepare for the
marriage encounter!" or "We went to your house to get prepared to get
married, and look, we have so many kids and we are very happy!"

In 1971, I was the first one to organize the Three Kings Celebration,
because you know that in Latin American countries, we don't have Santa
Claus. I didn't want our children to forget where we came from. And my
husband was the one who helped me. I talked to two big shopping malls:
I talked to Mayfair Mall in Milwaukee County and to Brookfield Square
in Waukesha County. They each had Christmas trees where organizations

could hang cards to ask people to provide Christmas gifts for needy families. We collected thousands of toys for our families and those were saved
for the Three Kings Celebration. We used the Carroll College gymnasium
because hundreds of families came. We sang Christmas carols in Spanish
as we went from one store to another, and then they would provide hot
chocolate and cookies that they cooked for us. At La Casa, we'd have Las
Posadas [mainly a Mexican community event to reenact the pilgrimage
to Bethlehem by Mary, Joseph, and Jesus]. We offered the drink *champur-
rado* [a warm, corn-based Mexican drink], and we'd have the games of *las
piñatas* for the children. I know the whole thing about Las Posadas even
though I'm from Puerto Rico because of my people.

Advocating for Children in the Waukesha Public Schools

Around 1971, Waukesha Public Schools had a very small bilingual program. They didn't have any counselors because they didn't see any need
for that. So our children were getting behind. Our parents were not active in the schools because of the language, so we had to organize. The
transportation for our children was not as good as it should have been.
So the only way we were able to get what was needed was by fighting for
it. What I mean about fighting was not hitting and punching, but making
our voices heard—*para escuchar a nuestras necesidades* [for them to hear
our needs]. The schools labeled our youth who didn't speak English as
mentally retarded. So we had to prove that our children were as smart as
the other children. A number of the children were not treated well either.

I'm going to use my own son as an example. My son has darker skin
and his hair is kinky. He went to Blair School and started kindergarten
in the bilingual program, but when he started first grade, in 1975, that
was hell for him! He came home crying every day. He didn't want to go
to school because the children pushed him and spit at him because of his
color; they viewed him as different. He was seven years old and was already having problems with his stomach from all the pressure. I decided
to meet with the school principal, Mr. Kota. I asked Edwin Maldonado,
who was a friend, to come with me. I even tape-recorded this meeting as
I explained to him that my son was born in Waukesha, but he was viewed

as different; he didn't have blond hair, blue eyes, or white skin. I then offered to go into the classroom and work with all the children, to share about our background. I knew how to approach the children in a positive way. And I said, "You know what? I can bring Spanish books; I can bring different things from home. I can bring different desserts, for the children to share!" His answer was, "Well, he has to learn how to live with that [the treatment by the children]." That was his answer! One day after that, my son came home without his jacket. It was spring, and he said, "Mom, my spring jacket is lost. I couldn't find it." I said, "It has to be somewhere in the school." So his spring jacket was found in the playground about two days later in the garbage; [the other kids] used it to clean a bloody nose. Yes! It was bad!

I used to go to the PTO meetings, even though I didn't know the language that well. I was the first one sitting in front at the PTO meetings. I wanted them to know that I was there because I cared for my kids. When they had festivals in the schools for fund-raising, I was one of the volunteers. Sometimes I didn't even know what they were asking me to do, but I was there. And, you know, today my son is a mechanical engineer and is very successful. And my daughter went to Syracuse University, where she graduated with a bachelor's degree in fine arts and continued her studies after that, so I think all of my efforts paid off!

Because the school issues were ongoing for many Latino families, we organized our parents and our children to have a walkout in 1973. We agreed that at eleven, we wanted all of the children to walk out of their classrooms. A number of parents and community supporters were outside waiting for them. It was very emotional to see our youth coming from different doors of the school. From there, we all marched to the school superintendent office of Russell Ranke. I remember we walked into the building and straight to his office. Our youth presented their needs to the superintendent. We had a lot of *cartas postales* [postcards] with the kinds of services we needed. And I remember there were TV channels 4 and 6, the *Waukesha Freeman*, I think there was the *Milwaukee Journal*. And we marched over to the school board president's office. Dr. [William] Carr was an African American and worked for the Social Security Administration to make similar demands. Afterward, we went to the next school board meeting, but they didn't allow us into their meeting room, so we opened the doors and walked in. We were told that there was no space on the agenda for us and [they] had the police take us out of the building, but nobody got arrested.

My involvement in all this was as a supporter, citizen, friend, and member of La Casa. I wore all of those different hats. My biggest concern was the children's education. Because of everyone's efforts, we were able to get more services for the children. We have what we have today because we had to fight—in a good way, because activism can be peaceful. We let our voices be heard and we marched; we were very peaceful. We were able to get a counselor, a liaison, and better transportation. The results were very productive. Before, the children had to walk, let's say, a block and wait for the bus on the corner. The weather was not good for that. And we demanded a bus stop in front of the children's homes because the other children were getting the service. Even at the high school they had bilingual teachers for the children that came new to the town.

Life Today

My husband died June 16, 2003. I think that we are here for such a short time. I don't want to spend my energy doing things that I don't like. You have to be productive; you have to enjoy life. Plus, if you complain, nobody listens to you, so why should you complain? So be happy; enjoy life. I love life. It is a gift.

My community service right now is not only for the Hispanic community, it is for whoever is in need. I mean, not all Hispanic people have needs. I feel proud to say that I have been able to develop some of these services and that the services have been provided to the people that really, really, really need the services.

Carmen De La Paz, 2017. CARMEN DE LA PAZ

Things are different in Waukesha today. The children are second or third generation. Some have become professionals. We don't have the language barrier like before. We have bilingual teachers because many of my students that came to Escuelita thirty to thirty-five years ago are the teachers in the public schools, or social workers. Today is different. Even the people that come to our agency are looking to learn English as a second language: "How can I enroll myself to learn English?" And the same people come and say, "Okay, what do I have to do to become a US citizen?" You know, the people today, they are more educated than way back. Activism is needed for the Dreamers.[2] They need our support.

Today, I continue to volunteer part-time at La Casa de Esperanza. Just recently, I received an award from *El Conquistador,* a long-standing community Latino newspaper. I was one of the twenty-five community leaders recognized for service to the community.

---

[2] The Development, Relief, and Education for Alien Minors Act, or DREAM Act, is a legislative proposal that would grant legal status to certain undocumented immigrants who were brought to the United States as children and went to school here (called Dreamers).

Gabriela Gamboa

Gabriela Gamboa González was born on November 29, 1970, in Guadalajara, Mexico. She moved to Green Bay, Wisconsin, in 2003 and immersed herself in volunteer and advocacy work. She helped create a scholarship program for high school graduates and has created programs to support the immigrant population in Green Bay. Gabriela is a general manager and on-air personality at a radio station, as well.

Ethnic identity: Latina.

Do you consider yourself an activist? *Sí, mi trabajo es apoyar organizaciones de todos tipos con mi trabajo voluntario. Puede ser considerado de una otra forma.* [My volunteer work is to support organizations of all kinds. It can be considered another form of community activism.]

How do you define community activism? *Apoyar a organizaciones de todo tipo con el único objetivo de ayudar. Todo lo haga de acuerdo a mis propias creencias.* [Assisting organizations of all types with the sole objective to assist. All that I'm doing is in alignment with my beliefs.]

Areas of activism: All!

Location of activism: Green Bay, Wisconsin.

Years of activism: 2007 to the present.

LIFE IN GREEN BAY

I came in December 2003, when I was thirty-three and not knowing any English, to reconnect with the father of my children. Once I got to Green Bay, it was horrible because it was December. I had no idea how cold it could be, and there was a lot of snow. I didn't know what kind of shoes or clothes to wear, so it was a horrible experience for me and my kids. It wasn't just my own personal or family experience. Being Latino in Green Bay could be one of the worst things that happened for some people. But as soon as I got here, I don't know, something happened. I don't come from a wealthy family; however, we lived pretty well. I always worked at our family business in Mexico. When I came here, I was with the father of my kids. I said that I wanted to be here and stay with him. He asked me to get a job. One of the first things I did was learn to drive in the snow. It was scary.

In a short time, my kids fell in love with Green Bay. I felt I needed to stay here because of them. I also felt they needed their dad. This was different, though, from what I knew. I came from a family with a dad who spoiled me and a mother who loved me. I was a big part of their world. My first job here was working in a factory. In Mexico, I went to work wearing nice skirts and looking pretty because I worked in an office where we sold cell phone contracts, so you had to look nice. After three months, my mother came for me and told me that I needed to come back, and I told her no. I decided to stay here because a lot of people were betting that I couldn't keep my job for more than three months—they said that I didn't belong in the United States, and that I wouldn't be able to work in a job where I had to wear bulky shoes and a hat like a laborer. But I wore makeup, and though I knew I didn't belong in a factory, I wanted to show them that I was able to do it, and I did it.

One day, I was working in the packaging line, and this lady came up to me and she said, "Hey, I heard you're taking English classes?" I had been taking English classes, and I said, "Oh, am I in trouble?" trying to be sassy right back. And she followed up by saying, "Hey, I heard you're just taking the classes to become a line leader." So I told her, "Oh, you know what, where I want to be is in that office right over there, and you're going to see me there soon." Six months later, they opened up a spot in quality control, and even though my English was very limited, I got the job. It was awesome; if you believe in something, just say it because it's going to happen if you want it. At that time, I needed to believe that I could do something, and I thought of the things that I was capable of doing. When you have your dad and mom to do everything for you, you don't realize it. In 2004, I began taking English classes at Literacy Green Bay and met some wonderful tutors.

ADVOCATING FOR CHILDREN'S EDUCATION

I want to tell you about a cool story, and this is just because it bothers me somehow. When I came to the United States with my two kids, Alex and Dalí, I sent them to school. Of course they are not very white, and you can tell that they are Latino. They automatically put my kids in a program called ESL [English as a Second Language]. I wasn't happy about that, but I didn't know what was going on because I just arrived. It was December 15, 2003, so I left them at this school. In January, after vacation break, I felt I needed my kids to have the full opportunities of the other students. I brought them to this country, but I wasn't sure they would get this full knowledge if I let them stay in the ESL program. I wondered how they were going to learn English, understand the culture, and those things.

A person I knew recommended another school, so I decided to take my sons there, but I was told that they could not attend because they were not bilingual. The oldest was somewhat bilingual, but my little one wasn't. The new school staff agreed that my older one could stay, but the little one could not. They said he would not learn well enough and that I would be "taking away the chance for him to learn his culture." So I said, "No, I will teach him about his heritage and his culture at home. He is in the United States. Please teach them how they live in the United States." I also wanted them to go to the same school. So they let [both kids] stay and they were some of the first Latinos in that school.

A lot of people looked at my younger son, Dalí, differently because he did not know the language too well, and that made it a struggle for us. I remember he would say, "Yo no voy a hablar ingles; a mi no me gusta tú cochino ingles [I'm not going to speak English; I don't want to speak your ugly English]." I told him that he had to. So he went to school and learned it. After three months at that school, he was 65 percent or more bilingual. I was lucky because my wonderful lady friend, Sandy Magolan, was able to talk to him. He was upset most of the time because of the way the kids at school would treat him. He could talk to her about what was going on at school, and Sandy would ask him if he wanted her to talk to [the kids] or the teacher. He told her, "No, just show me how to handle this." So she gave him ideas on how to handle the situations. It turned out that one of the boys who bullied him is now one of his best friends, to this day. So that's cool. Now it's hard for me to make Dalí speak Spanish. But it was cool, to be brave and tough, to say, "This is what I want for my kids, and this is what I need for my kids."

Sometimes parents have the problem that their kids are in ninth grade and the kids are confused. They don't know either English or Spanish very well. My idea is that you have to fight. If you consider that it's the best for your kids, then do it. They will never lose their heritage. My kids are bilingual, they can read and write in English and Spanish, they know who they are, and they love both of their cultures. They have Hmong, African American, Anglo friends; they are multicultural kids. So that makes them a part of this country.

Alex was nine years old; he's now twenty-three. And Dalí, who was four, is now looking at colleges, too. They were young when they came. They came to a place totally different. A new life, language, and school; kids who didn't know how to deal with Latinos in the school. It was a good thing that they were smart, and they learned how to handle life here. They didn't give up either. I am so proud of them.

Green Bay is a small city, so people who know me knew that my kids went to a school where most of the kids were Anglos. So this [Latino] lady wanted her daughter to go to that school, and somehow she communicated with them, but she was not bilingual. The school found someone to translate, to explain that [in the school's view] she was taking away the opportunity for her daughter to be with kids where she can learn more about her culture. So the lady told them that her daughter was born in the United States, so she needs to learn these things because she was born here, and she needs to be in that school. To me, the lady was right. And she knew that I was able to convince [the staff] to send my kids to that school. So she asked if I could be her interpreter because she felt that the interpreter that the school had provided didn't help her. So I told [the staff] that they could not deny her daughter from their school. The principal said, "No, I'm not denying this, but I'm telling you that you're taking this away from your daughter." And the lady said, "No, I'm not taking anything away from my child." The mother was short on words in both English and Spanish, so I knew I had to help her out and added that we, parents, are the ones to teach [our kids] their heritage at home; we want them to learn more languages. The school later decided to accept the woman's daughter, and that was a win for her family.

EXPERIENCING RACISM

In 2008, I volunteered at St. Peter and Paul Catholic Church. I used to be the manager of about sixty volunteers. They were Anglos, and most of them were Belgians. I was the only Latino. Some of them welcomed me, but I'll share one of my experiences when it was a challenge: I was getting ready to eat after a hard day's work, and all the volunteers got together at a table and they prayed. I decided to sit down with my boss, in one of the chairs in the corner. All the people opened a space for us, and they said, "Come here. Sit here with us." So I went there and sat down, but one of the guys said, "I'm not going to eat with her; she doesn't belong with us. She's not one of us." So everyone started whispering, and some of the ladies were crying. So the guy gets up and he leaves. And everyone else was trying to console me; they were worried for me, apologizing, and hugging me. So I told them that I wanted to talk, and I told them that I was not ashamed about this. And they said that I shouldn't be. I said, "I will never be ashamed about who I am because I don't have a problem with these types of things. That man has the problem." And they said that the priest was going to talk to him. I told them that I didn't need anyone to talk to him and that I would have him on my side pretty soon. After three months, he would give me friendly hugs, and he'd say, "You're lucky I am married." So he fell in love with me, and I would tease him and say, "Didn't you say you don't like Latinos? You used to be mean." He told me, "Oh, be quiet. I didn't know there were Mexicans like you." So I told him, "Because you didn't give us a chance. Give us a chance; don't judge us on the actions of others."

BECOMING A COMMUNITY VOLUNTEER

I started to volunteer for different organizations shortly after I came here. One of the organizations that I've been volunteering with since 2007 is the Hispanic Community Council (HCC) of Northeast Wisconsin. I was invited by Mayor Jim Schmitt to join. The HCC gave me the chance to help the students. There were a lot of volunteers that helped. We started a program in 2009 to raise money for scholarships. It's called Libertad, or Freedom, which helps high school girls go to college who don't have the money, or maybe the parents don't support them. It seems like a beauty pageant, but it's not. We are interested in Latinas who want to keep going academically. We support only girls in this program because women in our countries sometimes don't continue with school. They get married and have kids, and we are more than that. We need parents to know that there are other opportunities for their daughters. So that is why we created this program. This is one way to get a scholarship. Each young lady has to be involved in the community. Marisa Leza was our fourth queen in 2013. She belonged to Voces de le Frontera [a nonprofit immigration advocacy group in Wisconsin], and we were very proud of her. Others were Eva Cruz, also part of Boys and Girls Club, and Angélica Sánchez, now at a Milwaukee college. All of these girls continued with their education, and we are proud of them. We talk to parents about the importance of education, too. The HCC cares about the youth, and one of the things we try is to create programs for the parents, for them to have a better future. You have to look at the whole picture, the whole family. Somehow the whole community gave a level of support. With the money raised, working hard, and volunteering, we were able to give them a little bit of our help as Latinos, so it is cool.

I worked for a while as an interpreter for a company here in Green Bay, and it was a pretty good job because being an interpreter helped me to help people. I used to do it sometimes without pay, but later, as a full-time interpreter, the hospitals would pay so the patients didn't have to. They appreciated this service and would thank me for the help. It was my job, and it felt so cool.

I have been invited to different schools to talk to students about my life. And I wondered why these kids wanted to learn about my life. I didn't realize why, but now I know. If they know that people like me can create opportunities for themselves out of struggles, then they can do it, too, and it doesn't matter how old you are.

Working with the Greater Green Bay Chamber of Commerce

The Greater Green Bay Chamber of Commerce just gave me recognition because I have been so active in the community. The cool thing is that it was the Anglo community that nominated me, and this was awesome. It's like you're a grain of black rice in the whole pot with the white rice, and they can see you, and they saw me. I was blown away at the time. When they called me, I was in the process of becoming a permanent resident; I was in Mexico when I was given the notice. I was one of the twenty people recognized in *Current* magazine [published by the Green Bay Chamber of

Commerce]. Another Latina and I were in this group. A journalist interviewed me by phone and my son took a picture. That just made me want
to keep on going. The publicity is good so the people know what you are
doing because they might follow you or help you. Any recognition I get,
I feel humbled. It means I'm doing something good for my community.
I care for both the Latino and Anglo communities because I decided to
come to this country. I decided to be here, and I wanted to be one of the
best citizens. I'm working hard to be able to take my test soon and become
a citizen of the United States.

More Volunteer Work

Another event is the Information Fair. The fair helps provide information to Latinos when they come to Green Bay. Services are promoted by
nonprofits, since they usually don't have the money to advertise them.
The local radio station has helped share this information by promoting
the fair in the community. The radio station La Más Grande [96.9 FM in
Green Bay] helps to sponsor the event. For the Hispanic Information Fair,
we recruit volunteers, like students, to help with the event, and we invite
the public. We like to provide information to our community that looks
simple for some, but is not for the ones that are new here. An example is
the program for picking up the garbage. We need to know the time garbage will be picked up; otherwise they will have an infraction if they don't
take the garbage out at the right time. Another municipal rule would be,
maybe, you can't party in your front yard. Things that people who have
lived here their whole lives already know about.

Every year, we expect around one thousand people to come to the one-
day festival. It's cool having all these people come. Each year the cost of
this festival is about $13,000. We raised the money from underwriters and
charging for booth space to businesses and nonprofits. The entrance fee goes
toward scholarships for the students and to create programs for the parents
as well. I work with all my heart, like hard-knocking on doors and asking
people to donate some money. We pray and hope for good weather to have
a good turnout and cover our expenses. One of the cool things is La Más
Grande radio station became the lead sponsor in 2014. It was a blessing for us
as Latinos because so much information of community resources is shared.

Gabriela Gamboa with students after her Somos Latinas interview in 2014. From left to right: Steve Pereira, Sasha Reyes, Adee Guzman, Gabriela Gamboa, and Marcelo "Richie" Heredia. TESS ARENAS

The Hispanic Community Council also ran Consulado Móvil, a service for the Mexican community. This was a service for someone who, let's say, can't drive to Chicago or Milwaukee where the Mexican Consulate is located. So we provided the transportation, and many of us were volunteers who did this. I began to volunteer in 2007, so I took off from work and I didn't get paid. That was a sacrifice for me, but you do it because you care about your community.

Today I work full-time as the general manager and on-air personality for La Más Grande radio station. I started in 2013 in sales, based on the recommendation of a friend, and then I was offered a radio program. I was given equipment training and now I'm also a DJ. One program I was asked to start is called Nostros en América [We, in America], which is on Saturday mornings. I invite different speakers to talk on community topics. This has been a wonderful opportunity, and I love it. I get to promote programs and other resources so people in the Latino community know about them. I just bought my own home and will finalize my citizenship process sometime in 2017.

Sylvia Garcia

Sylvia Ruth Garcia was born on May 30, 1952, in Waukesha, Wisconsin, and, as a University of Wisconsin–Madison student, she helped to create the University's Chican@ and Latin@ Studies Program. Sylvia helped create the Latino Health Council of Madison and has been active with the Women of Color Network.

Ethnic identity: Chicana, Mexican American, and/or Latina.

Do you consider yourself an activist? Yes.

How do you define community activism? Activism has typically been associated with the whole notion of being out there rabble-rousing, challenging the system and all. Activism, for me, means that if you see something wrong in your community, it calls for a measure of your involvement. I think that activism is working toward a solution for that group affected by societal, economic, or political problems. In my case, that has been the Mexican American/Chicano/Latino communities.

Areas of activism: Education and health.

Location of activism: Madison.

Years of activism: Since 1973.

Early Years in Waukesha

I grew up in a community that was very insular, what might be considered the poor side of town. Ours was the barrio of Waukesha, which was surrounded by three or four factories. A lot of Latinos moved to the area because they were working poor. Almost every one of the Latino families had a connection with someone who was working at one of those places. And so it was geographically defined as an area of working-class individuals, though not necessarily a poor community. I think it was insulated to the point that people did not know a lot about the surrounding community, which would be the white community. Pretty much the original dominant culture was Mexican or Mexican American. Over the years, a lot of the Puerto Rican people moved into the area and also worked in the factories. The area was originally an Italian neighborhood, but as they started moving out, it became a Latino ghettoized neighborhood of Mexican Americans and Puerto Ricans.

I started in a public school called Hadfield. And then in about third grade, my parents switched my sister and me to St. Joseph's Catholic grade school. I attended fourth through the eighth grade. It was a racially mixed school. I think that's because of the school mission. The nuns, who were most of the teachers, enforced fairness. The student diversity helped to make us more understanding of each other. In other words, there weren't as many stereotypes or barriers as I would later feel in high school.

I think I always did identify myself as Mexican American and with the knowledge that my ethnicity made me different from the majority group. I remember sitting in my third grade class and looking at my arm and seeing that I was darker than the other kids in the room and thinking to myself, "Why?" I mean, I was just questioning: why the difference? And I think that even at that young age of a third grader, I began to question the issues of my color and why the way I looked was different. I tried to process what was my place as a result.

I had the biggest shock when I went from the eighth grade to Waukesha South public high school and began to interact more with individuals of the more dominant culture, and it became very apparent that we were walking on different paths and that there were inequities. I'll give an example. I became a part of our class Spanish club and they were picking the officers. Two white girls were elected to the positions of president and vice president. A white male student and I were both candidates for secretary, and even though I was more involved in the class than he was, he ended up being picked by my teacher, Mrs. Bowen. I don't know if it was discrimination or not, but it felt pretty bad to me. Her reason seemed to be a little flimsy. But those were the kinds of microaggressions that I experienced throughout my high school time. In an English class, I was made fun of by two white males for my opinion on a book review, and you know, there were snickers because of the terminology that I used; those were the kinds of things where you realize right from the beginning that things were not right.

I remember going also to the Brookfield mall, a mall in an even more white, suburban area, and my mother, who had a darker complexion, had just gotten a permanent; it was really tight. I remember two white guys going to their car and one of them actually called my mom "Aunt Jemima." I was so angry that I actually went over to their car and kicked it. That didn't help matters, because one of the guys came to my mom's car and kicked it. My anger just got the best of me.

Another remembrance of navigating race was trying to follow in the footsteps of a fellow student who was popular. She became one of the cheerleaders of our basketball or football team. I do know at that point I tried to be white, like her, to be able to gain benefits from the white culture, though I knew that I was living in two different worlds. I wasn't going to be white enough for the white community, and if I tried to embrace ideas from a white perspective, then I would not be acceptable in my Latino community. I didn't really fit into either world.

In 1968, I got involved with the Young Democrats from high school friends who were very active. Cathy and her brother, Robby, were both in the Young Democrats group, and their grandmother was very active in the Democratic Party. They were the ones who persuaded me to become more political in the issues of social policy-making for working-class people. That's when I kind of started realizing that a lot of Democrats were from the working class, and I began to be more involved in class issues. Through assessing the candidates and what they stood for and going to a state Democratic Party conference where they discussed issues and policies, I noticed the similarities between the white working class and our culture, which was all working class.

LIFE AT UW–MADISON

I had one or two girlfriends from Waukesha who were supposed to go to UW–Madison. One of my Latina friends and I applied together. We got accepted, and we tried to get housing together. For one reason or another, she was not allowed to come, and so I came up here looking for my place at the university. I didn't know how to navigate the system, and my parents didn't know anything about how to help, so I was really a mess in my freshman year. I didn't know my academics. You've seen those posters with those little kitties with their claws in the wall trying to hang on? That was me during my freshman year. It wasn't until my sophomore year that I became more attuned to the academic environment and more serious about my studies. I did find a group of Latino graduate students; we got together and found ways to celebrate our cultures, our identities, since we came from different ethnicities. It was at that point in time when I started integrating myself into the group.

Toward the end of that school year I got the internship to work with the US Department of Justice. Pancho Aviles hired me to work on this study of the political climate here in Madison. The Department of Justice wanted me and another person to try to get more information about the situation between police-community relations for the Latino populations in the Madison area. I reached out to the Organization of Hispanic America. It was the predecessor of Centro Hispano in Madison, a nonprofit agency working primarily with the Latino communities. We put the survey together and went to different households to ask them questions. This was hard at times because our communities are pretty private and did not want to share the incidents they had with the law in the Madison area. The results were supposedly used as the basis for obtaining funding for the Department of Justice to develop different types of programs to assist Latinos. I think this was my first awakening to what people in this community were going through and how there were similarities with my home community.

I started really getting serious about things with my introduction to the students affiliated with La Raza Unida (LRU) student organization [which was affiliated with the La Raza Unida Party (LRUP)]. They were primarily graduate students. One of them came from Racine, and he was studying to become a lawyer; another was a woman from Milwaukee. It wasn't until Carlos Reyes started recruiting from Racine and San Antonio, Texas, that the purpose of that group sort of shifted to be much more political. Many of those recruited were males. There was a certain amount of militancy they brought with them. I think their experiences of discrimination in their own communities are why they brought a sense of anger with them. I decided to become more involved because I wanted to make sure that I made a difference. I don't know if that's good or not, but that's when I started to feel a little bit more involved with our Latino/Chicano group.

The main influencers of our student group were Francisco Rodriguez,

Sylvia Garcia (center) participates in a La Raza Unida Student Organization demonstration at UW–Madison in the mid-1970s. SOMOS LATINAS PROJECT ORAL HISTORIES AND COLLECTED PAPERS

Jesus Salas, and some other Latino men who worked in state jobs. They were trying to get the group charged up with the notion that the university needed to provide a Chicano Studies department. I went to these meetings. We discussed things like the party's ideology and strategies of how to get a department and to increase access, retain students, and other services for Latino students. The group organized a picket line at South Hall, along with other highly visible protests. We sought a department of Chicano Studies; this was 1974.

When I returned to UW–Madison after my sophomore year, I found that there had been a division between the Latino men and most of the women students in our LRU student group. I remember women in the group, like Ramona Villarreal, who decided to leave the group. It was very disappointing because I knew they cared about the issues, and I went to them to see if we could work something out. By that point, they were too disenfranchised and would not even let me approach them. They did not return to our group during my last two years at the university. I made a decision to continue with LRUP, and later I was elected the president, although I felt as if I had little power. While I appreciated being elected to this role, it was clear that some of the Latino students seemed to have difficulty with a Latina as president. Others were very supportive. There were times, however, when I felt that I was placed in a token role. At the same time I was navigating the underlying, and sometimes strong, currents of sexism within my own Latino community. There was plenty that was unresolved.

Our organization was successful while I was president. UW–Madison started the Chicano Studies Program. Jesus Salas and others played a pivotal role in making this happen. Jesus had good connections with the state legislature, which allocated funds for the program in 1975. When I graduated from college that same year, I went back to my community in Waukesha and started working for La Casa de Esperanza in 1976, in job development and coordinating the ESL [English as a Second Language] and ABE [Adult Basic Education] classes. I started here because after my experience with the Latino students, it was clear to me that I wanted to serve the Latino community.

By 1986, I had already returned to Madison and was raising two children. That year, I joined the Wisconsin Women of Color Network. I was attracted to the organization because it was multiracial, multiethnic, and it had an empowerment mission for women to develop our skills and build alliances among us. Each year, the organization held an annual conference with many excellent workshops for women at all career levels, and it was held in different parts of the state. We brought in keynote speakers and other presenters. I became president of the network in 1994.

During that same year, two other Latina friends and I started Madison's Latino Health Council (LHC). I became involved because I was diagnosed with cancer in 1990, and I had finished my chemotherapy in 1992. That year, I joined the regional board of the American Cancer Society and advocated that the organization should have a greater presence in the Latino community. The LHC was first under the auspices of the American Cancer Society, which had provided some funds for our work. Eventually, it became self-sustaining. We organized annual health fairs to outreach and educate other Latinas about cancer—to look for the signs of cancer

Sylvia Garcia, 2014. ELOISA GÓMEZ

and to know about the resources available to them and their families. We branched out to address other health issues affecting Latinos, such as diabetes and heart disease.

For sixteen years, I worked for UW–Madison. In 2008, I began working for the Chican@ and Latin@ Studies Program as academic program administrator. I was also one of the advisors to the annual Mujer Latina Conference organized by UW–Madison Latina students. My cancer is in remission, and I continue to do what I can do. In 2016, I retired from the university. I received a very nice recognition from the university for my assistance to the students in the development and implementation of the Mujer Latina Conferences.

Yolanda Garza

*Yolanda Garza was born on March 5, 1955, on Chicago's South Side.
Yolanda moved to Wisconsin in 1983 and helped to form the Latina
Task Force, a Latina advocacy group in Wisconsin, and the Wisconsin
Hispanic Council on Higher Education. She later became an assistant
dean at UW–Madison and volunteered with various organizations on
and off campus, including the Madison Police and Fire Commission.
Throughout her professional career, she advocated for services for the
Latino communities in Madison, where she lived and worked.*

Ethnic identity: Mexican American or Chicana.

Do you consider yourself a community activist? Yes, I've worked on
issues directly impacting the community.

How do you define community activism? Working collaboratively to
address issues/concerns impacting the community.

Areas of activism: Education, health, civics, politics, Latina empowerment and racial/ethnic-specific (Native American, Asian, and African
American) issues.

Location of activism: Chicago, Whitewater, and Madison.

Years of activism: Since 1969.

EARLY INFLUENTIAL EXPERIENCES

I was fortunate in that my mother was very active on the South Side of Chicago, and so by attending meetings with my mother and others, I watched
them address issues way back then. As a young girl, I think that helped
me feel confident. I used some of their strategies when I first assisted in
organizing a walkout in my eighth grade class. I did that because I felt that
there were some injustices that were taking place. I saw my mother and her
friends and neighbors stand up to injustices. I was impressed because these
were women who were united on issues. They understood one another's

perspectives, even if they might not have agreed on every aspect of an issue. When they went forward, you didn't know that there were some disagreements among [them]. I thought that was really smart of them. I think oftentimes people get caught up on personal issues, and that means a response to a community issue doesn't move forward.

I can think of one example where the women were concerned about housing issues that were affecting Latinos on the South Side of Chicago. My mother and one of the other women contacted some high person in Chicago's Public Housing Authority; they asked to have a meeting with them. They went and talked about who was and wasn't getting access to public housing on the South Side. They were concerned that racial discrimination against Latinos was occurring. That was a long time ago, so I don't remember the outcome. What I do remember is that they were not afraid of taking on issues. If nothing else, they let [the Housing Authority] know that they were aware of some discrepancies and they would continue to monitor this issue. The South Side of Chicago is often considered the "forgotten" community because it is so far south. You'd hear about things that were going on in certain parts of the city, like the West Side and that. A lot of things were not happening for the people who lived on the far southeast side of Chicago. These women spoke up, and that was something I really admired. The other thing I learned from them was that one doesn't have to go banging on doors to be heard. Everybody has their own style of bringing issues to the forefront and making people aware of issues. So for some people it might be the appropriate approach to use, but these women didn't do that. They didn't have to raise their voices; they were just very united, and they wanted results.

I think my own activism started in eighth grade, because my community for me was my classroom. I was one of the active leaders in organizing a class walkout. It didn't happen because two minutes before we were supposed to walk out, my parents appeared at the door. Someone had leaked the information. My dad didn't necessarily think that that was being a great leader, because I went to a private school and was not obeying what the nuns thought was appropriate behavior. I just told my mother that I was following in her footsteps. She did not buy my reasoning!

Our actions were in response to our teacher, a nun, who we felt was overly strict, almost resentful as a teacher. We were predominately Mexican American students. She gave us a strong impression that she did not want to be with us, and that meant that she did not want to be around Mexican students. The last straw was when she was going to deprive us of our graduation party and other standard activities associated with graduation. She offered no explanation on this decision, and she didn't give us an opportunity to share our concerns. Most of us felt that we had a right to at least express our concerns, so our response was a planned walkout to get graduation privileges restored. There were about thirty classmates. Some of us agreed to take aside other classmates and get their support. We thought everybody was in agreement, but it turned out that someone leaked the plan. While the protest was prevented, I felt that the effort was well orchestrated. We did obtain a small compromise in the end.

I next went to St. Francis de Sales High School, which was predominately white. I often share this story because there was no doubt about the interpretation of this action. Once we had to work on a classroom project after school. I was told by one of my classmates that I was not allowed to go to her home because her parents didn't want any Mexicans coming over. I said, "That's okay, my mother is a great cook. I don't need to go to your home to eat or anything like that." So I never participated in any other projects after that. My father had told me early on that not everybody would be open-minded and I needed to understand that. Well, I experienced what being closed-minded meant in a very blatant way and it hurt, but I refused to accept that I was the problem; it was the closed-minded person's problem, not mine.

TEACHING ON CHICAGO'S SOUTH SIDE

With the undergraduate degree I received in 1977, I became a teacher. I taught at the same school that I attended myself, Our Lady of Guadalupe. Later, I became the assistant principal. I was the first Mexican assistant principal in the school's history. I got very involved with the community, making sure that our students were safe after school. That happened immediately after I became a teacher. A group of professionals came together that included a policeman, a fireman, teachers, social workers, and others. There were maybe eight of us. I mean, it was our generation that had gotten a college education. We formed a committee to find financing and promote athletic activities so that our students were off the streets because there was such a high crime rate. In the past, sports programs mainly targeted the boys. It was probably my first initiative to address opportunities for young girls. Sports was a vehicle to develop life skills, like working in a team, and to develop physical skills that could build confidence. I appreciated these years, but in 1981, I made a decision to go to graduate school to continue my studies.

CREATING COMMUNITY IN WISCONSIN

I moved to Wisconsin in 1983 after I accepted a job offer at the University of Wisconsin–Whitewater. I had already obtained my master's degree. About a year later, I found out that my male counterparts with the same or similar job responsibilities and with the same educational background and skills were making more money than me. I was raised to be grateful to have a job. No one told me about how to negotiate a salary. I never took a job because of the money, but I definitely was not going to accept inequality. I was not asking to get paid more, just the same. I also experienced harassment from a former [Latino] staff member who started false rumors about me, and he was being supported by several other Latino men. I confronted this man and told him that I would pursue a lawsuit if he didn't stop. He took me seriously and did, but by that time, I decided that I didn't want to be affiliated with a place that promoted inequality. When the administration discovered I was moving on, they wanted me to stay. I was one of the only females in that division and type of position, and was the lowest paid. I left in 1985.

When I first came to Wisconsin, I honestly didn't quite understand some Latino men from here, the way I was treated by some of them and how I saw them treat some women with various levels of hostility on and off campus, like not [inviting them] to important community meetings or not offering leadership opportunities. I remember calling my mother up and saying, "I'm not sure what is going on here, Mom. Is it because the men eat so much cheese?" I did not experience this level of sexism where I grew up. I am not saying men from Illinois supported us 100 percent. The main difference for me was that Mexicans and Puerto Ricans might have had big differences, but when it came to addressing issues facing Latinos, we united. My personal feeling is there was a nationalistic attitude by the Chicano/Tejano men in Wisconsin, and maybe they felt challenged by women leaders and those not willing to be confined by typical gender roles. Where I came from, we figured out, to a greater extent, how to get past gender and inter-ethnic conflict.

Working with the WHCHE and the Latina Task Force

I think two organizations that were very influential for me in continuing my activism were WHCHE, the Wisconsin Hispanic Council on Higher Education, and the Latina Task Force (LTF). I came to Wisconsin and I knew only one person who lived in Madison, and I lived in Whitewater, about forty-five miles south. Otherwise, I didn't know a soul. The people of these two organizations welcomed me to Wisconsin, and many of the LTF members were involved in WHCHE; that was really wonderful. I was involved with WHCHE at UW–Whitewater starting in 1983. One important thing about WHCHE was that the men affiliated with the group were very open to Latina leadership, such as Luis Garza, Eddie Guzman, Felipe Rodriguez, and others. WHCHE would hold meetings on various campuses throughout the state. Their contact on that campus would sponsor the meeting and recruit the chancellor or one of the high-level administrators to attend the meeting. This was an opportunity to talk about the importance of access and retention of both Latino students and staff. I helped to get WHCHE's visit organized at the UW–Whitewater campus sometime between 1983 and 1985. I also cochaired one of the WHCHE's student conferences, which occurred in 1985 at my campus.

The LTF was a perfect example of strong women who were not afraid of speaking up on issues that were important. I became a member, and we worked toward addressing issues like housing, employment, health, education, and civic issues. I helped specifically on health and education issues. We developed position papers to advocate for more services for Latinas and their families, hosted a weekend training, and were involved in other advocacy efforts. Many of the LTF meetings were held in the evenings, mostly in Milwaukee after work hours, and I would drive forty-five minutes each way. I didn't mind because we were not afraid to challenge the status quo. Even when the LTF ended, I maintained many of the friendships from those years of working together.

Life at UW–Madison

Dr. Vernon Lattin had been my supervisor when I was a graduate student. He and his wife encouraged me to apply at UW–Whitewater, as well as to join WHCHE. He later went to work for the UW system and was someone I looked up to. I started as an assistant dean at UW–Madison in 1985. There were very few Latinos on campus, and though small, we formed an organization, the Latino Academic Staff, for both men and women. WHCHE had started to slow down as a statewide organization as some of the leadership began changing jobs. I felt that a WHCHE-like organization needed to be on our campus. Just like students who needed support, Latino faculty and staff needed stronger connections; we networked among ourselves, and it really helped me stay sane. We first started as a way to share concerns and help each other problem solve, but then we started to observe that there were institutional issues, too. We met with the chancellor once or twice a year and were provided with a small budget to handle administrative costs. One thing that came out of our discussions with one of the chancellors was the lack of promotional opportunities for academic staff. We noticed that Latinos were mostly hired at entry-level positions and not at mid- to higher-level positions. Hiring improved, but overall, this requires ongoing attention and support. The organization still exists, but I am not a member since I retired.

Making a Strategic Decision

In 1989, I was recruited to serve on the Madison Police and Fire Commission by our dean of students, Mary Rouse. She had been asked by Madison police chief David Couper to recommend someone to serve as UW–Madison's designee, and Mary asked me. She knew I was familiar with the judicial process given my work helping students whose on- or off-campus experiences involved them with the criminal or judicial systems. I saw it as a great opportunity primarily because I wanted to see more racial and ethnic diversity among the fire and police department employees. I served seven and a half years altogether; this was between the years 1989 and 1996. The commission term was five years; however, in 1989, I first completed the remaining two years of Gladis Benavides's term, who left the commission due to health reasons. I then completed my own five-year term after. The appointment was extended an additional six months to help wrap up a pending case. I served as a vice president of the commission from 1995 to 1996. I felt diversity was important for both departments because the people of color communities in Madison were growing, particularly among the Hmong, African American, and Latino populations. I believed the workforce should reflect the community it served, as well as understand the culture of these communities and their languages.

When we hired the first Chicana fire chief [Debra Amesqua], there was a lot of resistance. It was a time when many of the men were opposed to it. She was the only female candidate that made it as a finalist. I felt that she had all the skills and experience that we were looking for. Yes, there were a couple of candidates that might have had some years more, but it wasn't

Yolanda Garza (center) with Debra Amesqua (left) after she was hired as fire chief in 1996. SOMOS LATINAS PROJECT ORAL HISTORIES AND COLLECTED PAPERS

like she didn't have any experience. Given what we were hearing from the employees of the fire department, we thought she was a good fit. It was unanimous with the commission as far as I recall.

When the decision was announced, it was horrible; there was a lot of media about her being a minority and an outsider; it seemed less focused on her skills and experiences. Historically, police and fire commission administrators were hired from within. Of course, you know, I was the only woman of color on the commission, and there was some discussion of whether I was pushing for her because she was a Latina. There were other things. I mean, she came from the outside, but it was more than that. It was more than her being from the outside. She was a woman and, God forbid, she was a woman of color. In the long run, she did fantastic. She won over most of the men who were opposed to her getting the position; they loved her. She had issues like anybody else would have had in this department. She did a great job. She has since retired. She started in 1993 or 1994 and retired in 2012.

I also helped start the Mujer Latina Conference that is held on campus at UW–Madison. In 1993, I encouraged and supported Latina student leadership to host this annual conference addressing issues that impact our Latina faculty, staff, and students and community members. The conferences have included difficult issues like date rape and domestic violence. Other topics presented have been to build leadership, and we brought in speakers from across the United States.

LIFE TODAY

I retired in 2011, but I'm still active. I have slowed down, but I am still working on issues that I think are important. I worked on my sister-in-law's [Susan Sadlowski Garza's] campaign. She ran for alderwoman in the largest ward in the city of Chicago and won against the political machine. I am working on my family's genealogy, and I help out at Mexican Fiesta in Milwaukee to help people learn how to research their genealogy online. People want to better connect with their heritage and culture.

I have been serving on the Somos Latinas Advisory Committee for the past five years, and I helped raise money in Madison for it in 2015. I have enjoyed this role immensely. I think it is important work because

I really believe our voices have not been sought after and have even been silenced. Very few of our women's contributions can be found in text or history books; we are just not there. Yet we know that we are hardworking women and have made tremendous contributions. It's time for the voices to be heard and for the younger generations to understand our history.

Yolanda Garza, 2010. © UNIVERSITY OF WISCONSIN–MADISON UNIVERSITY COMMUNICATIONS

I received the Our Lady of Guadalupe Distinguished Alumni Award in 1985. I was the first recipient of this award. Another award: the UW–Madison Students' MCSC [Multicultural Student/Student of Color], received in 2003. This was from students involved in student leadership; it was in recognition of the support I provided to them over the years. I received two of the highest awards that academic staff can receive on campus. One was the Chancellor's Award in 2006, sponsored by the Student Personnel Association, and the Chancellor's Award for Excellence to the University in 2008.

Debora Gil Casado

Debora Gil Rodriguez was born on December 1, 1957, in Ashland, Wisconsin, and has lived in Wisconsin since then. After her studies at UW–Madison, Debora became a high school teacher. She has taught in the Madison School District since 1982. In 2001, she helped cofound Nuestro Mundo Community School, Madison's first Spanish immersion charter school. She is an education advocate within the Madison School District.

Ethnic identity: I identify myself as Latina. I also think we need to be respectful of everyone's different community, so that self-identification can change. There may be multiple ways to define yourself.

Do you consider yourself an activist? Yes, I do.

How do you define community activism? My definition of a community activist is someone who takes on the role of leader or follower and gets involved in any way, shape, or form to change things in their community.

Areas of activism: Education, health, and politics.

Location of activism: Madison, Wisconsin.

Years of activism: Since 1975.

Early Influential Experiences

My parents are from Spain, and they were recruited to come to the United States. There was a national recruitment for people to teach foreign languages in rural communities. I think my father saw it as an opportunity to do something different. He worked at a bank and decided that he wanted to do something different. He heard about this program recruiting foreign language teachers, and he applied. They didn't really need special teaching degrees, so he ended up teaching in a grade school.

Since childhood, I was aware of an accumulation of things—an awareness that there were these differences among Latinos and non-Latinos.

My mother's English was not very good, so I had to spend a lot of time translating for her, which gave me a lot of power. I was aware of it from her point of view. She saw people, many who were trying to help, treat us differently because I spoke English perfectly well. We both saw the different intonations [with which] they talked to each of us, as if our roles were reversed. And then there were differences among Latino groups, in terms of country of origin. Most non-Latinos viewed us as all the same.

Another experience occurred in high school. One of my friends' parents decided to invite me to their country club. I remember her telling me, "You know, my parents are really worried about taking you out to dinner. They feel really strongly that they should help expose you to the real world, but they're concerned." So I asked, "Well, what are they talking about, not using the right fork? Or do they think I'm going to stand on a table and dance?" Her response was, "I don't know. I just wanted to let you know they're concerned." Well, that didn't help any, but she thought she was doing a good thing. Those were the kinds of things that showed the inequality among people. I'm sure I could come up with more, but I think those were kind of the defining moments, to say, "This is not okay, this needs to be changed."

To add to the complexity, I recognize white privilege, and yet, being white racially put me in a different place. For me, it really created a sense of a struggle of identity. Who am I? And I think the early struggles in college were really about defining identity, and I think that we Latinos were harsher on each other than many other people were.

Early Activism

My activism began in college. In high school, it was more about surviving. I was already living in Madison and went to Madison West High School. It wasn't until I got to campus that I learned political tools to understand things in a different way. Student activism against the Vietnam War and antiracism protests were occurring. I started at UW–Madison in 1975. Carlos Reyes had established a great recruiting program. He brought students from Texas, Puerto Rico, and lots of other places. When I arrived on campus, I started meeting people and heard about people already here who were doing organizing, and I said this was going to be my support system.

I first discovered a small group called MEChA [Movimiento Estudiantil Chican@ de Aztlan, a national Chicano college student organization]. There were about fifty to seventy-five students in it. I learned there was a schism in the group because the women said, "We've had it. We're tired of making all the tortillas and being in the background. We should have an equal say in what we are doing."

The women formed their own group called Las Adelitas.[1] I remember going along with that and being a part of the self-empowerment efforts, but it didn't quite fit me. I think that when we talked about self-discovery, there seemed to be a very small window of what it meant and didn't mean to be a Chicana. Lots of expectations, you know. Some people who were in the group had the right skin color but didn't speak any Spanish. I kind of felt marginalized. There was me that didn't quite fit in. Not that people didn't accept me, but in my search for identity, it wasn't quite the fit, and I didn't want to feel like I was pretending.

I sort of left the group and was looking around. At that time, there was another group that started up, called Eco Pan-Americano. These students were primarily Latin Americans and Central Americans, and other people like me in terms of a Spanish-oriented home country. The university was trying to set aside some funds to help people of color on campus, and so they asked the different groups to have a representative to help decide how to spend this little pot of money. I was the Eco Pan-Americano representative on this committee. Others on that committee were from MEChA, and Native American, African American, and Asian student organizations. That made a big difference.

Being on this committee gave me a broader perspective on racial/ethnic communities. There were two women who represented the Asian student group who were from New York. I had unconsciously accepted a stereotype of Asians being well-off and all smart. We took a trip to New York one semester because we were interested in starting a women of color class. So we went to New York to interview some professors. We did the road trip together, and we stayed in one of their families' houses, which was in the middle of the Asian ghetto. It was not like the stereotype I imagined,

---

[1] Las Adelitas is a historical term for female fighters during the Mexican Revolution of 1910, and Chicana student groups across the country later adopted this term.

so I realized I needed to build a different perspective about our ethnicities and what that means about relating to one another. About the same time, I became involved in an organization called Committee against Racism. It broadened my perspectives even more because they accepted people who were also white European Americans and were very committed to confronting racism publicly.

During the late 1970s into the early 1980s, I was involved on many different fronts, including antiracist efforts statewide and nationally. One involved a student campaign that started when the university decided to address retention on campus. They were going to require that anybody who graduated from a high school who had been in the bilingual program would have to pass an English test, as if they were a foreign student. Campus protests followed this decision. Students decided to take over a portion of South Hall. It still took a long time to convince the university that this was discriminatory. At that time, we didn't have any law students in our groups who could have brought a case, which probably would have been the saner way of doing it. There were also counterprotests to Nazi rallies. Once I responded to a request by chicken farmers who were a part of the Mississippi Poultry Workers Union; they were being targeted by the Ku Klux Klan. They needed people to come spend a couple weeks at a time helping them. Several of us spent a week down there helping to build houses and provide them support. Other people stayed longer to establish the union.

The years in college challenged me to think about my own ethnicity. Others were dealing with that, too. It was not easy on any of us. I often wondered, do we have to be stamped and marked by our ethnicity? Back then it was like, "I want you to see me, I want you to acknowledge me, and I want you to allow me into the power structures. I do not want to be marginalized."

During college, I taught myself how to organize. I was willing to put in the time, and ended up in these positions of being a representative. I learned lots of skills in terms of negotiating. How and when do you begin to confront? Is it okay to give in and just take what you can at that moment, knowing it's really a longtime war that you can win at lots of different places? Organizational skills I learned included getting people together on a bus to go to a protest. This included anticipating whether we needed to worry about the police and planning for people who could not get arrested for a variety of reasons. When you are organizing, you really need to take many things into account in your planning, and I see how that influenced my work on Nuestro Mundo [Our World] Community School.

FOUNDING THE LATINO TEACHERS ASSOCIATION

Around 1985, while I was teaching at Madison East High School, there were about four or five of us, including Karen Herrera and Tim Valdez, who were in the district and really concerned about the curriculum. We started out by trying to change the curriculum to be more culturally appropriate. So one of the things we did was to create these traveling educational kits of authentic artifacts that K–12 teachers could use in their classrooms. For instance, our most popular one was the United Farm Workers. We created three or four educational kits to be available to teachers. In this process, we found that there was a support system for us, that we could get together and do a variety of different things.

At East High School, I had started out working with an increasing number of settled migrant students and their families in the district. I traveled from school to school, so I knew where people were located and things like that. Back then, there was an expectation that a classroom teacher could be called out of a classroom and given the additional duty to translate. Once a secretary called me to translate. I remember going to the office, and she hands me the phone, and she tells me, "I want you to tell them that their child has lice and that this is what they have to do." I said, "Lice? I don't know how to say 'lice' in Spanish. I'm not walking around with a dictionary in my hands." There is the expectation that simply speaking the language gave you those kinds of translation skills. We wanted to help, but those who ended up in that position also wondered why the district didn't hire someone to handle this need and compensate those asked to do it.

As a group, we decided that what we really needed at East High School was a bilingual social worker. We got people from all over Madison, organized schoolkids, and, for the first time, got Latino parents to speak in front of the school board. We did the whole nine yards, and we got the position. It was the first dedicated position, and it took a community effort to make it happen. Next, we felt that written documents to parents needed to be translated into Spanish. If you have to send a note going to parents who speak little to no English, shouldn't it be in Spanish? It was this constant push and pull over many years.

Founding the Nuestro Mundo Charter School

Then around 2000–2001, there was a resurgence to organize because the number of non-English-speaking students was increasing. We had the English Language Learners (ELL) program, then it was called English as a Second Language. Another group of activist teachers from a Madison high school was coming forward. My friend Bryan Grau, who was also a high school teacher and had also been on the Committee against Racism at UW–Madison, called me and said, "I have a radical idea for you." I said, "Oh, that's not always a good sign." We were both involved in bilingual education advocacy and, in college, had a lot of experience of community organizing, so we knew each other very well.

He said, "We've been questioning ourselves as to why we are constantly asking for changes. [The system] makes us beg for them. We really need to do something different." He had been to a conference where he had been introduced to the concept of a charter school. State laws had passed, and so he said, "Let's sit down, start talking to people, and see what we can do. I think that we can start a school. The numbers are there." Graduation rates were just poor. Seventy percent of ELL learners were still dropping out in the Madison school district. And so we started having a conversation and got a group together, including Bryan's wife. I was cleaning out some of my old papers, and I found some old notes I had taken from the earlier protests. We had listed fifteen to twenty demands. Many of them from twelve years ago were still unmet.

A group of us convened and asked ourselves: What will this look like? What are our goals? What do we really want? One of the goals I had in mind was breaking the "glass ceiling" for our students and families. I wanted our Latino and other youth of color to complete the graduation requirements, which would break the language and academic glass ceilings and further integrate our youth into the general society. Based on my own personal experiences and my observations as an educator, I wanted to ensure that students would not have to feel different or less than others because of their language skills. Being proficient in two languages would give them greater options to be able to do worldwide travel or whatever they wanted to do in their lives. Overall, that's what the group also wanted.

We sifted through and studied various academic models, like weekend classes, and decided on a more structural approach. We came across this study that had been done nationally about different programs that followed students for twelve years in terms of their success rates: Latino students who either had no access to bilingual programming, just ELL programming, bilingual schools, and "immersion" programs. The students who were most successful, scoring the highest in English and in Spanish, had been in immersion programs. So we said, "Ah, well, that might be the ticket."

We met with community members and checked with them, and then coming back we said, "Well, if we open this charter school, what do we want it to be?" Another goal we established was that it would be community based, meaning the parents would have a level of control with the school. This was important for another critical reason: we did not want the school district to make decisions for the school. We knew that we could not always be assured that school board advocates, like Juan José Lopez, would be there to support us in the future. We needed the parents to be involved in the decision-making process of the school and to feel included in all aspects of the school community. We already knew parents who didn't work outside the home, but either did not feel welcomed in the schools or did not feel they had skills to offer the students or school.

Once we decided on the charter school path, we held numerous community events to explain and convince people that this was the way to go. Interestingly enough, we had more support from Anglos in the community, initially, than many in the Latino community. I think one fear was that this was for the university parents; this was going to help them. Second of all, there was a concern, particularly for Latino immigrant parents, who asked, "Why do I want to send them to a program that teaches Spanish?" So it took us maybe three years to build enough core support in the community to put this together. For these and the ten years that followed, I had a full-time job as a high school teacher, and, for the most part, it really was a second full-time job.

We also used the formation of the Latino Teachers Association to call upon the union to support the charter school proposal. We had a big stumbling block with MTI [Madison Teachers, Inc.], which is ironic because both Bryan and I had been deeply involved in the union for many years. Progressive Dane of Wisconsin [a labor-community coalition] was totally against us because they viewed charter schools as serving only the purpose of the right wing. We never got their support, even though we very patiently explained to them that charter schools are a tool and it depends on how you build them. We absolutely insisted we would not accept a school that didn't have union representation. Finally, the last time we met with John Matthews, MTI's executive director, I remember Bryan and I sat over coffee with John and he finally said, "Okay, I won't oppose you." But that took us a good two or three years to get the union's support.

We then went to the Madison School Board and the Madison School District administration and said, "We would like to apply for charter status. What do we have to do?" At that time, Arthur Rainwater was the superintendent, and he was just adamant that this was just not going to fly. I said, "We're going to do this with or without your help. There is a state law, so we want to know how to do this." The school board would not help us find the information, but did require us to cost out implementing a charter school. After much table pounding, they finally said, "Okay, here is the charter process, and in this application, you have to tell us how much the school is going to cost." And we said, "Well, we don't know the school costs." We had no idea what it cost to physically set up a new classroom! After some effort on our part, they mentioned that a school had recently opened and we could probably find records online to identify the cost of setting up a school. So my task was to look at this information and try to estimate the per classroom cost.

We then submitted a formal planning grant proposal to the school board for approval. At this meeting, we were there until 1:00 a.m. Parent after parent spoke in support of a charter school; most of their remarks had to be translated into English. Fortunately, Juan José Lopez was open to learning more about the proposal. Without his support, we would have been dead in the water. At one crucial meeting, Superintendent Rainwater said, "It's going to cost a million dollars to start this school up, just in terms of busing alone." And one of the school board members said, "It's going to cost a million dollars to bus kids? Can I have that contract?" There was an awareness that he meant to scare them off. And it was so unreasonable that some of the school board members supported the proposal.

We originally wanted our own building. Location was very important because it would convey who the school would be accessible to. In terms of student population, our ideal was to have one-third primarily Spanish speakers, one-third bilingual, and one-third English speakers. We believed the mixture would create a good atmosphere for all learners. Once we knew the school's location, we would have a team of twenty to thirty people going door-to-door canvassing on Saturday mornings in South Side Latino neighborhoods. We said we'd go there first, once we knew the school's location, and find people who might be interested in sending their children to the school. We very purposefully did not advertise in other communities. Our group explained the program to residents and encouraged them to become involved in the planning meetings. We really wanted parents to see themselves on an equal basis with those planning the school as we were conscious of our biases in terms of money, race, and different ethnicities.

For the final school board vote on the charter school proposal, we had charter school members from the Milwaukee area testify. The hallways of the school building where the meeting was held were crowded with people and parents who were there to speak or show their support by being present. We brought in treats. The kids were sitting in the hallway, and we hunkered down. We talked with one another, and some of us were helping people with speech writing. We had about eight hours of testimony from parents, students, and other supporters saying they wanted the school.

Running Nuestro Mundo

The charter school was approved by the school board with stipulations. We named our school Nuestro Mundo, and it started with just one grade, kindergarten, and then we added a grade each year until the fifth grade. It became a school within a school, and the charter was for five years. We were placed in the Frank Allis School. There were two principals: the existing principal and the Nuestro Mundo principal, who was bilingual. Some English-speaking teachers were laid off. Students who were at Frank Allis got priority to get into the program, and then there was a lottery for the rest of the people who wanted to get their kids in.

Nuestro Mundo had an impact in the district. We had a strong commitment to ensure that all parents had a voice, and we knew from the onset that the traditional communication model for non- or limited-English-speaking parents was for parents and their translator to sit in the back of a meeting room. The translator translates, then, everything that's going on. Or you have the translator up in front, and the meeting takes twice as long because everything has to be said in English and then everything has to be said in Spanish, and if someone needed to say something in Spanish, then you would go in the opposite direction. So you know meetings will take forever. We really wanted parents to be able to say things to each other, we are really talking about a community. You need to be able to speak to another person by looking them in the eyes. And so one of the things that we did was that we wrote a grant and got an interpreter machine. So afterward, whenever we had parent meetings, every parent would walk through the door and get a little headset. We had two translators, one who translated into English and the other who translated into Spanish. They would be in the back of the room with the equipment, and the parents could talk to each other, face to face, in their own language, while the other parents could listen to the translation. It made such an impact on community building in and outside the school.

We purposefully sought to build participation equally among all parents. We asked our Spanish-speaking parents to audio-record childhood songs or games. We asked them to record reading books on tape, too. This allowed their children to proudly say that this lesson or activity came from their parents. That gave them legitimacy and power. We wanted the different economic, racial, or ethnic groups of our parents to have equal values in the classroom. We knew that traditionally, if you are poor or if you don't speak the English language, it is very hard for you to be able to volunteer in the school or feel like you can help your children.

Where it was harder was when it came to getting school board members for Nuestro Mundo. We wanted to promote parent leadership, yet there needed to be a certain amount of reading and writing skills. Members had to review and discuss all the documentation from the school district, and this was in English, so it was harder to get that same level of equity. We kept plugging away and really trying to make sure that we had that community involvement at all levels in the school. Another role for parents was to serve on the parent committee that evaluated the principal. I became the first chairperson of Nuestro Mundo and, in some respects, the face of Nuestro Mundo, because of my skill set and being Latina.

After five years, the board of Nuestro Mundo rented a school building in the Monona district, which is very close to Frank Allis, so we now have our own building. They expanded the Nuestro Mundo program. From that, the school district has opened about four or five different dual-language immersion programs in Madison, but this is where the charter becomes important. The school board recently remapped their ELL program because it is so hard to find certified teachers. All the non-charter [ELL] programs have moved from a 90-10 model, [in which the ELL] kindergartens start with 90 percent Spanish. Every year they add on another 10 percent of English, so you know, first grade 80-20, until they get to 50-50. But all the school district [ELL] programs are now going 50-50, which is not as effective because they say that they can't find enough teachers. And so by doing it 50-50, they can have more English-speaking teachers in the program to be able to create that expansion.

Ending Direct Involvement with Nuestro Mundo

In 2009, I stopped being involved with Nuestro Mundo. Some of it was health reasons; some of it was exhaustion because, literally, for the previous ten years, it was a second full-time job. I mean, I was working all day and at night it would be phone calls, emails, writing pamphlets, and ongoing committee meetings. At a certain point, I just said, "I am not going to be involved in any committees, in terms of Nuestro Mundo." So I keep in touch, I see people; they shared with me that the school is going for their third five-year charter that may expand to the eighth grade.

Now I'm waiting for the next big thing. I will retire from the Madison School District in 2016 after thirty-two years of teaching. I'm thinking about doing small things, but things that are equally important. Part of that realization is that I don't always have to be the person with the megaphone, from my youth. There are other roles that are equally important. If you ever get a chance, there's a TED talk called "How to Start a Movement." You should see it. It's a three-minute video and this guy talks about it and he says, "You need people who take the chance. It's the follower. That is a form of leadership. Following and creating that base is also an equally important form of leadership." And so that's where I am right now, and I'm really kind of comfortable with that. I know that there are still many, many changes that need to happen. I hope that in my lifetime we truly embrace this concept of global citizens. We can accept each other, whatever our life experiences are, and not have to say, "You are this." Or you are black or you are brown. Or you are, you

Debora Gil Casado, 2014. AURORA WILLIAMSON

know, whatever, that we can take whatever it is. And I think we'll see more of that as people grow up in multiracial, multilingual communities, and embrace that.

In 2005, Nuestro Mundo was named the Charter School of the Year by the Wisconsin Charter School Association, and Madison Magazine Editor's Choice named Nuestro Mundo as a top charter school and recognized Bryan Grau and me for our roles with the school's development.

CARMEN IRELAND

Maria Del Carmen Villarreal González de Ireland was born in Monterrey, Nuevo Leon, Mexico, on July 16, 1941. Whether as a mother, teacher's aide, or college recruiter/advisor, Carmen used a variety of tools to improve educational opportunities for children, adults, and families in southeastern Wisconsin, especially in higher education.

Ethnic identity: Mexican American.

Do you consider yourself an activist? Yes, but I was not involved in much protesting.

How do you define community activism? Advocacy; being involved in the community and protecting our rights.

Areas of activism: Access to higher education, quality education, and equal opportunities.

Location of activism: Kenosha, Janesville, and southeastern Wisconsin.

Years of activism: Since 1972.

EARLY YEARS IN MEXICO

My parents met and got married in 1940, but my father died a few months before I was born, so it was really hard for me when I was growing up. I lived in Monterrey with my grandparents and my mother. She worked at Carta Blanca, a beer company. It was World War II, and there was a lot of work. She was one of the first women to go back to work after having a baby. In those days, once you got married, you couldn't go back to work.

Since my father had passed away, I was a fighter from the moment I was born. My mother would say that there were some things that I couldn't do because I didn't have a father. She always said, "You have to respect yourself so that others will respect you," so that made me upset and I would cry. At the same time, it gave me the character that I now have.

What may have influenced me from my childhood in Mexico was how

I learned at an early age the racial differences between who was wealthy and who was not. The school that I attended was a Catholic school that was supported by wealthy Catholics. There were things like, when we went to church, those girls would go in first. They would come in their white uniforms, and they looked like angels. Their families paid for some students like me, who could not afford the tuition at the school. Our uniforms were red. It was kind of upsetting that they needed to distinguish the two groups so visibly. I knew that I had to go to school and educate myself to move out of being in the middle/low-income class.

I was a bilingual secretary and had a very good position at the time I met my husband. I worked for two different accountants: one was for Allis-Chalmers de Mexico and the other was Hojalata y Lamina, SA, which was my last job. In both of them, I noticed I was doing the majority of the work, and I wasn't getting paid a quarter of what others were getting. I thought to myself, this isn't right. I am of an age where I should go back to school. So I started going at night until I graduated from preparatory school.

I met my husband and we married in Mexico. We had three children in three years, and I had my fourth child three years later. My husband kept saying that we could choose a place in the South [of the US]. I wanted to be closer to my family, but I knew I would not be happy to be in Texas. There was still overt racism. We were a mixed couple, so either he would come live with me in the Mexican community, or I would have to go live with him with the Americans but not be welcomed. I tanned so dark in summer that I didn't know which segregated bubbler [water fountain] to go to—the black or the white one. So finally I said let's go to Wisconsin, because my husband was born there. It's colder in Wisconsin, but the people are a little warmer than in the South, and I didn't like the racism this country was facing at the time.

Advocating for Youth and Families

At the very beginning, when I came here to Kenosha, my husband wanted me to stay home because he was always working. So I started volunteering. I was president of the Welcome Wagon Club, which was a good program for newcomers to know what's in the city. Some time later, I was volunteering at the church we belonged to, St. Mark's Catholic Church in Kenosha. I taught CCD classes [Confraternity of Christian Doctrine is a religious education program of the Roman Catholic Church] on Sundays. As my kids were growing up, I was growing up together with them and volunteering in the programs that they were part of. I also volunteered to teach migrant children English offered at a church location through Kenosha's social services department. Later, I started to integrate my children's lives with the children I worked with in sports programs. I encouraged them to join the basketball team or the soccer team because I wanted them to have the same opportunities. I also started what was probably the only Hispanic Girl Scout troop at the time. I also directed the whole Girl Scout program at the Catholic school my children attended.

So I was doing advocacy work even while volunteering. While my children were in a CYO [Catholic Youth Organization], I noticed something was going on that favored programming for boys. I had two girls and two boys, so I said to the boys' sports director, "How come there are no CYO sports programs for girls?" Their response was that the girls had cheerleading and volleyball, so they didn't need it. I said, "Well, soccer's coming, and there's other sports that the girls can do, like basketball and softball." They said, "Well, do you want to be the director for the girls?" So I became the director of that. I enjoyed getting sports programs for the students and my own children.

Life at UW–Milwaukee

When I went to college in the late 1980s, I was able to go to UW–Milwaukee (UWM) first, with a scholarship. I have a good friend in Kenosha. Her name is Ruby Gemmell, and she was already working for the Kenosha Unified School [District]. One time she told me to quit complaining about not being able to teach and to go back and get my degree. She said to do it now because UWM was offering a scholarship, which I was able to get, but I still could not go in the front door. My ACT score was not high enough, so I was not accepted into the particular school that I wanted to major in at UWM. There were all kinds of problems to get into that school. But then I met Dr. Salomon Flores. He was a professor there, and he said, "Come on, Carmen, you got the scholarship, so we are going to have to do something good with it. Take my class, you're going to take

Chicano history." I wasn't too happy about this, but then he explained to me that I would learn the college entrance process by being in his class. So I took his class. I really enjoyed it. Then Dr. Flores said, "Okay, now let's take a history class of Latinos in the USA. So I did that. I took those two classes and did well in them. I learned from him that if I got good grades in courses that accumulated to sixteen credits, [I could be] accepted by the school [I] wanted to major in. That's the way I started college.

Dr. Flores inspired me. I used this same approach right here at UW–Parkside. I told students that somehow I was going to get them admitted to Parkside, but we would never lie to do it. I said I learned some time ago that there's more than one door to the university, and somehow we are going to get in through one of them. It was easier here for me at Parkside because it was a smaller school.

Working for Kenosha Unified School District

In 1979, I started working for the Kenosha Unified School District. The district was looking for bilingual people who could work in the schools. I had been a volunteer in the Kenosha County social services department. There was a program that was in one of the church basements, and we used to get together with migrant students and work with them on their language skills. I thought, well, if I could do this, I could go to work in the bilingual program for Kenosha Unified, and that's how I started working there.

Once I started working in Kenosha Unified School District (KUSD), I became very close with Señora Santos from the Racine/Kenosha Spanish Center. I started to volunteer in 1979 and became vice president for many years. It was through KUSD that I could work with the center for anything that the parents of the students needed. I stayed on the board for ten to fifteen years. I also served as the treasurer for about five years, and twice I filled the president's position for interim periods, until the next election. In those days, we accepted that the president should always be a man. It was the way we thought at the time.

I started doing some training for the teachers in the school to help them address the cultural and economic differences and, in some cases, their own biases. An example of the need for the training was when I became aware of a teacher saying that she was going to have this little boy, who was right there, tested because she did not think he could hear. So I said, "What do you mean? He listens to me and understands me." I asked if it might be because of the language, and she said no. She told me that every time she called him Leo, he never responded. I said, "Well, his name is not Leo; it's Leonardo." And she said, "Well, that's a long name." I was quick to respond that I had to learn her name, which was Mrs. Lewandowski. I suggested that since her name was also a long name, that she could learn to say Leonardo. That happened quite often at that time. Teachers would change names, but for the most part, they didn't do it on purpose. I did need to speak up, like this time. I felt I needed to support *mi raza* [my people], my own kids, when there were troubles like that.

Then my next job with KUSD was as a migrant recruiter. That was a beautiful program. The migrants would come from El Valle de Tejas [the Rio Grande Valley of Texas], and they would come from different states, to Kenosha, where there was a UMOS [United Migrant Opportunity Services] office. I worked for KUSD to make sure the school districts those students came from were notified that they were here, and that the schools they attended here in Wisconsin were also notified, because those students used to leave places like Texas in April or May, so they didn't finish the school year there. There were disagreements between the districts as to the students' placement. But once the program was put in place, [the students] were able to finish high school and leave the fields and go to college, so it was a very successful program.

One year, I went to Madison for training and to a conference in Texas. I always included parents in all of this. One of the parents who was involved was a mother who went with me to the Texas conference. We learned that having a parent group would help the students academically, so we started a parent group. I moved to the bilingual program with KUSD and became the community liaison between the community and the parents. At that time, I was the leader of the bilingual and migrant parent groups. By the time I left, I passed on the job to one of the migrant mothers.

I started taking groups of parents to the Wisconsin Association for Bilingual Education (WIABE) conference, which was held in different areas of the state. There was a conference in Madison where I decided to take a bus full of parents from Kenosha. At that time, there was a different kind of immigration occurring. There were Puerto Ricans and Palestinians coming into Kenosha. Many did not speak English. So I went and talked to them and offered the bilingual program, and they accepted. The Palestinian group said they wanted to show their dances at the conference, so all the girls had their own beautiful outfits from Palestine and long, bright, colored dresses. So not only did I have a group of Latinas dancing, but I also had a group of Palestinians dancing. At the end of the conference, people had to vote for the new president for WIABE, and all of them got a piece of paper. Well, these parents didn't know anybody, so they wrote down my name, so that led to my becoming the WIABE president. It was pre-president, president, and then past-president, so I was involved with that for three years. It was very nice, and I really enjoyed it.

I was also working on my degree, and all these people were doctors and had master's degrees in education, so I tried to hurry and get my degree done so that I could be up to their level. I finally graduated in 1991 from Carthage College. Carthage College had a teaching program at night, so I was able to complete my studies. I got a bachelor of arts in education and a minor in Spanish. I graduated summa cum laude, which is funny because I didn't know what that meant. When they called my name and said summa cum laude, I said, "What is that?" My kids were jumping up and down and applauding. My husband was very proud that I finally finished my degree. There were many times that I tried to do everything. Every day after the kitchen was cleaned, I would sit down and start my homework for a class that I was taking.

WORKING AT UW–PARKSIDE

I was fortunate enough to know Lucia Herrera Delgadillo, who has since passed away. Lucia was my good friend, and she was already here at UW–Parkside as an English proficiency [ESL] teacher. Lucia met me at a conference at Kenosha Unified that I organized. She was one of the speakers. She told me of an opening at Parkside. I applied in 1992 and was invited to interview. Lucia was on the committee and the only familiar face I knew on it. There were some awful questions. One person asked me if my blond hair would limit my connection to Latino people. I remember answering that I only needed to open my mouth and they would know I was a Latina. I mean, I have an accent, and I will speak to them in Spanish as well as English. "It's not only the appearance that will attract the students," I added. I shared that I knew the community of Kenosha. In fact, I had a group of students that I planned to take to a precollege program at UW–Madison and later to UW–Parkside whether I was hired or not.

The committee offered me the job. Once I started, I was able to bring in some of the high school students I already knew from Kenosha, Racine, and many other cities. One very funny experience early on came from a group of parents who migrated from Jalisco. They were used to leaving the United States for Guadalajara every year to be in Mexico for the first *posada*, just before the sixteenth of December. Well, you can't do that in college because that's the week of finals, so I had to go to their homes and talk to their parents about why they could not take their children at that time. Little by little, the parents started learning that they had to leave later.

Supporting Latino Students

I was advisor to the Latino student group. First it was called HOP [Hispanic Organization of Parkside], but later the students said they didn't want to be called Hispanics any longer, as it was a name given by the government. They chose Latinos Unidos [United Latinos]. At that time, it got a little contagious because even UW–Whitewater wanted to have a Latinos Unidos, as well as Milwaukee and others. I said, "Two things are going to be very important for your group's budget: the US Hispanic Leadership Conference (USHLC) and your open house." We were able to get money for both. Our best speakers who came to Parkside's open house were speakers from this conference.

At first we started with ten in the group, and [then we] grew to thirty students who attended the USHLC in Chicago. The main thing I wanted them to learn was that at eighteen, you should learn how to select your elected officials and how to vote. All these things they were learning in the classroom didn't make sense to them unless they did this. Maybe you memorize it for the test, but you don't know exactly how it works. I kept insisting that on the application they had to register to vote in order to go to the conference. I was a chaperone and advisor for the three-day conference. I think the first time President Clinton ran, we met him and Hillary.

It was a great experience for the students and me. I hope they are still voting. I remember the first time they said, "Mrs. Ireland, we know who the presidential candidates are, but we didn't know all the names of the others on the ballots." I said, "Well, it's time to learn about that, and I think this leadership conference can help us."

We expanded the concept of representation to include how many Latinos were on campus and how many Latinos were instructors. We went to the police and fire departments and local government to determine who represented the Latinos. We went to the mayor, and it was the first time that he was on the ballot. They needed to go and see all of this, and it was a learning experience. Kind of hard for me because I was not a citizen and I took them to do all these things. Finally when George W. Bush came, I said, "I better become a US citizen so I can vote." Sometimes I think we are kind of isolated, and there was a process to be learned by us, because in Mexico it was always just the PRI [Partido Revolucionario Institucional].

In my position at UW–Parkside, I created a program where the parents could bring their financial papers because they didn't want anybody else to look at them, and I helped them complete the FAFSA [Free Application for Federal Student Aid] form. I used this time to explain the difference between grants and loans. I encouraged them to accept the grant money because it was free, and I encouraged them to be extra careful if their child needed loan money. I offered the sessions on Saturdays, and later I involved others from the multicultural office to help out.

I worked eight years in the admissions office and then the next eight years I worked in the multicultural office. I had more freedom in the admissions office because I could bring the students in the door and get them admitted. There was a system that I learned where you added a high student's ranking [percentile of senior class rank] with their ACT score. If the ranking and the ACT score added up to one hundred (for example, an ACT score of fifteen plus an 85 percent ranking would equal one hundred), the student was admitted. They took that away from us later, but that program was really good. One time, I had a student from South Division High School in Milwaukee who came to Parkside. She said that she only had a fifteen on the ACT and wouldn't be admitted. I said that maybe at UW–Madison or UW–Milwaukee you wouldn't be admitted, but at Parkside you would because we will add that to the 85th percentile of your rankings. I had many other students who qualified that way. Over the years, some of those students became engineers, doctors, and lawyers—with a fifteen on their ACT.

My strongest advocacy role was finding ways to bring the students into the university. I did not break rules but was able to get students in with the least amount of problems. This included dealing with undocumented students. I had a valedictorian from South Division who asked how to get financial aid. He was in the middle of completing his citizenship process. I told him to bring in the financial aid forms to the financial aid department. If they don't say anything, you don't say anything. And sure enough, in his first year he became a citizen. The scholarship continued, and he got his degree. Another thing, when students did not have papers but they had their high school diploma, we used that. Most had four years of attending school in Wisconsin. The university's residency requirement was one year, so admissions interpreted it as if they were Wisconsin residents.

It was interesting to work with them. I tried to help them figure out which way they were going to swim out and be successful. And so that's the kind of activism that I did. However, when it came to the DREAM Act, Latinos Unidos and myself went to the government building and demonstrated in support of the program, because by that time I had so many undocumented students in school. We got together with UW–Madison and some other campuses with those same issues.

Another thing that comes to my mind is the way Latinos Unidos was able to change the way it received its budget. I tried to explain to them that the power was in the student government body. The minority students weren't able to get money for their requests, and the nonminority got to go to conferences and things like that. An African American student wanted to be nominated for president. When he ran, he said he would like to have one representative from each of the minority groups, so that he would have support to propose that these groups have their own budget. It would eliminate writing for every penny that each minority group asked for. The plan was that each would issue their own budget and the student body would approve or disapprove it. That's how we were able to go to all these conferences and learn more about the politics. The different student groups accepted this proposal. The groups had representatives from Latinos Unidos, Asian, Native American, and gay/lesbian students, and they all started coming together when the budget was made. We were the first university that was able to have these kinds of budgets, because at one time we had a budget of $30,000 for Latinos Unidos for culture programming, going to conferences, and other things.

That was kind of radical because my African American colleague Bridget Johnson and I were student advisors in the multicultural office. She said, "Carmen, we are going to have to go to the meeting and have to be right in front of the administration and the students so that they can get what they are asking." We felt our jobs might be on the line, but we did it. We wanted to make sure the students were being heard. From that experience, the students learned how politics worked.

There was a particular multicultural conference that we used to go to. It's not in existence anymore, but we used to have a joke. Someone would ask, "Where is the conference this time? Superior? Okay, let's bring 'color' to Superior." Next, it might have been in Eau Claire. We'd say, "Okay, let's bring color there." About fifteen African Americans and fifteen Latinos would go and make presentations. This was a very good conference because it required a paper presentation. In order to qualify, the students had to write a paper or a poem, [create] artwork, or use some other talent they had.

Latinos Unidos is the big umbrella; under it are the fraternities and sororities and other areas of interest for the students. I remember the first dance they sponsored to bring in a fraternity. It was Hispanic Heritage Month. I was a supervisor at the dance. All of a sudden, one student came in and said, "Mrs. Ireland, you gotta help us." And I said, "What's the problem?" "The police wouldn't let us in; they said we are a gang because of what we are wearing." So I talked to the police, and they said the kids could not go in, that they did not belong to the university and were members of a gang. I told them that I could tell them the names of each student and all were registered at UW–Parkside. They were wearing different kinds of clothes because they were trying to bring the fraternity on campus, and there were certain rules in order to do so. I added that I would talk to the officer later to bring in training so they could learn more about what was going on. They finally agreed.

Two fraternities started on campus, and a sorority. I was the campus advisor for all three and for the multicultural sorority we added. I was very proud that we added that on campus. These fraternities and sororities are important. Each brother or sister is supposed to help another. I learned that even the president of the United States [Barack Obama] belonged to one. I feel that when you graduate from Parkside and have a good job, you should help a brother or sister who just graduated get a job.

Carmen Ireland, 2017.
CARMEN IRELAND

In 2008, I retired from UW–Parkside. That same year, I received the Living Legend Award, an award for leadership in education. It was named for Mary Lou Mahone, an African American activist in Kenosha. I knew her and her children. The award subtitle says, "Reaching for Rainbows in Pursuit of Excellence."

I am now traveling with my husband, who has also retired, and we are enjoying our family and friends.

Barbara Medina

Barbara Medina was born on April 22, 1956, in Uvalde, Texas. Her parents, who were migrant workers, came to Wisconsin for better opportunities in the late 1950s, when she was a child. As an adult, Barbara became actively involved in community coalition building, especially in electoral politics and Latina empowerment.

Ethnic identity: Chicana.

Do you consider yourself an activist? Yes.

How do you define community activism? Any action that leads to change as a result of goals one has set for oneself.

Areas of activism: Electoral politics, community empowerment through financial literacy, women, and people of color empowerment.

Location of activism: Milwaukee, Wisconsin.

Years of activism: Since the mid-1960s.

Early Influential Experiences

My father was from Cotulla, Texas, and my mother was from Crystal City, Texas, the birthplace of La Raza Unida Party (LRUP); my family very much supported its emergence as a political party. Some of the LRUP activists were migrant workers, too. People like my parents came to Wisconsin to work, and they settled. My mother, Genevieve, remained involved in change as soon as she arrived. She became one of the founders of United Migrant Opportunity Services (UMOS), a nonprofit organization that started off serving migrant workers in Wisconsin. As I was an only child, she would take me to many community meetings. I was exposed to different organizations that were involved in addressing migrant labor and civil rights. My mother was in the middle of it. I think I was raised with a sense of being able to impact change, being able to address the inequalities of institutional racism. I was in a great place of observing and learning the different techniques that La Raza played in trying to address the injustices. So, all of that said, that led me to know that by being part of the Chicano movement, we could mobilize and impact change. That's how I got my identity as a Chicana—knowing that there was a lot of power inherent in that, even though the leadership positions were held by men.

I was exposed to the different stages of organizational development needed to reach certain goals. The strategy ultimately led toward electoral politics: exercising your vote for representation. When I was eight years old, I remember my mom, UMOS, and LRUP, which shared much of their leadership, ran Hispanic candidates for office in Milwaukee, Wisconsin, in the early 1960s, but they were not successful. I remember going door to door with the campaign literature for several local races, the most prominent being Dante Navarro, who had been a union steward and Spanish-speaking DJ [the program was called Corazón Latino, or Latino Heart] on Milwaukee's South Side, but he didn't win. Each time it was a learning experience! It was never a waste of time because there was always a way to mobilize people, outreach, and educate. So then the leadership decided, "Okay, we didn't win this time; maybe the community is not ready for a Hispanic candidate. Let's find a candidate who is winnable, and who would work with us." That's how we were able to get Mary Ann McNulty elected as alderwoman in 1983 on the near South Side from a special election.

Grassroots Economic Empowerment Effort

I got involved in the 1980s to bring some economic stimulus to the near South Side of Milwaukee. I helped with a newly started credit union called La Cooperativa [the Cooperative], which was run out of St. Patrick's Church on Seventh and Washington Streets. The credit union was very small, but it was right in the neighborhood. When I came on board, they had asked me if I would be chair of the credit committee, and I said, "Credit committee? What does it do?" They explained that I would take loan applications from members, and then the committee would review each application to see if it had merit. I thought that would be interesting, so I told them I'd do it. I was first a member, then I became committee chair. One person who was very instrumental in the operations of La Cooperativa was David Espinoza, who was also very active in the community and had many great ideas. He was great to work with, and we spent time trying to recruit people to help in various ways. One of our efforts was to ask people to invest their money in the credit union, and we would loan it back out to community people. I liked the idea that we, as Latinos, created our own economic option. Our loans, to hundreds of people, ranged from $500 to $10,000, but mostly it was small amounts of money, more like micro-lending. I had an economics background from college, so this recirculation of money was really exciting and needed. People's loans went for down payments on houses, emergency needs, or their businesses, and our interest rates were very reasonable.

So I'm surprised, at this point, by how much we did without thought to obvious concerns. For example, we'd be open most weekday nights and on Saturday mornings. We had no paid staff, so the members themselves took turns handling transactions (after they received some training), like taking payments. We sometimes had a lot of money on-site with just a little vault. Mostly, there was only one person a night. Many times, I was there by myself until ten p.m. At nine p.m., I had to close the books, and sometimes I had to stay much later until accounts were reconciled. At St. Patrick's, other agencies were housed there, but the credit union was on the first floor and not very big; anybody could've come in and robbed us! But we didn't think about it at the time. We knew we were providing a service to the neighborhood. I'm very proud of that because we gave out a lot of loans that maybe would not have been able to happen without us. And then it just got to the point where we weren't able to sustain it, so eventually it was combined with another credit union.

Involvement with the Latina Task Force and the Sí Se Puede Latina Women's Conference

The LTF [Latina Task Force] was really one of the highlights of my activism. We began in the early 1980s in Milwaukee as a group of Hispanic women, many of whom were single at the time, and most of us were college educated to varying degrees. We lived mostly in the Milwaukee County area, but some of our members came from southeastern Wisconsin and

Madison. We worked for either South Side nonprofit organizations or were volunteers with them. At first we were informal, just having lunches or going out after work, and then began sharing ideas and concerns about the community. Some had already tried volunteering with different community causes, which were led by Hispanic men, but there was a level of frustration. We didn't feel our voices were being heard, largely because [we] were women. We all wanted to see improvements for Hispanic families, but there didn't seem to be the vehicle to use our talents and energy, so at some point we decided that we were going to make things happen on our own. After work and on weekends, we began to create a framework for our work. By consensus, we agreed that education, employment, and health were the most critical issues for Latinas and their families. We thought that once we gathered good data, we could influence the institutions, particularly government agencies.

We broke up into groups on these three key needs. We wrote proposals and searched for funds to support programs we wanted to undertake, but in that process, we realized that we needed a nonprofit status to receive funds, and we struggled with that. We wanted to remain a collective; we didn't want to re-create a hierarchy, yet standard bylaws required you to have officers, like president, vice president, etc., so we never became a nonprofit organization. In the meantime, we tried to connect with administrators of government programs and other advocacy groups, like the Wisconsin Women's Council, to seek their support for increased programming for Hispanic women. As we made more connections, we realized that government agency directors were also influenced by elected officials, and so we decided to get involved in electoral politics, too. When we learned of people running for office, we invited them to come talk to us because we wanted to know how they were going to help improve our community. About a year into our group, we met other women from southeastern Wisconsin and Dane County, like Irma Guerra, Gladis Benavides, and Anita Herrera. We were never a large group, but we were fairly dedicated, and we did gain support from many of our men, too.

We believed it was important to develop and support other Hispanic women leaders. We agreed that a leadership training was needed, so we applied for funds from the Wisconsin Community Fund in 1983. The conference title was Sí Se Puede [Yes You Can]. We held it at the Benedict

Center in Madison. And we were able to invite grassroots women. Aurora Weier from El Centro de Enriquecimiento brought several women from Milwaukee. I can't recall where our other women came from. I remember we offered scholarships to women who would not be able to afford it. It wasn't very expensive, but we wanted to make sure it was accessible to the women. We brought in a Latina organizer out of Chicago, Mary Garcia, from the Gamaliel Foundation. As part of this weekend-long training, some of our Latino men who supported LTF volunteered to provide child care. That was pretty special to us that they did this. I remember one of the women's children had the measles, and so all the children were exposed.

It was an interesting training. Advocacy and organizing strategies, such as Get Out the Vote, were shared and discussed. We also created space to talk about how we struggled with our needs and identities as women, and about being, or becoming, a leader and managing the expectations by others, such as husbands. I think a lot of the more critical issues happened afterward, when we were able to sit down and network and just share ideas and experiences. We knew what they were going through. We went through much of the same, like growing up poor and not finding enough resources to help our families. We hoped they saw us as a resource for their own empowerment, along with an attitude of *sí se puede*, because *sí se puede!*

Over time, a number of the women moved to different cities, got higher responsibilities, and got jobs, so we had less personal time and our group finally disbanded. But our networking

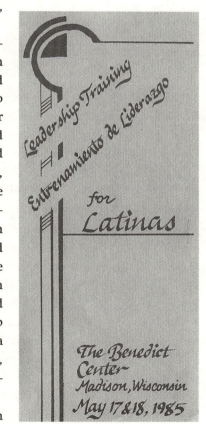

A brochure for leadership training offered by the Latina Task Force for current and new Latina activists in 1985. SOMOS LATINAS PROJECT ORAL HISTORIES AND COLLECTED PAPERS

remained strong, and this turned out to be very good at a personal level as we moved into nontraditional roles, like working for elected officials or government administrative positions. Maybe three of the best things we did, besides creating special lifelong friendships, was to let our Latino men know that we were going to have a credible and visible leadership role in the community on our terms from that point on; I think advocacy groups who were supportive of Latina empowerment made connections with the Latino community that they might not otherwise have had; and finally, we used our connections over years to continue Latina empowerment goals that none of us gave up, even as we transitioned in our careers.

Organizing and Mobilizing around the 1990 Redistricting Process

The opportunity to get a Hispanic elected [in Milwaukee] came right after the 1990 census results were known. It led to the redistricting of elected seats statewide. I was working as the associate director of La Causa, Inc., at the time. I had already been involved in electoral politics and felt this was such a key opportunity to grow the Hispanic voice in politics. People knew my history of involvement, so they were receptive to my organizing role. I helped lead a volunteer team of people [who] were equally committed to ensuring that we maximized our influence in order to get the best district available, to be able to elect a Hispanic candidate in the near future. At the same time, there was a climate of people believing that government was too big and should be reduced. Our goal was to increase the number of representatives and, at the very least, maintain it.

We decided we wanted to draw the district lines ourselves. I knew that we needed to build a coalition to be successful. We had to be strategic, and we needed to start with the people from the near South Side—those who would be most affected. To make people aware of what we were doing, I started knocking on doors and calling people. I explained that we should be the ones to determine the district lines to meet our needs. I didn't want people to think we were from the outside. I knew that one of my biggest prerequisites for whoever would be the official point person in seeking the new boundaries had to live in the area; we did not want to be thought of as being carpetbaggers. One person I sought was Leonor Rosas, who lived in the area and was also the director of the state job service office in Milwaukee. She had unimpeachable qualities, had worked as an assistant to the county executive, and had also worked on different campaigns, so she knew the ropes. We also asked Miguel Berry, who worked for SER [Service, Employment, Redevelopment] Jobs for Progress, a South Side Latino nonprofit agency, who helped in many ways that included being one of our number crunchers; Marilyn Figueroa was a known organizer from the area, and she was asked and accepted. All lived on the near South Side.

When I first started thinking about trying to get this type of coalition together, I wanted to see who else was out there. I found out that attorney and community volunteer José Olivieri was already planning to be involved and organize the effort. We met and agreed that our Hispanic leadership needed to come together as one. I also wanted to make sure that we didn't get Hispanic agency directors to take a lead role if they did not live in the community. I had to smooth ruffled feathers because our official representatives needed to be from the area. We created a redistricting committee so that we could have that larger level of support and involvement.

Once the redistricting committee came together, [what] we had to do was to educate ourselves on the process, and let me tell you, it was no easy task because you have to know the population counts in the different districts, block by block. We had to select which ones we wanted included in the district to maximize the number of voting-age Hispanics. We were able to look at the information that was necessary to create the best possible map. The stars were aligned because at that time we had access to people in power that allowed us access to the latest technology. Eloisa Gómez was working for Mayor Norquist; Maria Rodríguez was in charge of the Elections Commission. They were able to help us get into the technical computer system that the city had, in order for us to look at and crunch the numbers.

COALITION BUILDING

And at the same time, we outreached to the African American community to make sure we were looking for the same thing for our constituencies and not at odds with our goals. Fortunately, I had past collaborations with a number of African Americans. We also had to coordinate and organize around the public hearings on the different plans. We had to make sure we had people at the hearings, discuss the key message points, and help prepare our people to speak at these hearings. We wanted to make sure that we were best prepared to advocate our positions. We did this at the city, county, and state levels. We had to know when the subcommittees were meeting and sometimes they didn't give much advance notice, so we had to make sure we got supporters to them and make sure we had the right person to talk.

We had to identify who had what relationships with elected officials. This was a key strategic step because of how quickly the process had to occur. Someone was assigned to be a lead and work with the existing elected officials to make sure he or she would be able to take ownership. We helped to build up support from their constituents. It was no easy task, and each one has their own dynamics. I mean, you might have an easier time at the city but not necessarily the county. And then at the county, you might have competing factions. So it really was an intense, time-consuming process. It all happened, like, within 120 days. We were up against people who were trying to downsize government, and each time the number of representatives was reduced, that meant that people of color would have less *voz* [voice], less vote. We knew this, so our strategy was at the very least to try and maintain representatives.

Gaining an Aldermanic Seat and Getting Out the Vote

And we were successful with the city. We were able to gain an additional seat at the city level. Milwaukee's Common Council went from sixteen to seventeen seats. People were talking to each other [who] maybe never would have talked to each other before. Communities of color shared the same goal. And so I think that was an incredible experience. Our goal was to get the best demographic district to be able to elect a Hispanic in the future, which we did. And we gained additional voices eventually. So I'm particularly proud of that.

With this victory, the next step was electing a Hispanic to office. So we looked at different potential candidates and ran some campaigns, but our Hispanic candidates did not win. We went through this a couple of times, so then we assessed other strategies to ensure Hispanic representation. This led us to consider advocating candidates for political appointments and, more specifically, judicial seats. We started looking at the pool of people who were credible, and we came to a consensus of approaching Elsa Lamelas, who was an attorney at the time. We talked to her, and she agreed that she would be interested in seeking an appointment when, and if, the opportunity occurred.

Sure enough, there was a judicial seat that was vacated at Milwaukee County. At that moment, we started laying a campaign groundwork, including proposing Elsa Lamelas to the governor as our candidate. No Hispanic had ever been appointed to a judiciary seat in Milwaukee County, and we felt it was time for the governor to appoint one, and he did. She had to face election within the year, but by then we already had much of the work done; she was already there and was reelected. From a strategy that had never occurred to us before, it worked!

Next, we looked at our South Side assembly seat. So the same group began to look for a qualified candidate and the name of Pedro Colón, who grew up on the South Side and was an attorney, was brought up. We met with him, and he agreed that when a seat opened, he would run. He did and won, becoming the first Latino state representative. He won reelection and is now a judge in Milwaukee County. In between Elsa Lamelas and Pedro Colón being judges, other judges were appointed as candidates who courted the Hispanic community vote.

CONSIDERING A RUN FOR THE TWELFTH DISTRICT ALDERMANIC SEAT

I made a decision in 1993 to run for the aldermanic seat in the heart of the Hispanic community. Let me tell you, it was all-consuming. I don't care what they say, electoral politics is very grassroots. Candidates have to go door-to-door to win. That is the only thing that really works, or would work at the time. You needed to identify the hard-core voters and start from there. It was very intense, and ultimately I found out that after doing all that work with the redistricting committee and this campaign work, I really had to have a heart-to-heart talk with myself. And you know what I discovered? I didn't have the fire in the belly, meaning being willing to do anything and everything to the exclusion of everything else. My skill was more about getting people involved, creating and supporting a unified political strategy, but it didn't necessarily have to be me. So that's what I learned. It's better to have people who really want it. They're the ones [who] will do a great job.

STATEWIDE EMPOWERMENT PHILANTHROPY

I keep coming back to the same theme of self-determination. How we really need to provide, give ourselves, the opportunities—because nobody else will. Through Tess Arenas, I was able

Barbara Medina, 1996. SOMOS LATINAS PROJECT ORAL HISTORIES AND COLLECTED PAPERS

to get involved in the Wisconsin Community Fund, which is a statewide philanthropic organization in Wisconsin. It was not part of the mainstream foundation community. Several individuals with inherited wealth started a progressive social-change fund, and the board continued to raise funds for it. We also would distribute it to organizations that weren't necessarily being funded by the United Way or other traditional foundations. We involved the past grantees and their staff, as well as community organizers to make sure that when we would have proposals, the ones that would review them would be the actual people who were involved in the community, because they were the ones who would know what the need would be and what projects could work. We had applications of Native Americans from the north, to farmers' rights out in the west, to urban issues in Milwaukee, Kenosha, and Racine. This was about a ten-year commitment.

Through that opportunity, I got to know the rest of the state, their needs, and their issues. We were making sure that there was room for them to be heard. We traveled statewide to raise funds for the organization, too. And it wasn't the only one by itself; there were sister funds across the country. So it was the go-to place for people, for organizations in Wisconsin who may not have been eligible for funding from other sources. And it could be something as small as maybe they needed a computer, or they needed something small like that, that maybe other places wouldn't review, but we would because we knew it could make a critical difference.

I have recently retired and am focused on assisting my father and my stepmother. They live in the house, in the heart of the Latino community, which we've owned for over forty years, and I'm there often, daily. I stay involved as I can. I recently coordinated an event for a Hmong American woman candidate for a County Circuit judge position in Milwaukee [Kashoua "Kristy" Yang]. She won her election in the spring of 2017 to become the first female Hmong American judge in this country.

MARIA LUISA MORALES

*Maria Luisa Morales was born on July 4, 1944, in Cotulla, Texas.
She started her life as a farmworker with her family. They settled in
Racine, Wisconsin, in 1949. She became a community activist while
raising her children in response to injustices she witnessed in her community. She has largely been a farmworker and immigration rights
advocate in Racine since the 1970s. Maria became active in her union
and the Racine Labor Council and worked for Voces de La Frontera, an
immigrant rights advocacy organization.*

Ethnic identity: *Soy* Mexicana [I am Mexican].

How do you define a community activist? I would define an activist as
someone who has the heart to want to be a part of the community, to seek
changes, and doesn't ask for a penny for it.

Areas of activism: Voter registration, immigration rights, welfare and
labor rights.

Location of activism: Racine, Milwaukee, Madison, Waukesha, and
Chicago.

Years of activism: Since the late 1960s.

EARLY INFLUENTIAL EXPERIENCES

I came to Racine in 1949. I was five years old. My father came from Mexico.
He was a migrant worker, and my mother was a homemaker. We lived
in Cotulla, Texas. As migrant workers, we traveled to different northern
states to work, like Michigan, Indiana, Iowa, and elsewhere. My family
picked tomatoes, cabbage, potatoes, cherries, and other crops across the
Midwest. We also picked cotton in Texas. At that time, I didn't understand
why migrant workers were not treated very well. We accepted it as part
of life. Sometimes we would live in a barn with cows almost next to us, or

we would have a little building for the whole family. Sometimes we slept in our truck, in a tent, or houses that were more like shacks. We had no indoor toilet; we had no place to wash our hands.

I saw how hard my dad worked. My mom washed clothes by hand, like heavy blue jeans. She washed clothes until her hands were all red. She made sure the tortillas were made when the family came home. We had a lot of brothers, sisters; sometimes cousins were with us. I saw her making tons of tortillas for everybody. I would see the big houses and people with their children, drinking their lemonades, and we didn't have water. Our education was cut short because we would leave to come up north in March and then we would head back around October. So we missed out on our education, and in Cotulla everybody spoke Spanish, so we really didn't pick up a lot of English.

When we finally settled here, my father still continued taking us to migrant camps to work on farms; we picked whatever was in season. So when we'd go back to school, I would see the kids talking about their vacations, like going up north, and we worked in the fields so we had nothing to talk about. And when they required us to take lunch, we saw the kids taking out sandwiches, and we would take out rolled-up tortillas and hide in the corner so they wouldn't see us eating our food.

The teachers changed our names at the Racine public school. My name is Maria Luisa, and they changed it to Mary Lou. My brother's name, José Guadalupe, was changed to Joe. It was confusing. There was discrimination back then that is just as bad as it is now. This is one reason why I had to speak up for the immigrants today, because we went through that. We suffered discrimination, like being told that there were certain parts of town we couldn't live in.

Early Community Involvement

I got married in 1963, and I moved to the north side of Racine. I didn't work in the fields anymore. I wasn't always as radical as they say that I am. When my kids were young, I was actually a den mother for a Cub Scout troop. We had the meetings at my house. And then I assisted with the Girl Scouts. I took them camping and stayed overnight at the different campsites. I was a catechism teacher. I helped formulate Las Posadas at St. Patrick's Church and the Virgin of Guadalupe Days. We're Catholics. I got married at St. Patrick's Church.

Later on, I helped to petition for another Spanish-speaking parish to be renamed Cristo Rey [Christ King]. I worked with others to get a center in Racine because we didn't have one. I helped them get the Fiestas Patrias, a traditional Mexican heritage festival, which we didn't have before. My kids and I also helped with area breakfast programs. During this time, a group of us worked to get rights for people who were in our state prison, and gave rides to their mothers and their wives so they [could] visit their family members, so it wasn't all that radical.

ADVOCATING FOR MIGRANT FAMILIES

During this same time, the late 1960s, I realized that many people from a nearby barrio came from Cotulla, too. They called that place the Mexican Beach. The reason they called it that was because when it rained, it became one big mud puddle. It was just mud—no paved sidewalks or paved streets. The bathrooms were outside of the homes, and so was the water; there was no running water inside the homes. So the heavy rain made it difficult to get in there because of all the mud; that was something that really blew my mind. I was still pretty young, though.

A group of us came together and started asking questions like: why don't they have the basic necessities there, like indoor plumbing and sanitation? The girls would have their babies, and they would be washing the diapers outside, breaking the ice, so they could get the water to wash the diapers; there were no Pampers in those days. In the middle of the night, they would have to form a line so they could walk to the toilet because they were scared to go alone. My husband, Tómas Avila, was a member of the American GI Forum. LULAC [League of United Latin American Citizens] members; Arturo González, Gilbert Delgado, and Julio Robles, who were with Local 180; me; and others formed a campaign around these issues. We went to the Racine City Council and asked them why [they] allowed for these conditions and to make the necessary improvements.

The council seemed to think that because the migrant workers didn't ask for anything, they were okay with the conditions. They didn't bother to ask the people if this was okay, so they did not do anything. Our coalition prepared ourselves to go back again. This time, I got ahold of people who were pretty active in Milwaukee. I invited the Brown Berets to join our effort. The Brown Berets [a Chicano youth organization established in the 1960s in response to police brutality and other civil rights violations] stood behind us as some of us made presentations to the council; they didn't say a word. The council members seemed shocked by their presence and this time voted to provide indoor plumbing and paved streets and sidewalks. Now it has become a pretty nice neighborhood; some people still live there from back in the day.

Since I saw what was happening to migrants in Racine, I started getting involved with the migrant movement in other parts of the state. I became involved in some marches and rallies. Our biggest march was in the 1970s when Governor Lucey was in power. We fought for better conditions at the migrant camps. There were several migrant camps here in Racine, and in the nearby town of Wind Lake, the last ones around here. In the 1970s, we had a big march, and Governor Lucey signed a migrant bill where the state would require more sanitary conditions at the migrant camps, and it also made them eligible for in-state tuition.

I went to a community meeting that discussed the *Brown v. Board of Education* decision; I said that there was really no difference today because our neighborhood schools were still racially segregated. I visited one school in Racine, and 90 percent of the population was African Americans; I went to another inner [city] school and maybe 80 percent were Hispanics; and then I went to another school and maybe another 90 percent were African American and Hispanic.

In my neighborhood in the 1970s, I would see the police help the Immigration and Naturalization Service (INS) officers to circle a whole block and just round everybody up. Sometimes they would do this at night when most people were asleep. I saw how people left everything behind—houses, their cars, their checks—and nobody would know what happened to them. I just made a statement to the police, "So why don't you tell somebody something?" When a dog gets picked up, you try to find the owner, but when these people are taken away in the middle of the night, you tell no one. That's when I started getting involved, to see if we could make some changes. People were also being picked up at work or the places where they would go cash their checks, and, at one point, some were picked up in the stairwell of a church.

I organized our first immigration summit at St. Patrick's Church in Racine in 1977. A lot of people attended. Representatives from organizations like LULAC, American GI Forum, and the Mexican American Educational Party were there. We wanted to understand what they were doing with the roundups, and we wanted them to be more humane when they took people. Mr. Ron Swan from the Milwaukee Office of Immigration and Naturalization Service came. I always thought that if we are going to do something, we should hear it from the horse's mouth, so that's why we asked him to come. INS did make some changes as a result. We got them at least to stop the way they did roundups. We didn't think it was legal for the INS to use the police to assist the immigration officers, so they stopped that. They started telling us when somebody was going to be taken away, so we could at least help them get their paycheck so they had money to go back. Some of them married here, so we would help them by telling their wives what happened to them. Things seemed to die down a little bit, but as you can see, we are having way too many deportations.

My husband and I became active with social service programs and welfare rights. We enrolled our children in Head Start, and I started volunteering through the parent program. They put me on their policy council. I also became active with the Kenosha Community Action Program, and I led their council, too.

Little by little, I started getting a little more radical working with the mothers of the Head Start and the AFDC [Aid to Families with Dependent Children] programs. I was volunteering with Welfare Mothers, an advocacy organization, when the AFDC benefits were cut. One of the major cuts was the stipend that allowed mothers to purchase school clothing and supplies for their school-age children each year. About one hundred women marched from the Franklyn [now called the George Bray] Center to the Ellwood Store. We got our carts full of school supplies, and we put them on the counter; once they rung us up, we told them we didn't have the money to pay and left everything there. That was a good one.

Then I went on to help this one young lady. A school board member went to her school, and they were talking about funding for Head Start.

The school board member made derogatory comments, like AFDC recipients were overweight, ate doughnuts, and wasted government money, so the young girl got up and replied, "Who are you calling lazy?" and the school board member slapped the girl in the face.

I asked a friend who was a lawyer if the young lady had a case against the school board member, and he thought she did, so he told me how much money it would cost to represent her. Head Start parents and other supporters started making and selling tacos at Cristo Rey and the Spanish Center as a way to pay for her legal representation. I'm not sure, but it may have been over $2,000. We won the suit, and afterward the school board was instructed not to let the board member talk at school meetings. She could vote, but she could not state her opinions. The sad thing was the school board member won reelection. With that mentality, it makes you think that the people who voted for her may have the same way of thinking. We have a lot of work to do. It was a long time ago. Racism has been there since the beginning of time. It has been chopped away little by little, but it's still there and can be very toxic and contagious.

Involvement in the Labor Movement

I have always been pro-union. I was a part of Local 347, and my husband was a United Auto Workers [UAW, Local 553] union member at Racine Steel Casting. We actually worked there at the same time, but in different departments. I left there and started working for Racine County government in 1982 as an eligibility worker; our group of employees were represented by the machinists union. At the first meeting I attended, I started raising questions. The women members hadn't brought these questions up before, so right away they asked me to be their rep. I then started getting appointed to different committees, and eventually I became appointed to the AFL-CIO [American Federation of Labor and Congress of Industrial Organizations] Racine Labor Council from our local. I served on the council from 1981 to 1989. It was more like fate because another woman was supposed to be president but she moved, so I was appointed and became the very first Hispanic woman in the AFL-CIO to become president of the Racine Labor Council. Later on, I was elected. I served as president

Maria Luisa Morales at an AFL-CIO demonstration in the 1980s. SOMOS LATINAS PROJECT
ORAL HISTORIES AND COLLECTED PAPERS

from 1982 or 1983 until 1989. When I left the council in 2003, I served on
the Labor Advisory Council and Labor Fest Committee until 2014. Due to
health reasons, I ended my involvement.

During my years on the council, I was very involved and served on
different committees. I started going to conferences and conventions and
became a COPE [Committee on Political Education] delegate. My husband became a union steward. He went to steward school at the Walter
Luther Educational Center for union workers. We were able to get county
supervisors to make a proclamation supporting the union workers and the
farmworkers who were coming here for a protest. I supported the sanctuary movement in the 1980s and became part of a coalition called CASC
[Central American Solidarity Coalition] to provide sanctuary for people
coming from El Salvador and Nicaragua. I envisioned the union not just
as a union, but as workers being a part of a whole community. Another
action I remember was when the council protested apartheid in South

Africa when one of their rugby teams had a game here at the John Bryant Community Center Park. I think it was in 1981. It seemed unfair to me that our community members had to go through a lengthy process to get permission to use the space for our Mexican Fiesta event, but the sponsors of this rugby event got permission so quickly or without notice.

This was the same weekend as the Million Man March in DC, so many of the African American leaders were out of town. Several of us who went to protest their use of our space were white, Latino, and black. I was scared because there were big rugby players coming at us, and we were trying to make the game stop. When we could, we'd kick the ball away from the players. A couple of our people, Mike and Joe, got arrested for trying to stop the game. We also raised funds for the Zapatistas in Chiapas, Mexico. Those were the kinds of things that we did as a union. I was pretty excited to be a part of it. I saw so many things happen.

In 1991, César Chávez joined one of the worker marches in the union's strike against Rainfair Corporation [a garment manufacturing company in Racine]. I believe he heard about Rainfair through union activist Gilbert Delgado. He was sort of our contact person with the United Farm Workers. It was exciting to have César Chávez with us. I was able to stand next to him and talk to him. Racine wasn't all that big, but he was here marching with the people at Rainfair. Several of the workers and union members went on a hunger strike. We were fighting for a good cause: to seek better wages. The workers did get the raise, but unfortunately the company later moved to another location.

Involvement with Voces de la Frontera

I heard about some workshops on labor issues sponsored by Voces de la Frontera [Voices from the Frontiers], a Milwaukee immigrant rights organization, so I attended them and got other people to go. There I learned about the "No Match" Social Security Administration (SSA) letters. This matter was about employers being sent letters from the SSA that stated to the employer that it could not verify the social security number of one or more of their employees. What some of the employers did was to fire them as a result. The group felt this was wrong because the error could have been with SSA or for other reasons that may have had nothing to do with the employee being undocumented. They wanted this employer practice stopped. Then I heard about the 2003 Immigrant Workers Freedom Ride Rally in Washington, DC. I could not go, so I started a rally here. It was my very first event in support of Voces de la Frontera, which is often just called Voces. For the rally, I sent messages to the schools. My granddaughters attended one of the high schools. A teacher, Mr. Levy, heard about it, so he got all the students to go. Afterward, he asked me to speak to his class. That's how it started. It was called Students United for Immigrant Rights. So, from then on, I became involved with Voces. It was going to be an election year, so they hired me to do voter registration. I got the whole family involved: my kids, my grandkids, nephews, and nieces. We went out and got a little over two thousand [people] registered.

Waukegan, Illinois [thirty miles south of Racine], passed a city council resolution in 2007 in support of federal law 287G that gave police power to arrest people who were undocumented. I was at that rally when the resolution passed. The turnout was huge; there were at least two thousand people there. I recall being in this large crowd and I saw a wall of police officers and other military men who were fully geared with the helmets and shields and billy clubs and rifles and dogs slowly heading toward us. No physical violence occurred, but right after the event, the police department and immigration went through all the people's records, and found people who had three or more misdemeanors and went to their houses and arrested them. They rounded them up around Waukegan Lake, and one particular girl was crying. She was thirteen years old and had been adopted as a baby. They asked her if her father was there, and she said yes and they took him away. Even though he had minor traffic violations, it was more than three. He wasn't one of the "undesirables," like the president had said would only be deported, but they did take him away.

Regarding one of the Day without Latinos marches, we tried to get the word out about the anti-immigration legislation to supporters, like unions and faith groups and Jewish communities. Racine itself had eighteen buses filled to attend the Milwaukee protest. We had people from Racine, Kenosha, and Delavan and had a rally first in downtown Racine, and then we went over to the march and rally in Milwaukee. I think we did change things. For that event, I worked a lot with the kids. I told them, yes, there were a lot of people, but it doesn't always take a lot of people to make change.

The anger and racism toward undocumented workers is real. Before my work with Voces and during my years with them, I saw it. I'll give you an example of it. I help people who come from other countries, and they tend to come to my house. I have little welcoming things for them sometimes. I put little gifts together for them, like toothpaste, underwear, shirts, stuff like that. In 2011, this one young man came, and he brought a bumper sticker to show to me. The bumper sticker read, "Illegal Immigrant Hunting Permit. No Bag Limit – No Tagging Required." I was so mad. I asked, "Where did you get this?" So he told me it came from a Citgo gas station in Racine. I called them, and I said, "Why are you selling this?" Well, he didn't even know it was there. So then I told Christine Neumann-Ortiz, director of Voces, and I told my son, "We gotta do something." So we decided to have a rally.

First, we asked them to stop selling it. I asked my Racine friends to get involved. Christine Neumann-Ortiz came from Milwaukee from Voces. We had a rally here, and it turned out that the owner, when confronted about selling them, removed them. It turned out that the owner was married to a girl from Guanajuato, Mexico. Quietly we thanked the guy, because we started calling other businesses and asked them to take these stickers off their shelves. This was not just about Mexicans, since the sticker targeted all undocumented immigrants. I ended up receiving a letter in the mail. It wasn't a hate letter, but [it] said that selling the item was freedom of speech, and that the store owner had the right to do it. The person added a couple of other names for me that I won't mention. A short while later, there was a television story about a family suing someone because their child was being harassed at school for having that sticker.

Unfortunately, I took a little break because of heart failure, then right afterward, I went back to work with Voces. I worked there until I was laid off in 2011.

FIGHTING FOR IMMIGRANTS' RIGHTS

In October 2013, I found out that immigration officers were at the Racine Courthouse picking up anybody that did not have [lawful status] papers.

They were in the waiting room asking people if they had papers. On October 2, one person in particular went in to pay a ticket, and he had no papers. They took him away with twenty other people, including a woman. So I found out about it, and I tried telling people about it. I wasn't getting attention, so I told my son, Steve, that we needed a rally to let people know what was going on. I rented a Grinch's costume for my son because of the symbolism. I called people to a rally and, despite the cold, they showed up. The symbol of the Grinch was that Christmas was being taken away from immigrant families. We rallied in front of the courthouse and went inside for a while. After that, a coalition was formed by Voces and some public defenders from Racine. They got in contact with different legislators. I wanted to find out what immigration officers were doing [in the courthouse] and how they were finding out when immigrant Hispanics were there. It seemed they knew that when the court interpreters were there, immigrant Hispanics could be there, too. Someone was tipping off immigration. The rally was just to kick-start a campaign. The coalition started writing letters to the legislators for a couple of months, and the INS practice ended quickly.

TARGETING CONGRESSMAN PAUL RYAN ON IMMIGRATION

Around 2000 was the first time I talked to our district congressman, Paul Ryan, and I was naïve. I met him at a *quinceañera* [a coming-out event for girls turning fifteen]. He was there with some family members, and I was introduced to him. At that time, I was trying to get people to sign up to go to the protest rally in November for the School of the Americas, a taxpayer-funded program that trains other countries' soldiers in war and torture tactics. So I asked him if he didn't think that was wrong. He denied [that] we were doing this and was pretty defensive. When I got involved with Voces de la Frontera, [Ryan] seemed pretty anti-immigrant, too. I started going to his rallies and forums. I kept this up because he was a key national legislator on immigration reform, and he covered my county and many of the nearby counties. He did a forum for Hispanics once, and I tried to ask questions, then realized I wasn't getting any answers. We had a forum where, first, he was sort of pro the DREAM Act, then all of a sudden he said he wasn't going to talk about it anymore. I asked him why he wasn't supporting it any longer. He said he would study it, but that this was not something he would support at this time.

So later on we had another rally. I wanted a specific answer on immigrant reform, so I asked this young girl if she would ask the question. At some point, he stopped answering me at forums when I raised my hand, so I asked this girl if she would ask the question. I raised my hand, too, and he called on me. I was surprised, so I told him that I wanted to give the floor to this young lady from high school. He just gave her the same answer, too, which was still unclear.

I once tried to meet with him at his Washington, DC, office with a coalition on the same issue, and I conducted rallies and sit-ins locally. When he decided to run for vice president, the newspaper quoted one of his staff as saying that I was a professional protester. I found that offensive because I didn't learn how to be a protester, but I did learn to speak up for others. I'm just there bringing a voice for people who can't speak for themselves. I'm in there to tell them what these people feel. Now that I know that I'm on a conservative right watch list, it doesn't bother me. I mean, what I'm doing is right.

I don't think we are going to get an immigration reform in my lifetime, unless we actually hit them in their pockets. The protesting, screaming and yelling, letters, petitions, faxes, prayers, jumping up and down haven't gotten a reform yet, but I think if we do a boycott, something that is going to hurt them like we are hurting, that would be effective. Just like César Chávez with the boycotts; they were very effective. And I think we are at a time right now when we could actually do a boycott. Unless something more radical is done, we are not going to get it in my lifetime. I continuously tell people to make themselves legal any way they can; too many people's hopes depend on it.

The way I see working on issues is that they are all related, all one circle. Whether you are working on immigrant issues or workers' rights, criminal justice rights, courts, people doing drugs—it's all one big circle; one touches the other. You can't separate immigrants' need to work, so you have worker rights; if there is no work they go into criminal activity, drugs, etc. So they all go around each other, and they all touch each other, even

Maria Luisa Morales volunteering at a voter registration event in the 2000s. SOMOS LATINAS PROJECT ORAL HISTORIES AND COLLECTED PAPERS

health-care issues. Like for me right now, I am getting my insurance cut off, and I'm going to have to make a choice whether I am going to go buy my prescriptions or buy a gallon of milk. Everything touches everything else.

I am still involved in justice issues, such as voter registration, but I need to pay more attention to my health. I recently left the board of the Urban League. I served on it for four years. I feel honored that I was included in a mural that was unveiled in 2014.

TERESITA NERIS

Teresita Neris Ortiz was born on March 28, 1952, in Puerto Rico. She moved to Sheboygan with her family in 1994 and started the nonprofit organization Latinas Unidas of Wisconsin, Inc. in 2002 with a group of twelve other Latinas with no financial resources.

Ethnic identity: I know I am Puerto Rican, but I have studied and gotten involved with people from other Latino countries and their cultures, so for me, I identify as Latina.

Do you consider yourself an activist? Yes.

How do you define a community activist? For me an activist is a person that is vigorously passionate about creating a positive change in the workplace, school, or community; this can happen through educational, legal, and/or government systems. A group can make positive changes with a goal in mind to make a better life through freedom, justice, and a sustainable society.

Areas of activism: Translation/interpretation services, education assistance in the areas of English as a Second Language, GED [General Equivalency Diploma] and HSED [High School Equivalency Diploma] assistance, and other advocacy.

Location of activism: I've been able to assist as a volunteer in the communities where I've lived (Puerto Rico; Chicago, Illinois; San Diego, California; Sheboygan, Wisconsin).

Years of activism: Since the late 1990s.

EARLY INFLUENTIAL EXPERIENCES

My parents brought their twelve kids to Chicago, Illinois, in 1966 to escape the economic hardships in Puerto Rico. They had an elementary school education, but knew that with hard work they could strive for the American dream. In those early years, I saw the passion that my mother had to protect and guide us to do well; they both supported us to accomplish what we set out to do through education. Growing up in a rough area of Chicago, I saw a lot of things: drugs, abused women, and different kinds of crimes. It was a blessing that we survived those tough times. My family moved often, so we were always looking for resources to be able to help ourselves and neighbors who would ask for help. In Chicago I went to Tuley High School, what is today part of Roberto Clemente High School. I married very early in life and started a family at age eighteen.

Life in Sheboygan

Over the years, I have been working with the Hispanic community, starting in Chicago, then in San Diego, California, and Puerto Rico. Throughout this time, it became clearer that people needed access to education of all kinds, and I helped as I could because I continued to always learn about the resources in a community and to share this information with others. I moved to Sheboygan in 1994 because my son's wife is from Sheboygan. They married here and found it to be a very good place to raise kids. I was in Puerto Rico at that time, and we lived in an area that was not conducive to raising children, so I sold my home and moved to Sheboygan; I wanted the best for my children. The Hispanic community in Sheboygan, though its population is small, has similar needs [to the Hispanic communities in Chicago, San Diego, and Puerto Rico], especially the immigrant people. There were those without social security numbers, so there was a need to obtain them in order to work, get a driver's license, and become citizens so they could vote. Economically, many had to work two to three jobs to be able to support themselves and their families. Access to education programs and the ability to apply for the different state or federal programs are huge issues. Many do not have enough money to send their children to college, so we have lots of needs and barriers.

Founding Latinas Unidas of Wisconsin, Inc.

I helped found the organization Latinas Unidas [United Latina Women] of Wisconsin in 2002. I was working at the Sheboygan County Job Center at the time. I was working with Hispanic clients because I was bilingual. So

I noticed that the Hispanics were coming with maybe four or five issues at once. They needed education in computer skills, English language, and obtaining a high school diploma. They also needed translations and interpretation at the doctors' and dentists' offices, immigration offices, clinics and hospitals, courthouse, jails, and lawyers' offices; and they also needed referrals, but referrals to someone who would speak Spanish. When I saw this larger picture of so many individuals needing all types of services, that's when I called the Latino women who were already working in various agencies throughout the Sheboygan and Manitowoc counties and told them that we should do something.

I knew of only about five Hispanic professional working women in the community in different areas, such as a nurse friend and someone from Silver Lake College. I set up a meeting for us and encouraged them to bring others who could help; I also invited other Latino women who were not employed but were bilingual. About eighteen of us attended. I recall saying, "I have brought you here today to make you aware that we need to establish an organization that will back up and support the Hispanic community." I explained to the group that there was a breakdown in the way we were referring the Spanish-speaking community to services they needed. Some needed food stamps, so they were sent over there. This person needed some type of documentation, so we showed them where to go. This person needed to see a doctor, so we sent him/her to a doctor; and so on with the referrals. But they would come back! The referral system was not working well for them because at the agencies where we were sending them, they had no Spanish speakers, so they were all going around in circles, completely confused! The message, real or perceived, was, "You don't speak English, and I don't speak Spanish, so I can't help you." Many of the women there already knew of the problems; that is why we agreed to start the organization by the end of that first meeting. We elected officers, and I became the board president.

We decided as a group to concentrate our focus on the needs of Latino women. We wanted to look at the woman's whole life and provide a safe space to be understood, so we decided it would only be for Latinas. We also knew that there were men, husbands of these women, who would say, "No, I don't want you to go to a man and tell him about your problems or your health issues. I want you to go to a woman. She will understand you better." Some of the women at the meeting agreed, because their husbands would not allow them to participate in an organization where there would be men involved. We also made the decision to have the board and the staff all women, and then we selected our name as Latinas Unidas of Wisconsin, Inc.

We informed women of all the available resources in Spanish, and would identify the Spanish speaker at a particular agency, or send someone to help with interpretations. Access to learning the English language, obtaining a GED, classes, and computer skills were huge needs in order to get a decent job. In those days, most immigrant Hispanics did not know how to use a computer, so we made this a key part of our work as a nonprofit organization. Silver Lake donated some computers they no longer needed, and we provided some basic computer training to people.

Teresita Neris in her office at Latinas Unidas. SOMOS LATINAS PROJECT ORAL HISTORIES AND COLLECTED PAPERS

LATINAS UNIDAS AS A NONPROFIT

Latinas Unidas of Wisconsin specializes in providing a bilingual bridge between the Hispanic/Latino client and the agencies from which they need services. We accompany the people to the job centers, health and human services agencies, lawyers, clinics, chiropractors, dentists, as either an interpreter, translator, and/or advocate. In Sheboygan, the private and the public sectors did not have enough people who were bilingual or offered bilingual services. The courts and the jails especially—they expected you to find interpreters. We provided this service. We did not have any money to start our organization and did not think anyone else would fund us, so women gave us what they thought they could afford, and we received it as a donation. An important understanding that all volunteer staff had was that everything we did for the people was confidential. We took this very seriously.

Another project was our GED and HSED assistance. Everything connected with practicing for and taking this test became computerized, but many did not know how to use a computer. Since I had more knowledge than some of the rest of the volunteer staff, I taught some computer skills every day. In 2014, I learned that the Department of Public Instruction changed the GED/HSED book that year, but there was no Spanish version. So I called the Department of Public Instruction, and I also called Joseph Leibham, our state senator. I asked how they failed to make a book for the Hispanic community and that my students would be on hold because they didn't have a book in Spanish to study. Their office said that one would be finished at the end of the year. So I asked them, "How could you forget forty million Hispanics in this country?" Then I asked the director of the GED/HSED department if they had the test in Spanish. "Oh, we do have it. People can come and take the test in Spanish," she said. My response was, "So if you don't have the Spanish study book, why do you have the test? This is like setting them up for failure." They did not have an answer to that, so I tried to bring together Spanish speakers to see if we could start translating the book to help people prepare themselves so they can go to Lakeshore Technical College and get their GED/HSED tests.

Being Called "Too Radical"

I went to look for a job because my job at Latinas Unidas didn't have funds, and I wanted to keep the organization going. A Hispanic man who interviewed me for a position as a Hispanic liaison said he did not want me to continue supporting the Latinas Unidas group because he did not want all these "radical women" around his agency. I felt insulted when he told me that in a bad tone of voice. He didn't understand what we were doing, and it kind of offended me; I'm sure it would offend all caring people. He probably felt intimidated. If the definition of radical is advocating to accomplish something better for women, then I can accept this term to describe me. He did not hire me for the job; and, personally, I had lost interest in the job because the agency contradicted its purpose.

Running for the School Board and Continuing Education

I became a school board member of the Sheboygan Public School District from 2004 to 2007. I actually went to see the school superintendent, Dr. Joseph Sheehan, in 2004 because I planned to file a complaint against the school my son attended because I believed they were discriminating against my son. There were instances when they picked on him because of his ethnicity. He was also a very active boy, so they started loading him with project assignments. At one point, he had five projects in one month. It created stress on him and with me, too. After the meeting with Dr. Sheehan, he asked me if I would consider running for a school board position because he heard about the good things that I was doing with the Hispanic community. I responded, "Yes, what do I need to do?" I had no idea what the position involved. He explained the procedure to me, so I collected about four hundred signatures needed to be a candidate and other requirements. The day after the elections, I learned that I had won. I was the first Hispanic woman to serve on the Sheboygan Public School District Board. I participated for three years and felt that I contributed in many ways. Unfortunately, I left the school board due to personal issues. I had a surgery, and my husband, Bob, was diagnosed with a terminal illness. I helped him with everything until the day he died; my children and I were deeply affected by the loss.

SERVING ON LAKESHORE TECHNICAL COLLEGE'S ADVISORY COUNCIL

I became a member of the Multicultural Community Advisory Council at Lakeshore Technical College from 2009 to 2011. They did not have staff that represented the Hispanic community. The council already had representation from the Hmong, German, and other Anglo communities, but they did not have anyone from the Hispanic community, so my input on the council filled a very high need. I shared information with council members and the other staff about Hispanic cultures and our needs. My ideas helped them come up with programs for the Hispanic community and to hire a Spanish-speaking liaison.

I was invited to join the council because I was already attending school there. I had a bachelor's degree from Universidad del Turabo in Puerto Rico in business administration in 1996, and so from 2009 to 2011 I was in Lakeshore's criminal justice program, and later switched to civil litigation classes. I obtained an individualized technical studies degree as a community legal specialist and a certificate as a paralegal post-baccalaureate. I studied in an effort to help myself, my family, and the Hispanic community with better understanding of the government and legal systems in the United States.

Part of my "radical" work was to support the operations of Latinas Unidas when we had no funds. Often the services, like translation, interpretation, or transportation, came out of my own pockets. I helped connect women to public services like Alliant Energy Co., WPS Gas Co., food stamps, immigration services, courts, and job searching all through my computer. I printed off the legal forms from my computer, helped women fill out the forms to submit to court. I am a notary public, too. Some of the women, when they come in, if I detect they are hungry, I make them a sandwich and give them some coffee, tea, or water. I am glad that I got the degree as a community legal specialist because that way I am able to better help the community.

Life Today

Latinas Unidas continues today, though it has scaled back. We still have our board, and it's still all women. We continue as volunteers as we are able. I have an office in my home, helping the community members as best I can as a volunteer. I sometimes have to charge them the basics, like paper (legal forms that I print out for them), ink for the printer, gasoline if I need to take them somewhere. For interpretations/translations services, I may sometimes need to charge them according to their income.

A group of friends are working on a new project. We are establishing groups for Spanish Bible studies/community support in four different points in Sheboygan: north, south, east, and west. Our goals are: 1) to contact Spanish-speaking men and women (all men and women—senior citizens, disabled, lonely, depressed, young, etc.) and inform them of these groups so they can attend, and provide them with transportation; this is a huge issue for the area; 2) to learn more about God and enhance their hope and faith; and 3) to let us know if there is a personal need (emotional, physical, or social) with which we can provide help in some way. We already have a room at Campus Life in Sheboygan (south), and two rooms at First Congregational Church in Sheboygan (east).

I have gone through a lot of grieving since my husband died in 2007, but I have had good moments, too. I traveled to the Czech Republic and nearby countries to be with my daughter, who was sent there for work. She thought it would be a good idea to help with the healing process. The trip was awesome, and I learned a lot about other countries. I am well now and back on my feet.

LUCÍA NUÑEZ

Lucía Nuñez was born on January 3, 1960, in Guantánamo, Cuba. She has lived in Madison, Wisconsin, since 1999. Foremost, she views herself as an educator. She has held the role of executive director of Centro Hispano in Madison, director of the Department of Civil Rights for the city of Madison, and vice president of equity, inclusion, and community engagement at Madison Area Technical College.

Ethnic identity: Cuban; Latina.

Do you consider yourself a community activist? Yes and no. I have been more of a community activist in the past, mostly around educational issues and students. I would label myself as more of an educator now. For me, education has been the driving force and has changed the course of my life.

What is your definition of community activism? Giving voice to a community of people who at times are not heard.

Areas of activism/education advocacy: Education and voting rights. I was a teacher in Holyoke, Massachusetts, and in the Bay Area in California. Most of my students were Puerto Rican or recent immigrants from Mexico.

Cities and areas of activism/education advocacy: Holyoke, Massachusetts; San Francisco and the Bay Area, California; Madison, Wisconsin.

Years of activism/education advocacy: Since my college years, the early 1980s.

FROM CUBA TO NEW ENGLAND

In 1965, my family left Cuba after the Freedom Flights to Miami, Florida, had been suspended. We left through Spain. We went to live on the US naval base on Cuba. We lived there for five years, and then we went to live in St. Thomas in the Virgin Islands since we were not able to obtain US citizenship living on the naval base. I'm the first in my family to get a college education. My mom has a fifth grade education and my dad an

151

eighth grade. Education was something that was valued by my family, though it wasn't valued for females as much as males. It wasn't even considered that I would go to college. The expectation for the only daughter was that I would get married and wouldn't need a college education. My mother's friends questioned why a girl would need to go to school when she needed to learn to cook or to clean house. Those were the things that were important and expected of a mother and a wife.

Teachers have always played a significant role in my life. There were influential teachers who saw potential and encouraged me to do more, so I wanted to get more out of my education. That's one of the reasons I left the island at sixteen. I secretly applied to a boarding school in Massachusetts. I saw a brochure in my counselor's office and it looked pretty cool, and that's how I picked the school. I was fairly shocked when I learned that I was accepted. Only then did I tell my parents about what I had done. My mom fell apart; a sixteen-year-old daughter wasn't supposed to leave home. My dad wasn't happy at first, and then he became one of the people who most encouraged me in high school, college, and graduate school. He flew up with me at the beginning of my school year. I think he lived vicariously through me because he didn't get that kind of education and I think he should have. He's a very smart man who didn't have those opportunities.

I started in 1976 at the Williston Northampton School in New England, where I finished my last two years of high school. My parents sent me $5 once a week, and I was able to get work study, and that's how I made it financially for those two years. A teacher at the school drove me to visit the different colleges and may have even paid for me to take my SATs, since now I know that these tests cost money. I did my undergraduate studies at Connecticut College and graduated in 1982. I was a Hispanic studies and political science major. So, ironically, I walked into Connecticut College, a predominantly white school, and found a great deal of support for what it meant to be Hispanic, and an understanding of the complexity of race and ethnicity. Not that there wasn't racism and homophobia at Connecticut College, but I was able to find a safe space to explore my identities. I reclaimed the Spanish language in college because like many immigrants, I spoke Spanish, but I never learned to read or write the language properly. I never had read any literature from Latin America or Spain, and so I embraced all of that; it was a major awakening. What incredibly rich cultures exist in this world, not just Cuban culture, but so many other cultures. I couldn't get enough. Connecticut College offered a unique environment to students, with small classes and the opportunity to really get to know my professors. That's why I still believe that education can be so powerful in our lives.

I went to graduate school at the University of Massachusetts in Amherst. My graduate degree was in international education. There have been a lot of different things I have done that have contributed to my professional and personal worlds.

In 1985, I joined the Peace Corps, where I met my partner, Heidi Vargas. We were assigned to Honduras, and we lived in a village of about twelve families. That was it. There was no electricity, no running water; you had to cross the river in order to get to this village. You know, every once in a while you could buy a hot Coca-Cola, and that was a treat. We were both assigned to work with the Federación Hondureña de Mujeres Campesinas, the Honduran Federation of Rural Women. They were a very active women's group from small villages who wanted to start schools for their children. We traveled to some of the poorest and most isolated areas of the province.

The 1980s were extremely charged times in Central America with the war in El Salvador and the fighting against the Sandinistas by the United States. Honduras was in the middle of all this conflict. Though the United States government claimed that there wasn't a US military presence in Honduras, in the years we were there we saw an increasing presence of military personnel. It was so common to bump into US military in the capital and even in my small village. We stayed in the Peace Corps until 1989. The village where we stayed needed better access to neighboring areas. I worked with the village residents and other Corps members to design and build a footbridge. We applied for funding and received it. My time in the Corps ended before the bridge was built, but one of the Corps members left prematurely, so we stayed until it was built.

I've done other community work in education, like helping at-risk girls obtain their GEDs. We, teachers, took a holistic approach to support them and didn't just look at their educational needs. It was the most creative work I've ever done. I remember the girls would call me Maestra [Teacher], and they wanted to know why I wasn't married. I'm glad they saw that women didn't have to fit into one prescribed role and that there were many roles available to them. These experiences have shaped who I am and my beliefs.

Until I lived in California, I had not fully embraced what being Latino meant. It's taken a long time for me to think about what those labels mean. I understand now the power of these umbrella terms to unite diverse groups. My identity as a Latina is different than my identity as being Cuban and even as a lesbian. The combination of being a Latina lesbian stands apart from the other identities. It's interesting for me to play with all of these in terms of what it means and the politics behind it, but I can't separate them out.

In California, I worked with teachers at Stanford University. In California, [some] classrooms in the early 1990s were 100 percent immigrant populations. The atmosphere in California in those years was very anti-immigrant with Governor Pete Wilson and many of the initiatives against all immigrants.

CREATING COMMUNITY IN MADISON

I came to Wisconsin with my partner in 1999 in response to getting a job offer from Centro Hispano [Spanish Center] of Dane County. When we arrived, I didn't know there were so many Latinos in Madison. As the director of Centro Hispano during a boom of growth in the Latino community, not just here in Wisconsin but throughout the Midwest, I watched how this community dealt with the influx of this population. I saw reactions from fear to curiosity. In 2003, I accepted the position of deputy secretary of the Department of Workforce Development. This position exposed me to statewide issues facing not just Latinos but rural women and the Native American communities around the state.

I then became the administrator of the Equal Rights Division for the state of Wisconsin. In 2006, I became the first director of the Department of Civil Rights for the city of Madison. I learned a lot from my positions in government. Those were crucial years to figure out how government worked, not just in this community but everywhere—in Milwaukee, in Green Bay and Appleton. During my work with the Equal Rights Division, my identity took a backseat; I learned about fair employment and housing laws and the process of investigations.

SUPPORTING IMMIGRANTS IN MADISON

In 1999, with the growth of the population of immigrant children in the school district, they weren't ready for that. In my role as the director of Centro, I spent a lot of time educating them. I developed a relationship with the superintendent in those years that was unusual. Art Rainwater spent a lot of time listening. He didn't see me as a token. I had many conversations working with employers to understand immigration, working with the police and fire departments, too. People became fearful of calling the police for fear of deportation. I met some young women who had been brought to Madison by a coyote and who were being controlled and manipulated by this coyote and her family. They came to us at Centro to ask for help, and a Madison police captain and I drove to the house to talk to the coyote. These partnerships were important.

Wearing my community hat, I remember marching at the Latino immigrant rally in 2006 with Mayor Dave [Cieslewicz], from West Washington Street to the State Capitol, and that was significant. There were a large number of people who participated in the rally. To see the busloads of people arrive, the young people who attended; it was so powerful to witness all this energy and support for immigrants. I was overwhelmed with hope for our future.

LIFE TODAY

As a lesbian who has been in a relationship for over twenty years, I feel like we have made such progress and am hopeful about that. When we first got together, my partner, Heidi, and I never dreamed that same-sex marriage would be legal. Three years ago, we drove to Minnesota so that we could get married, and now same-sex marriage is legal in Wisconsin.

I made the decision to explain being lesbian to my parents by bringing home my partner, Heidi. I was raised traditional Cuban and Catholic; being a lesbian didn't fit into either framework. I didn't know what to expect, but one Christmas I brought Heidi to my parents' home. There wasn't a direct conversation about us, but my parents figured it out and accepted my relationship and me with Heidi. There was a gift-giving practice at Christmas that my parents had with the spouses of my siblings. The second time Heidi was with my family for Christmas, she received the spouse's gifts. It was a wonderful surprise and symbol of their acceptance.

My children motivate me to be involved and to keep learning. My daughter is away at college but my son is at East High School, so we are still invested in the Madison school district.

Lucía Nuñez, 2016. MADISON COLLEGE

HEALTH AND WELL-BEING

I'm a pancreatic cancer survivor. My brother passed away with the same cancer in 2006, and I was diagnosed not two years later. That's a new identity and something that changes the way you look at life, the importance of things, and what I need to think about. Just because one is cancer free does not take away this bizarre relationship with cancer. Very few pancreatic cancer patients reach the five-year mark. I expect the cancer will come back; it hasn't, but the fear still is present. I live with that and have learned to manage the uncertainty of living with cancer. How unbelievably precious my time is, and how I value this time. Facing cancer is an experience that slowed me down, and it's something I've had to do since facing mortality. So that's a difference. I've started to embroider. I've made peace with my mom. I'm so glad she taught me all of those womanly arts because they're a huge part of my peace.

Nelia Olivencia

Nelia Olivencia was born on June 21, 1941, in New York City (East Harlem). She was involved in the antiwar movement and fought for Chicano and ethnic studies while living in California. She has lived in Wisconsin for forty-five years. As a higher education administrator and instructor, she focused her energy on creating a global awareness at UW–Whitewater with the help of Latino and other students. In 2015, she served as chair of the National Chicana & Chicano Studies Association.

Ethnic identity: Puerto Rican and Latina.

Do you consider yourself an activist? Yes.

What is your definition of community activism? It involves working with the community to address issues of equal opportunity and anti-discrimination in multiple areas (e.g., voting rights, employment, housing, education, immigration rights, and health care). You provide programs to the community that are pertinent to them (e.g., immigration, voting, education, health care, nutrition, birth control) and financing (e.g., financial literacy, obtaining credit).

Areas of activism: Bilingual and ESL [English as a Second Language] education; immigration rights; access to higher education; freedom of choice; health care for women of color; women's rights; Chicano, Puerto Rican, and ethnic studies.

Location of activism: New York, New York; St. Louis, Missouri; East Palo Alto and San Jose, California; Madison, La Crosse, and Whitewater, Wisconsin.

Years of activism: 1959 to the present.

Early Life in New York

As a child and teenager [in East Harlem], I was exposed to poverty and discrimination in school and feared the streets in which I walked. There were multiple gangs in the neighborhood controlling certain blocks. One of my parents' moves unknowingly placed us in the center of where the area was controlled by an Italian gang, the May Rose. As a Puerto Rican girl of fifteen, I was subjected to sexual molestation almost every day as I made my way into the apartment building where I lived. The gang members hung in the candy store next to my building entrance, which was located at the street corner. Instead of coming home the short way, I would take a very long way around to bypass the candy store to enter my apartment building without being harassed and molested by them. One day, when I came home from high school, some gang members followed me into the building. I threw my books at them because I knew their intent. They intended to push me toward the basement to rape me. I started screaming; my mother heard me and started screaming back. She had a broom with her to push them away, which helped, and we ran up the stairs. I lived in constant fear of them the entire time we were there.

EARLY ACTIVISM

Because of my good grades, I was admitted directly to and graduated from City University of New York, Brooklyn College. I attended between 1959 and 1962. In undergraduate school, I became very pro-Puerto Rican and very pro-black and tried to join a black sorority, but I could not afford the entry fee required to join. I became a member of the NAACP because there were no Latino organizations. I did attend black fraternity dances and went to some of the black sorority meetings. After graduating, I was interviewed in NYC by the chairperson of the Department of Romance Languages at Washington University [in St. Louis] and received a scholarship to attend there between 1963 and 1967. I had not visited St. Louis until I started my studies, and I seemed to be the only Puerto Rican on that campus, so I hung around with international students, with whom I had more in common than the rest of the student body. I think it's interesting to note that that was what Barack Obama did in his college years. I met my husband, Glen, during these years. We were both students, and we married in 1967.

Becoming a Political Activist

I became much more politicized when I moved to California. We went in 1967, and I started as an assistant professor at San José State College. Shortly after I started, in 1968, the students wanted open admissions, and the four Latino faculty, of which I was one, joined the strike. Together, we fought for the creation of a Chicano Studies program. It was a very tumultuous time. When we were not picketing, we were meeting for hours on end. I picketed with three other Latino faculty with whom I became close friends. They were all Mexican Americans who were from Arizona, Michigan, and New Mexico.

The chancellor's office refused to listen to our requests. I didn't want to get arrested, but I was willing to take that chance because I felt so strongly about all having the right to attend college and to study subjects that addressed our history and our needs. This was at a time when we, as Chicanos and Latinos, were practically nonexistent on college campuses. The strike also required that none of us teach as a form of protest. We would march back and forth in picket lines all day, trying to close the college down. I didn't think it was my right to deprive the students if they didn't want to strike, so I held classes off campus. The atmosphere was very intense. We would spend all day—from nine o'clock in the morning till three a.m.—negotiating, but eventually we lost. We also went to Sacramento to demonstrate at the state's capitol to advocate for an ethnic studies program with state legislators, starting with Chicano Studies. It made sense to me to have a Chicano Studies out on the West Coast. At other protests in the San Francisco Bay area, we also demonstrated for Black, Native American, and Asian Studies.

My antiwar activism during the Vietnam War came from a combination of personal beliefs and personal impact. I was against the war, and my husband was notified that he had been drafted in 1967, shortly after we married. He did not believe in the war and fought the decision. The process took some time, and eventually he won his appeal. We were activists to keep others from getting drafted. When we first participated in the demonstrations, we decided to make a pact: when I went to a demonstration, he wouldn't go because then one of us could bail out the other if thrown in jail. I remember a particularly scary instance when we went to the first anti-draft resistance movement demonstration in Oakland, California. Draft cards were being burned, which I think was a criminal offense, and the Oakland police marched in phalanx formations toward us. These men were big and burly; they were at least six feet tall and white. I recall they came at us with big rectangular shields to protect their bodies, and they carried billy clubs; they came toward us. At one point they surrounded the group I was with. I thought I was going to be hit and beaten. I was caught between the wedges and was terrified. Fortunately, we were not harmed, but I realized this was part of seeking an end to the war in Vietnam. Other demonstrations and marches included two in Oakland in support of the Black Panthers—I got to see Bobby Seale, Eldridge Cleaver, and Kathleen Cleaver speak—and another in Palo Alto against the use of napalm. Much of our time was spent running up and down the San Francisco Bay Area supporting our brothers and sisters on different campuses.

In the 1960s, I also participated in the grape boycott strike. One day, while I walked the picket line with others in front of a supermarket, a car tried to run me over. That was a frightening experience, but it made me more determined to support the boycott. Some of the students I taught at San José were involved in El Teatro Campesino, a Chicano political theater company whose plays were centered on themes of inequalities and injustices, particularly for Chicanos and migrant workers.

CREATING COMMUNITY IN WISCONSIN

We left San José in 1970 and moved to La Crosse, Wisconsin. We were seeking a less intense life, and that brought us to Wisconsin. In 1976, I took a position on the UW–Madison campus. I was first hired as a recruiter and then competed for and became an assistant dean of students; this included serving as dean and director for multicultural programming. Part of my duties included working with the multicultural student organizations, which included five groups: Chicano, Puerto Rican, Asian, Native American, and African American. I also wrote and administered multicultural programming for the funding of cultural, historical, and other events on campus.

My activism transitioned in Wisconsin. In the late 1970s into the early 1980s, I was involved in a Madison group called Alianza Cívica Cultural [Cultural Civic Alliance]. I was president for three years. I didn't want to be president for that long, but no one else was willing to take it on. We were made up of different professionals, from different Hispanic backgrounds. We had people from Spain, Mexico, Bolivia, and Argentina. The group tried to do things for our rights. We did a lot of work with Los Marielitos [who were part of the mass emigration from Cuba to the US in 1980[1]]. When they first came here from Cuba, they didn't have a home. We had fund-raisers for them with food and helped them to settle here.

I served as chair of Governor Schreiber's Committee on Hispanic Affairs in 1978 before they eliminated it. We wrote one of the last reports on services being provided to Hispanics by the different state agencies. I also testified before the legislature's Joint Finance Committee to try to continue it, but it was defunded.

From 1976 to 1979, I also served on Governor Dreyfus's Commission on the Status of Women, which worked on issues such as marital property reform [and] women in penal institutions. The council was also defunded under a Republican administration, so a group of women, including myself, started the Wisconsin Women's Network, a nonprofit statewide women's leadership organization. I was the only Latina founding member. It took a lot of hours in the evenings and on the weekends. It was an incredible group that is still in existence. I'm still a member, but I'm not active. I became friends with some of the original founders who played key roles in the national and Wisconsin women's movements. I also joined the Wisconsin Women of Color Network and am currently the president.

WORKING AT UW–WHITEWATER

In 1991, I took a position at UW–Whitewater (UW–W) as director of Latino student programs and held this position for nineteen and a half years. I was responsible for academic advising as well as advocating for increased

---

[1] Terry Rindfleisch, "When Cubans and Chaos Came to Fort McCoy," *La Crosse Tribune*, May 29, 2005. http://host.madison.com/news/local/when-cubans-and-chaos-came-to-fort-mccoy-that-was/article_457bd8e1-8018-53cd-a28a-6ae83011c3f3.html.

admissions of Latinos. I worked with students to put on educational activities for the annual Latino Heritage Month program and celebrated the Day of the Dead through dance and theater performances. I developed the first travel study course for Latinos and other students. In total, I taught fourteen travel study courses to Puerto Rico, Jamaica, Mexico, Peru, Spain, France, Italy, Cuba, Morocco, Egypt, Turkey, and Greece. I wrote proposals, created course syllabi, recruited the students, and prepared the travel portion of the trips, and much more. From these travels and my national connections, I brought onto campus exceptional speakers from Peru, Mexico, Cuba, Puerto Rico, other countries, and from the United States. I believe our students benefited greatly from this exposure to different perspectives, cultures, and histories. I saw travel abroad as an important way to learn about the world. Students could find out about their backgrounds, learn about the world, and discover commonalities we share as people.

I was also an advocate for students to present their research at national conferences, such as at the Puerto Rican Studies Association and National Association for Chicana & Chicano Studies national and international conferences. I took as few as five and as many as twenty students to present at conferences in Los Angeles, Miami, Albuquerque, New York, Mexico City, Puerto Rico, New Brunswick, and many other places. They attended the United States Hispanic Leadership Institute Conference and the American Multicultural Student Leadership Conference. I wrote a student exchange agreement between el Tec, Instituto Tecnologico y de Estudios Superiores de Monterrey [Monterrey Institute of Technology and Higher Education], and UW–W, which was approved because I believed that students should become totally bilingual in English and Spanish. As the UW–W coordinator for this exchange, I felt proud to have sixty-six-plus students participate in it over a fifteen- to sixteen-year period. All these were possible because I sought funding for the programs; the supervisor of the area in which I worked refused to fund most of my requests, so I wrote proposals to other campus departments and outside organizations, many of which were funded.

I joined the Coordinating Committee of the National Association of Chicana & Chicano Studies from 1992 to 1994, and I became chair-elect in 2014, the chairperson the following year, and then past chair in 2016. It was a positive and rewarding experience. I also joined the Puerto Rican

Studies Association and served on the national executive committee. I was just elected board secretary. It was very demanding, but I thought it would be a very good experience for me and I could represent the perspectives of the Midwest.

I worked at UW–W when September 11 happened. When I saw it on television, it broke my heart. I was devastated for three months. Like other people, I didn't want our government to invade countries or start another war over this tragedy. A week later or so, I saw some students on campus wearing black and white bows made from ribbons. I asked them what those were for, and they told me they were for peace and for mourning the loss of people who were killed in the Twin Towers. I thought that spoke to exactly the way I felt, so I put it on the jacket I used all the time. One day I was asked what the bow stood for, and when I responded, I was told, "You come from New York. How could you be for peace?" I explained that this whole situation was created because of the way that we saw and treated the rest of the world. We have little to no understanding of their conditions, like poverty, or their cultures, and how our economic and political policies affect the rest of the world.

INVOLVEMENT IN STATE CAMPAIGNS AND NATIONAL ELECTIONS

In the first year of Governor Scott Walker's term, I became involved with political issues affecting Wisconsin (e.g., ending collective bargaining for state unions). Regarding his 2011 recall effort, I demonstrated at the state capitol, attended hearings, and helped get petitions signed. I also worked on President Obama's reelection campaign in 2012. I volunteered at the campaign headquarters because I thought it was critical that he be reelected. I wanted racial and ethnic minority groups to have a voice and also a say in what this country will be like, now and in the future. The cultural face of the United States has changed immensely. It's no longer white only; it is browning and will continue to become more and more so. In 2016, this country is not as obsessed about dating across racial/ethnic lines. It's no longer a taboo to date a person of another race or ethnicity. I grew up in a world that saw the mingling of races as a taboo. I remember that happening to me—people's stares. When I would board a subway with my African

American boyfriend, those stares would cut right through us. And this was in New York in the early 1960s. My boyfriend was middle-class and came from a better background than I did. People would just stare at us everywhere we went together.

I received more than nine different awards and recognitions, and I'll mention two of them: the 2009 University of Wisconsin System Board of Regents' Diversity Award in the individual category and the UW–W Non-Instructional Staff Award in 2003.

Nelia Olivencia, 2016. MARINA OLIVENCIA

MARIA RODRÍGUEZ

*Maria Isabel Rodríguez was born in Milwaukee on September 11,
1952. She became active in community organizing efforts at an early
age through her involvement with the Latin American Union for
Civil Rights as an education advocate. In 1990, she became executive
director of the City of Milwaukee Election Commission and became a
founding member in 2003 of Latinas en Acción, a philanthropic fund
of the Women's Fund of Greater Milwaukee.*

Ethnic identity: Mexican.

Do you consider yourself an activist? Over the course of my life, yes.

How do you define community activism? A person who advocates for
more resources. There are many ways to do this. As I have aged, my ways
of advocacy have changed.

Areas of activism: Education and cultural knowledge advocacy.

Location of activism: Milwaukee.

Years of activism: Early 1970s, starting right after high school.

ACTIVISM AFTER HIGH SCHOOL

I was pretty young when I became aware of the social unrest in Milwaukee's
Latino community. I was hired part-time by the Latin American Union for
Civil Rights (LAUCR) in 1970, while I was a junior in high school, for their
Bilingual-Bicultural Education Program. The organization was involved in
many civil rights causes affecting the Latino community. If Latino members were trying to organize a strike or a walkout or something of that sort,
LAUCR was likely involved. They wanted better enforcement of civil rights
for Latinos, and to make people see that we were all human beings, just like
anybody else. The underlying work was always about equality and justice,
whether it was for the improvements of migrant workers on the farms in
Wisconsin, job access in the tanneries or breweries, or addressing police

brutality toward our youth. The organization really took a front-line role on these issues.

The LAUCR Bilingual-Bicultural Program

The LAUCR Bilingual-Bicultural Education Program (BBEP) had about twenty part-time staff during the school year and twice the number for our summer camp programs. It was an academic program for children of migrant families who settled in Milwaukee. We served about one hundred families during the school year and about two hundred during the summer. The academic part of the BBEP was really about helping children meet their benchmarks in school, and so we worked very closely with the schools, too. Children were attending neighborhood schools, so it was easier to work with the schools because the children had to live in a certain radius to attend. We followed their academics throughout the year. After high school, I ran the program.

The BBEP offered the cultural arts, too. We actually had dancers, musicians, and artists to help children understand their heritage and culture, to strengthen their resiliency, and, hopefully, to do well in school. We created dance groups and annually I coordinated Fiesta Navideña [Christmas Party]. It was an event at the downtown Performing Arts Center. In this beautiful facility, we featured many of our children, and the event was usually sold out; a couple thousand people attended each year. Our children danced *la botella*, *la bamba*, *el merengue*, and other folkloric dances. It was great.

I stayed with LAUCR until 1980. During these years, I also learned from working with high school students who we hired that many had feelings of being treated "less than," with lower expectations by teachers and administrators in the schools. I think their poverty was a part of feeling frustrated and angry. This may have led to our Latino students' high dropout rate, but I also saw their resistance to this treatment.

Supporting Parents, Schools, and Community Advocates

Fortunately for BBEP staff, our access into the schools was with the permission of the parents, and so we were able to get information and work with the teachers. We really didn't have any problems. There were some stubborn teachers, individuals who would not give us any updates or help us in any way, but most were caring individuals and did work with us. We were helping them do their jobs to see student improvements. Now bilingual-bicultural education, as a whole movement, is seen as a little more threatening.

In my second or third year with LAUCR, I took a part-time job as a teacher's aide in Milwaukee Public Schools (MPS) and I worked with only bilingual children—all bilingual children: Yugoslavian, Latino, anybody who didn't speak English. One time, I went to the principal to meet with him because parents had asked for bilingual services. He was a good principal and agreed to a meeting. As it was occurring, the union steward of that school rushed into the meeting and objected to us meeting with the principal. She objected to the principal even listening to what we had to say. At one point, I recall her saying, "This is about us [the teachers]!" Certain teachers were fearful that a bilingual program was going to be coming to that school. In fact, several of the teachers refused to talk to me for the rest of the school year. So, you know, a couple years down the road the bilingual program became available for the entire school because the majority of the school population was Latino.

My role included support for the advocacy efforts of the Citywide Bilingual-Bicultural Advisory Committee (CWBBAC). They were mostly Latino parents who wanted a bilingual program implemented in the MPS. I helped them organize demonstrations before the MPS administration and the school board to advocate for bilingual education. The parents were not the experts but knew there was a need. We formed an alliance with two academics, in particular, to speak on strengths of the program based on research findings; they were Dr. Tony Baez and Dr. Ricardo Fernández, who came from UW–Milwaukee, though Tony played a much greater activist role in our overall efforts. They helped the parents, who were primarily women, understand the need, and offered strategies. We had, in some cases, busloads of families going to school board meetings, staying at school board meetings until one or two o'clock in the morning until our agenda items were addressed. My job was to help them stay organized and help them in any way that I could. The administration's acceptance of the program took four to five years.

There were three major community leaders in that citywide organization, and those women were dynamic in bringing together Latinos of many backgrounds. They were Mercedes Rivas, Amparo Jiménez, and Aurora Weier. They led the effort to motivate and mobilize hundreds of parents to attend community strategy meetings, and school board and administrator meetings. By doing so, they were successful in making the CWBBAC the recognized group to negotiate with administration on the program's development. These women, and others, worked hard. Amparo and Mercedes were doing this as volunteers, and Aurora did this work through her nonprofit organization. The grassroots work was a large part of what led to the bilingual education program in MPS, to make it happen.

INVOLVEMENT WITH LA RAZA UNIDA PARTY AND LATINA FEMINIST ISSUES

One of the organizations LAUCR collaborated with was La Raza Unida Party (LRUP). They both were creating awareness of the social, political, and economic oppression and our need to organize for change. Both groups, along with the whole national Chicano movement, believed that Chicano people were a nation within a nation. I became more involved since I worked for LAUCR and participated in meetings, conferences, and workshops for women involved with La Raza Unida. There were not that many LRUP women members in Milwaukee or Wisconsin. I attended three mini-conferences of LRUP women. One was in Illinois and another in Indiana. I was amazed by these strong, smart Chicana leaders, but also somewhat unsettled because, while we discussed many women-focused issues, the overarching effort was about how to support our men's roles within LRUP.

I became the selected delegate from Wisconsin's LRUP to the United Nations Conference on Women in Mexico City in 1975, and I can't remember how I was selected! LRUP was recognized by the UN as a nation within a nation, so that's why LRUP delegates could attend. Although I was the only official delegate, two women from Wisconsin affiliated with LRUP attended. Our delegates came from several states, such as California, Texas, Arizona, New Mexico, Indiana, Illinois, and Wisconsin.

UNITED NATIONS CONFERENCE ON WOMEN IN MEXICO CITY

Delegates came from all over the world. LRUP delegates met with the Third World women who were organizing in their countries of Bolivia, Vietnam, and elsewhere. We had the opportunity to learn about their backgrounds and struggles. I recall there was a woman from Bolivia who had been jailed and raped for simply organizing the women working in the mines. Now she came to the conference by way of her priest. He helped pay her way to the conference to build awareness about the struggles of women in that country and what the government was refusing to do in terms of their safety, equity, pay, and things of that nature. I didn't realize how much it really affected me. I was struck by her. She was a small, indigenous-looking woman who experienced horrible treatment in her own country, and she was willing to speak out against the injustices against not just her, but other women; that really hit home to a lot of other women, too. One of my initial reflections was, "Those are not the things that happen back home." And then I thought about the mistreatment of our own women and thought that, to some extent, we were victims of injustice, and we needed things to change, too.

LATINA MUJERES CONFERENCE IN NEW MEXICO

Sometime between 1974 and 1976, we were invited to a LRUP *mujeres*-sponsored conference in Montezuma, New Mexico, and some of us from Wisconsin decided to go, including Patricia Goodson. We met with women from all across the States, talking about Latina issues and building a group consciousness about our roles as women in the movement and how to support ourselves in becoming better organizers of our own communities. We didn't see ourselves as the Gloria Steinem feminists; we saw our men as participants of community change. We wanted to identify ways to help our men see how they could help the movement by sharing leadership responsibilities and power. By doing this together, we would all gain more in the end, so that was kind of our philosophy. The other thing about that conference that has stayed with me was that our protection seemed necessary. Our Latino men served as armed guards at the conference because there had been a rash of killings in New Mexico of Latinos and Native Americans at that time. So there we were, driving up to an old building, which I think had been a convent, and seeing our men with guns. It was kind of an eye-opener because every day that I was there, the newspaper reported that several people had been killed the night before. It was very eye-opening to see how dangerous it was to be a Latino or Native American and how little our lives mattered to some.

HELPING TO FOUND THE LATINA TASK FORCE

The idea for starting the Latina Task Force (LTF) came from several Latinas in the early 1980s; some of them are close friends of mine. Patricia Villarreal, Barbara Medina, Eloisa Gómez, and several others were looking to improve the conditions for Latinas in Milwaukee and elsewhere in Wisconsin. We thought that by working together we could better advocate for more services for women and their families. I became a member, and other women were attracted to the idea of a Latina-led advocacy group. A number of the women had tried to work with various community leaders, who were almost all men, but they felt limited in what they could do largely based on their gender.

One of the very first activities that we organized under our group was a weekend training for grassroots women from various neighborhoods in Milwaukee, Racine, and Madison who really did not understand their power or potential. Through a grant we obtained, the women, their children, and LTF members came together at a former convent in Madison. We offered child care, organized by some of our male supporters, while the women took part in different trainings. Many didn't speak English, so our sessions were bilingual or all in Spanish. We attempted to affirm that they were already leaders in certain ways and that they had the abilities to further develop their organizing skills in order to make change in their neighborhoods and cities. It was this effort that clearly said to me that there's so much potential in women. That experience has stayed with me. They were amazing women, and I think they recognized their strengths, too.

For several years, the LTF worked on different advocacy projects. We gathered research information so we could better articulate the issues of

Latinas to policy makers. We dealt with local and state government, as they were the largest service providers to the Latino community. Eventually, we became politically involved because we saw that elected officials had a say in how government resources were distributed and how programs could be directed toward different populations. We would interview candidates based on their level of support for the Latino community and fund-raised for them once we decided to back them.

I think we walked away from our time in the LTF with a better understanding of who we were individually; we saw the different strengths we

(Left to right) Margaret Zarate, Gloria Rodriguez, and Maria Rodríguez attend a LAUCR Sixteenth of September Community Event, ca. 1975. SOMOS LATINAS PROJECT ORAL HISTORIES AND COLLECTED PAPERS

could contribute and the power of our collective force. This was certainly needed, as we were viewed by Latino men as being dangerous; we were viewed by heads of different organizations as being ball-busting. Watch out for those Latina Task Force women! But that's not what we were about. We were not anti-men, even though some of our men couldn't understand why their leadership wasn't fine as it was. In the process of exerting our power, some [men] did hurtful things to us. There were verbal attacks, and direct and indirect intimidating statements, but for the most part, it did not go beyond that. Electoral politics was one way our power became visible in the community. We would meet with politicians as a group and show that there was strength in organizing voters. In the process, many of us ended up working for [the politicians]. I think good contributions were made by all these women. Even after we moved on, we stayed connected and helped each other out personally and professionally. We continued to team up from time to time as certain issues arose. Some of the fruits of that can be seen at the university, within MPS, and in a better relationship with politicians—and also in understanding our relationship to our men, Latino men. Many of them continue to make contributions and, hopefully, can continue to influence younger people.

SUPPORTING REPRODUCTIVE RIGHTS

I was offered a job with Planned Parenthood in 1985. I talked to my mother before I took that job, and I asked, "Mom, what do you think I should do?" And she said, "Women in my time didn't know anything about their bodies; they didn't control how many children they wanted. You know, this is a good thing. Women, especially Latina women, need to know about this kind of stuff." At first, I thought she would be mad at me or say, "Don't go," or "Oh, don't take that job," but she was very in tune to what had happened to women in her day and what women had done to themselves. So I was like, "Wow, Mom." She was very supportive. She was the one that all along kind of said, "There are injustices in this world, and we have to do what we can for those that don't have the support, knowledge, or capacity." She would say that there is always something you can do to help and somebody that needs help." I took the job with Planned Parenthood, and I promoted the many educational and health services for anyone, but particularly girls and women.

HELPING TO START LATINAS EN ACCIÓN

Around 2000, I started to serve on the Women's Fund of Greater Milwaukee (WFoGM). I sat on the Grants Advisory Committee for six years, and I felt out of place among the women, and that felt very strange to me. But again, I learned that you have to know how to work with people different than yourself or those that aren't aware of their own biases.

In either 2004 or 2005, Cecilia Vallejo and I decided to formalize a fund specific to Latina girls and women within the WFoGM [called Latinas en Acción (LEA)]. Since then, we've raised over $70,000 and started awarding small grants just a few years ago; we have already given out over $35,000. So it is small, but it is growing. I saw this as an extension of the work of the Latina Task Force and so did Patricia Villarreal, who was very involved in the LTF and is now active with LEA. We developed a steering committee for fund development and grant making. By LEA being part of the WFoGM, it sort of gave us an edge, because we were part of an institution, and they had a bigger reach that we didn't have in terms of philanthropy. Broadening the understanding of Latina issues and concerns with a group that traditionally just deals with reproductive health added another layer of education. I've had some reflection on my role to support Latinas and my community. Right now, it's about broadening the knowledge with others as to who we are as Latinas, that we are a vital part of this community now and in the near future, even more so as our population grows, and we need to make sure that our girls and women are advancing.

Some older members of our original group and myself have begun to step back and let the younger members of our committee take over. Formalizing a group was one thing. Getting it started, building the fund, having it as part of the WFoGM, and negotiating how we use those dollars in the community was all part of the steering committee. But in the last couple of years we really wanted, very strategically, to bring in young women, and we've done that. I think we are better, we are stronger, and they are going to carry out the mission of LEA into the next generation.

Life Today

In 1990, I was hired by Mayor John Norquist to be the executive director of the Election Commission. I always thought that voting was so important. When I was in high school, I volunteered as a poll worker and translated for Spanish speakers who came to vote. In 1994, I transferred to the city's Housing Authority, where I have been ever since. The agency has a strong philosophy of supporting the person toward greater economic independence, which includes resident leadership and supporting parents to see that their children do well in school.

Maria Rodríguez, 2014. ELOISA GÓMEZ

As I can, I enjoy time with my husband, Emilio Lopez, and expanding family. I'm now a grandmother of ten grandchildren. It's a wonderful experience, and when I retire, I plan to enjoy time with all of them even more.

One award that I'd like to mention is the Gwen T. Jackson Community Service Award from United Way of Greater Milwaukee in 2014. I felt honored to receive this award. My mother, who has since passed on, was able to be present when I received it, so it's even more special to me.

LEONOR ROSAS

Born Leonor Rosas Pinzón on August 12, 1947, in Bogota, Colombia,
Leonor came to Milwaukee in 1958. Following her grandmother's
examples of service, Leonor sought employment in the Latinx commu-
nity and worked to increase fairness for women and the poor. Leonor
became involved in electoral politics to strengthen the collective voice
of the Latinx community.

Ethnic identity: Hispanic/Native American.

Do you consider yourself an activist? Somewhat.

How do you define community activism? Knowing the issues in the community and advocating for equality as an individual and as part of a group.

Areas of activism: Economic and political.

Location of activism: Milwaukee, Racine, Kenosha, and Madison.

Years of activism: Since the late 1970s.

EMIGRATING TO THE US

How I arrived in Milwaukee comes down to my uncle's death in 1952. He
was in a bicycle race in Colombia, which was a big sport, such as football
is in the United States. He was competing in the national Colombian
race, and he went over a cliff and died. It was traumatic for the family. It
was so traumatic that my two aunts joined a convent. They couldn't take
the pain and devastation, so they joined a convent and ended up in the
convent of the Sacred Heart in Milwaukee. They stayed in the convent
until 1956, when one left first, then the other. One worked as an elementary teacher, and my other aunt worked at St. Michael's Hospital. They
wrote home and said Milwaukee was a nice place to live. Colombia, at
that time, was under the dictatorship of President Gustavo Rojas Pinilla,
and we lived under martial law. So my aunts wrote to my mother and

urged her to sell the house and move to Milwaukee. My uncle, who was twenty-one, and I came first because of the cost to emigrate, but by 1959, my mother, grandmother, little sister, and brother arrived. A year later, my dad arrived, too.

LIFE IN MILWAUKEE

We didn't know that on the South Side of Milwaukee there was a pocket of Hispanics living there. So we found a place on the East Side, which is now called Riverwest. It was mostly a Polish community at the time, and we felt accepted. My mother worked for Lappin Electric Company. When I was eleven, I would go to the bank and cash her check. I could go to the corner grocery store and buy my father his cigarettes. My mother had two babies, and I went to all her OB/GYN appointments and translated everything for her. When they bought a house, I translated all their papers.

It wasn't until I was a teenager that I started experiencing discrimination. I know the day that I felt discrimination for the first time was on my sixteenth birthday. We went to the suburb of West Allis to go to the state fair with my uncle, and I went to the bathroom with my two younger sisters. I always told my little sister to put toilet paper on the toilet seat before she sat down. So my little sister went and she came out and said, "Lee, I put the toilet paper on the toilet like you told me." I said, "Excellent, *mi'ja* [child]!" The cleaning woman in the bathroom heard this. Now, in my country of Colombia, we didn't have racial stereotypes, but we had economic segregation. So a woman that cleans your bathroom is not viewed the same as someone who works in an office. So maybe I was looking down on her. The woman said, "But did you flush the toilet? You people never flush the toilet." I was confused. I walked outside and my middle sister said to the woman, "Why don't you flush yourself down the toilet?" I was still very confused. I said, "What kind of people did she mean? What is she talking about?" My middle sister knew. She said to me, "She was saying that because we're Latino." I was like, "Oh, we're Latino!" It was like a revelation. It was the first time I found someone looking down on me just because of how I looked. So that's the first time I found prejudice.

LOSING A PARENT

My family valued education, and my plans were definitely to go beyond secondary education. I did graduate in the upper 10 percent of my class, even though Spanish was my first language. I tried very hard, and I always excelled. I even went on a weekend visit to Carroll College and had my heart set on going there, but on November 27, 1965, the day after Thanksgiving Day, my father killed himself. It was too difficult for him to live in this country. He was a good mechanic in Colombia, and my mother was a secretary. Those were middle-class positions. When she came here, even though she didn't speak English, she started working at Lappin Electric. She did filing, and she was quickly moving up. My dad started working at Donaldson Oldsmobile as a janitor, but they made him do all the tune-ups on all the cars and paid him as a janitor. Everything may have seemed too much for him. My little sister was only two months old when this occurred.

Three visitors arrived at our house from St. Vincent de Paul Society shortly after. They were three men in gray suits with hats. They came in and brought us a basket full of groceries. I translated for them as they told us that we could go to the county welfare office to apply for food, or we can go to a government employment office and look for a job. They wrote down the addresses and then left. My mom, my *abuelita* [grandmother], and I sat down and talked. I had just graduated from high school and was enrolled at Carroll College the following semester. My mom said that we were not going to the county because that didn't sound right. She said we were going to get jobs.

The next day we went to the Plankinton Building and lined up with a lot of people. There was a little box with job information; to this day I remember the little box. We met with this case manager who looked through the little box for job leads. They found a job for my mom at the First Wisconsin Bank downtown, in the mailroom. I got a job at Brills Colony Menswear store in the unit control, working with inventory. We each started work the following day. I then took some bookkeeping classes at MATC [Milwaukee Area Technical College]. After Brills, I went to work for Johnson Controls and continued to take classes. I married shortly afterward and had a baby.

I continued with accounting and bookkeeping classes and anything I could at night. I had a second son and continued to pursue my education.

During the 1970s, I decided to participate in the citywide Take Back the Night march. I made some posters for the march and participated in it. Women were being attacked on the streets, and women, in particular, were advocating for more police protection. I had little children and didn't drive at the time, so I walked much and relied on the bus; I saw it as a personal and community issue.

In 1978, when I was thirty years old, I got my bachelor's degree. I worked for Miller Brewing Company at this time. At a certain point, I knew that it was not what I wanted to do. So I left, and I sent my resume all over the place. I had an interview at La Guadalupana, a senior day care program on the South Side. I remember Mrs. Renteria interviewed me, and she said, "No, you don't have any experience." I didn't! I thought, "But how am I going to get experience if no one gives me a chance?" So I had a college degree and a lot of experience in the private sector, but no community experience. Mr. Murguia, the director of Centro Hispano [Spanish Center; its formal title is Council for the Spanish Speaking], gave me an interview, and I started working as a prevocational coordinator. That's where I really started learning about the Latino community and community issues.

WORKING AT CENTRO HISPANO

In this position, I started working with women who were displaced homemakers. I worked to prepare people for a second vocation. I was working with three groups of people: displaced homemakers, at-risk youth who had dropped out of high school, and ex-offenders. I started seeing that there were so many issues that young people and displaced homemakers were facing. One of the women in her forties was abused by her husband, who went back to Mexico. He left her with the children. She needed to find a career, so I helped her polish up her resume, referred her for typing classes, and encouraged her along the way. She was finally placed in the courthouse as a translator. I saw other barriers for her, like finding decent child care for her children, and her older children were beginning to get involved with gangs. Then there was another woman who was maybe fifty or fifty-five, but she didn't qualify for anything. Her husband had died, and she really could not type, so we thought she could get a clerk position, but math was difficult for her. One day, we started to talk about cooking because I knew she loved cooking. I said, "Okay, how much flour do you put when you make tortillas? How do you measure it?" Well, all of a sudden she had a breakthrough. She understood fractions, and I was happy for her, and we were able to place her in a job right afterward.

Life was very complicated for the families. We had women coming from Mexico who were undocumented. If a person is undocumented, almost every door is closed to them. They are not able to apply for many services, like health care, dental care. They didn't go to the police if they were robbed or if they were abused, for fear of deportation. Landlords abused them and charged awful prices, maybe thousands of dollars for a two-bedroom that they have to share with five or six families. We saw things that were atrocious because of the inability of someone to call the police or report it, because they didn't want to be deported. Then we saw other people, like Puerto Rican families. Many who came to our office had low education levels. The economic conditions in Puerto Rico were also very bad. So we would see them because even though they could legally apply for things, they didn't. Sometimes there were issues with drug and alcohol abuse, or sometimes the children fell into gang activities, so they had to deal with the juvenile justice system.

At the Spanish Center, I saw two things that I had never personally seen before. I saw a young man, who was about seventeen years old, in a room being taught to read. He was in our adult basic education program. As I passed by him, I noticed that the book he was using was very similar to the book that my seven-year-old son was using. Later on, I asked the teacher, "Why is he using a second grade textbook?" And she said, "It's because he doesn't know how to read." Then later I saw a young woman also at the Spanish Center and she was bruised black and purple all over. I had never seen that before. There was trauma in seeing this and feeling ill equipped to handle this. I kept thinking, "What do I do now?" I knew I couldn't lose my composure while taking her to the police and then the hospital. My plan was to provide help to address the crisis at hand, but at the same time, evaluate ways to make it better for the next woman, should it happen again, like what to do if there are no translators? All of these places that I'm talking about finally now have bilingual counselors.

We have bilingual police officers. We didn't have that then. There was the issue of languages and translation and services that weren't available. So I think my role has been mostly from the inside advocating to make the system better, like creating bilingual positions so that people could move through the system easier.

I wasn't involved officially with any formal women's group. Mine were mostly unofficial groups. One was a group of Latinas who got together in the late 1980s. Some of the women included Patricia Villarreal, Elisa Romero, Maria Rodríguez, and Gladis Benavides. We shared with each other issues that were taking place, like the atrocious conditions that were taking place in the migrant camps and the way that young people of color were being treated by the police force. We would then discuss what to do, and this might include political work. We became involved in supporting political candidates [who] supported our views and would work with us. We wanted more jobs for our families and better education. We wanted bilingual education. We wanted bilingual-bicultural teachers to help our kids move forward. We tried to work with parents to educate them on their rights. Many of the parents didn't know that they had rights to have their children tested or not have their children expelled from school without sufficient cause. We wanted to meet with educators to have equal access to education, equal access to jobs, and housing was a big issue for us because there was segregation.

The Chicano Movement and Marriage

Well, I fell in love with a Chicano. The Chicano movement that began in the 1960s was a cry for justice, which leads me to the man I would marry, Alex de Leon. He was one of twelve children. He went and fought in Vietnam because it was the right thing to do. He received quite a few awards for fighting in Vietnam. That's where he said he learned about racial injustice—when the Vietnamese people and Vietnamese children would go up to him and say, "Same. Same. Same." They would show him their skin. He said they would rub his skin and show their skin and say "Same, same." He started seeing that we were in Vietnam for the wrong reasons. When he returned, he went to look for the revolution; that took him to Denver, one of the centers of Chicano activism. He was there for maybe two years working with the schools, being a part of the movement. Then he came back here. The movement came first with the African American community, and the injustices and Martin Luther King, and it quickly, simultaneously, woke up the Chicanos, which are Mexican Americans who were born in the United States. That's how I would define a Chicano: someone who found him- or herself struggling with injustice and wanted to do something for a better life for their children. Some of them sacrificed themselves, like going to jail, and some of them died. But the Chicano movement that Alex was involved in was not what I was involved in. Mine was more passive. Maybe I didn't have the passion that he had, but I had the same philosophy, and we supported each other's efforts for many years.

The Chicano movement seems to be gone. It emerged because it was needed. The 1960s was called the Decade of Discontent. It was the awakening of the baby boomers, who come in different shapes and colors. The baby boomers were saying, "This isn't right. This isn't fair for the African Americans, and it isn't right for the Latinos." You needed to identify yourself as something—that word "Chicano," because you weren't Mexican. People sometimes ask me, for example, if I like Mexican music. Alex and I didn't listen to Mexican music. We listened to the Beatles, the Who, and the Doors. That's who we were. We didn't really have identities with Mexico or Colombia. We had identity with our people, our neighbors, and our friends who looked like us, who were going through the same issues.

INVOLVEMENT IN ELECTORAL POLITICS

I worked at the Spanish Center in Racine, and I was commuting back and forth to Milwaukee. Alex and I had just adopted our little girl, and this commute was time-consuming. So in the 1980s, I called Mary Ann McNulty, a close friend, and told her that I needed to find a job in Milwaukee, and asked if she had any job leads. She was the alderwoman of the district that had the highest concentration of Latinos in the city. I had helped in her campaign. I found early on, if you help people with their campaigns it's a good thing because you can get your issues addressed. So I asked her if she knew of any jobs. She said, "You can come work for me." So I worked for her as a legislative assistant, but I was really involved with helping her introduce and pass resolutions. I spoke before the Common Council and got to know all the aldermen in the city. I helped her with her reelection and helped the political movement learn how they formed their caucuses and their clusters, how they voted together, how they passed each other's resolutions. So that was very helpful.

From this involvement, I met her network of supporters and advocates. Many were other elected officials, judges, and attorneys. Many of us started working on Dave Schulz's campaign for Milwaukee county executive. I've always been involved with progressive issues, and his campaign was definitely not old school. The old county executive targeted county money and services to the same people, all the time. We needed money coming to our communities and jobs being available for our folks. So a big cluster of us worked diligently on Dave's campaign, and in 1988, he won the election. Right after, he asked me to be his assistant chief of staff. That was an exciting thing. I was put in charge of the Private Industry Council. It wasn't called that at the time, but it was the office that dealt with the dollars that came to the county for the area of economic development. I also worked with the office of veteran's issues, whose director reported to me, as did the office of emergency management and economic development.

So one of the first things that the county executive asked me to do was to detach the Office of Employment and Economic Self-Sufficiency and create the Private Industry Council, which would be an arm of the county that dealt with CETA [Comprehensive Employment and Training Act] and other federal dollars, so it could become its own nonprofit organization. He wanted to end the patronage system and make it independent. It was a difficult thing to do, but I got it done. He was the best supervisor I ever had because he always empowered me. I used to say, "I'm just a little kid!" He'd always be like, "You got to do this. You got to get out there. You can do it!" Whenever I brought him a problem, he always told me, "You don't bring me a problem without a solution." He empowered you to research that solution and form possible outcomes and work forward, so that's what I did.

At the end of four years, he said, "I'm not running for reelection." Toward the end of his term, I ran the Private Industry Council once I had separated it from the county. He put me there until the board did a national search and found a director. I ran it for eight months. That experience helped me when I applied to become the Job Service district director for Milwaukee County. I did that for eight years. During that time, every position that I could add bilingual as a needed skill, I did. You can make it as a skill if you could show need. This was not an easy task, as it involved the civil service process, so there was plenty of bureaucracy involved, but I maneuvered through it successfully many times.

I was appointed by governors of both political parties onto councils, such as Patrick Lucey to the Criminal Justice Council; Tommy Thompson, twice, to different councils; and I was appointed by James Doyle, also.

Leonor Rosas, 2014. ELOISA GÓMEZ

Through my employment and training I ended up back in the community. Even though I did my part with the government, I always wanted to finish the circle and come back to the community. I worked for United Migrant Opportunity Services (UMOS) for fifteen years. I held three positions there: director of fund development and research, director of family services, and director of employment.

I retired from UMOS in 2016 and remain involved in volunteer work. My son, Bayardo, and I have been members of Congregation of the Great Spirit for the past eleven years. The parish is part of the Catholic Church and offers services to the Native American community. I have been on the Elders [Parish] Council and volunteer on many fund-raisers so they can offer a food and clothing bank, and emergency funds for families in financial and spiritual need.

Irene Santos

Irene Santos was born on April 5, 1931, in Crystal City, Texas. Her parents were migrant workers. They came to Wisconsin in 1943 to work on farms in Kenosha and elsewhere. Irene settled in Kenosha in 1965. She began her advocacy work in 1965 when she started as an outreach worker for the United Migrant Opportunities Services. She eventually expanded her leadership role as director of the Racine/Kenosha Spanish Center in the 1980s; while there, Irene built black/Latino alliances to increase services for both communities.

Ethnic identity: Mexican.

Do you consider yourself an activist? Yes.

How do you define community activism? Present yourself and get involved with others. We have rights, and we have the right to speak up.

Areas of activism: Migrant rights, racial justice.

Location of activism: Racine and Kenosha.

Years of activism: Since the 1960s.

Early Years in Texas

I experienced the harshness of life in second grade when my teachers would use a big wooden paddle with a little narrow handle so that they could hit us better. We had a really nice teacher, but she would come at me because we had to know the colors. She made us repeat all the colors, like red and yellow, but I couldn't remember purple. Time after time I couldn't get it, and eventually she gave up on me. She put me in the last back seat and once paddled me so much that my legs were purple. I remember walking home like that. My grandmother had been visiting from Mexico, and I was late because I had difficulty walking. When I arrived home, she asked why I was so late, and I told her that I was paddled. When she and my parents saw the back of my legs, she was so mad. She said, "Desgcraciada maestra [Disgraceful teacher]." "Let's go and kill her," she told my father. I said, "No, mama, we can't do that. She is the teacher." In the back of my mind, the color purple meant that the day was so sad, hurtful, and shameful. Even the kids laughed because I couldn't walk right. So purple is right here, in my heart.

LA RAZA UNIDA PARTY AND ELECTORAL POLITICS

Things started to change in Crystal City, Texas, where I mostly grew up. At the time, many of us worked at the Del Monte cannery in town. This was around the time when the La Raza Unida Party started. At that time, a small group questioned why we didn't have any Hispanics on the city council—or as mayor, since we had the same mayor for thirty-five years. Back then, Hispanics had to pay a poll tax—I think it was $1.76—to vote, and that prevented many of us from voting because we did not have the money. We knew it was wrong, and one time in the early 1960s, we held a protest about our right to vote. We said, "Vámonos [let's go], let's work together." We urged our friends, "Vénganse [come on]," and held meetings at people's houses. Some of the gringos came to our homes to intimidate us, but we didn't know how far they would go, so when we held our meetings, we put blankets on the windows so no one could see inside. We used kerosene lamps for dim lighting as we met. Once there was one or two men waiting outside in the back of this house where we were, and we were scared about what he or they might do. They meant to intimidate us so we would stop organizing, but we didn't give up. At the same time, our people came out of college, so they knew the rules, and then we better understood that we had the same rights as a gringo. We decided that we had to vote and have our own candidates run for local offices, like mayor or the city council.

We started getting excited once we understood our rights better. Finally five people said that they would run for office. The Teamsters came and helped guide and advise the group. Then we also had to deal with Los Rinches, the Texas Rangers. They came, and they beat up the few young men who were advocating for our rights. Dr. José Ángel Gutiérrez, who was from the university, was one of the leaders. He knew more than the rest of us and came with a lot of ideas. One night, the Rangers were waiting for him outside his house. They were beating him up until his mom came out with a rifle, and that's why they left. They did many things to intimidate us, but we pushed back. As Election Day got closer, we were scared to death, but we said, "No, we can do this; we deserved this like anybody else."

On Election Day in 1963, we won all five seats that we ran for. The gringo mayor and everybody else lost. Juan Cornejo, who was a member of the Teamsters union and one of the leaders of the group, became mayor of Crystal City. I still have the original cards and everything. For many years after that, the positions were being filled by Mexican Americans. Now we have congressmen. Hispanic people now know they have rights to choose political leaders.

EDUCATION AND FIELD WORK IN WISCONSIN

Getting educated was really hard for us because we were a migrant family. I only went up to fifth grade because we moved back and forth. We first came here to Wisconsin in 1943. I was thirteen or fourteen years old. Wherever we arrived, I would go straight to work in the fields. School was not a priority of the family because the wages were very low, so everyone had to help out. My aunt, Genoveva Medina, had also lived in Crystal City, but she and her family moved to the Kenosha area. She had been a migrant worker, too. She was also influenced by the work of La Raza Unida Party in Crystal City, and some of those people moved up to Wisconsin. Several of them, including my aunt, started the organization United Migrant Opportunity Services (UMOS). She became the first woman organizer in the fields and helped change the conditions on the farms.

My aunt was one of us. She tried to do things a few steps ahead of others. She met with people who came to work on the farms. From her, we started learning that we weren't supposed to live in the poor conditions on these farms. Sometimes we were housed on farms where animals used to live. Back then, some of our men talked about the hay that was still there where they slept, but those things did change. Why? Because there were organizers like my *tia* [aunt] and her bosses and friends who organized a march to Madison to protest these conditions. There were three hundred or so people who went on the march. This was in the 1960s. We protested for the services we needed. I remember that on one of the marches, I heard someone yell out at us, "Go back to Mexico, dirty Mexicans!" I just waved back. Because of these efforts and others, state inspectors were sent to inspect the houses where migrant workers lived, so the worst conditions improved over time. Afterward, my aunt was worried about how we were going to protect the farmworkers from harm in case there was a backlash.

UMOS wanted workers to go and do outreach in the farms, to see if the workers were getting assistance and things like that, so they hired me as an outreach worker. At the farms, I would go and talk to the fieldworkers and their families. We would talk about the conditions and the pay. We talked about not coming here every year from Texas in April and going back to our cities in November. We let them know about UMOS services, like information about more permanent jobs and relocating here. This was why a lot of us are here. I think when I came to Kenosha, there were ten Hispanic families working the farms here. But right now, we are thousands. This is why we are here, because of UMOS and my aunt. At that time, there were a lot of jobs at the American Motors plant and not enough workers, so when we contacted them, they took our referrals and said they needed even more people.

WORKING FOR THE KENOSHA SPANISH CENTER

I was in an accident, so I left for a long while. After I was okay, I went to work in Burlington [in Racine County] in the 1980s. By then, the Spanish Center had started up. The director called me and asked if I wanted to work for the Spanish Center in Kenosha. They already had a Spanish Center in Racine but planned to open one in Kenosha. The services helped people who settled there and we helped with the educational needs of the children. We continued to do all sorts of advocacy work.

While at the Kenosha Spanish Center, we helped Aurora, a bilingual person, who had applied for a job with the Kenosha Social Services office. We were concerned that she was being discriminated against. She was told they weren't hiring, but she had a good education. I thought we should protest against the city council. Fifty to sixty people showed up at one of the committee meetings. We asked to be heard, but we were told that we weren't on the agenda. People waited inside and outside of the meeting room until they gave us time on their agenda. Then I introduced Aurora and explained that she had applied and reapplied for a position. I reminded them that Kenosha Social Services had clients who didn't speak English, but their workers didn't speak Spanish, so how were they going to get the services? The committee said that in a few weeks they would let us know their decision. They did hire her, and this was the way that we got power for the Spanish Center and the way that we got a voice.

Working for UMOS

I returned later to work for UMOS in the 1990s. One time, there was a Latino male who had a problem with me early on. The agency received government funds to help relocate migrant workers, such as for car repairs. It was money to get them here to Kenosha if they had problems. Mr. [William] Kruse was the director of UMOS at the time. I was responsible for these funds, a few thousand dollars. We kept records of how the money was spent, and we did it very honestly. One day, I got a call from Mr. Kruse, who said, "Mrs. Santos, I think you gave two checks to the same person." I said, "Really?" He said, "Yes, and we have to talk about it; it's bad." He was accusing me of giving two checks to the same person, but I knew this was not true. They gave me the dates, and so I contacted both men, Luis García and Luis Gonzáles, to come over and I told them what was going on. I asked them to wait in the office downstairs. Mr. Kruse came with the books and he said, "You lied to me; here are the two persons: Luis G. and Luis G., different addresses, but the same last name." I said, "He is here. Luis Gonzáles, puedes venir para'ca por favor? [Can you come here, please?]" Mr. Gonzáles responded, "Sí, Señora Santos, ay voy. [Yes, Mrs. Santos, I'm coming.]" The director asked him, "Did you get a check from Mrs. Santos?" He said, "Oh, yes sir; here is the copy for two tires." The director's response was, "And did you get a second check?" I asked him to wait a minute and asked Mr. García to come upstairs. Mr. Kruse asked Mr. García if he received a check from me, and Mr. García said, "Yes, and here is a copy of a receipt." The initial of their last names were the same, like the first name. The director said, "I am so, so sorry." I told him, "Never do that to me again. Never. I would never take a penny from an agency if I didn't earn it." I am not sure if you have seen a picture with a lot of dogs playing cards, sitting and passing the cards to the other one. We bought a picture of that. I put his name on it and wrote, "With a lot of love from Kenosha, Wisconsin." I signed my name, and the other people signed their names, and we sent it to him. We were honest. And from then on our team was beautiful. It was fine.

THE WOMEN'S BLACK-BROWN ALLIANCE

I also worked with the Urban League, and they offered English as a Second Language classes. We had many issues in common, and we served similar people. When issues came up that we shared, their staff would say, "Let's go to the meetings at city hall," or "Let's go to the meeting of the school board." They knew that things weren't right. It was a wonderful time.

Ms. Elma Or was the director with the Urban League for a time. We found ways to help each other and became friends. At one time, [the Urban League] ran a lunch program for seniors that was very important. The city was trying to shift the funds, so she had invited me to go with her. The snow had come early in the afternoon; it was real cold. She said, "Mrs. Santos, I don't have my car, so I am going to use my grandson's car." It was a sports car and had a stick shift. We were late to the meeting because of the storm. We went to the second floor of the city hall, and everyone was already sitting. This assistant came to us and told us we were late. I said, "Ma'am, when you are our age, and there is a storm outside, and you are using your grandson's car with a stick shift, you tell me that you'd get to a place on time?" She said nothing. So we sat, and they all said, "Welcome, Mrs. Santos." We had a good friendship until she passed away.

THE SANTOS FUND

Sometime between 1994 and 1997, a good group of Hispanic ladies who were friends and I donated a few dollars every month, and we would give it to the needy. It expanded because of the support of a former Racine mayor who also became my friend. When John [Antaramian] first ran, I worked at the Spanish Center. He called me to help him with his campaign. And I said, "Yes, and can you help me, too?" And he said, "Well, what do you need?" I said I wanted his help to tear down a four-unit apartment [building] that was in terrible condition, but people still lived there. Even a skunk lived there. It would go up the stairways and sneak in all the rooms. He asked to see the apartment, so one day I took him there. While we were in a back room, the skunk jumped out. He had been in a garbage can. It was so unexpected that it caught him off guard. He didn't expect that.

Then I took him to meet all the people who were waiting to meet him since I told them that he was coming. They said, "Mrs. Santos, bring him over so that he can see the conditions of the building." He saw the other problems with the apartment, like water leaks here and there. He said, "Mrs. Santos, if I were to win as mayor, this house will be torn down, I promise, and I will help you." So we did our best. John won, and one day shortly after, I was contacted by a man. He said, "Mrs. Santos, they need you at this place" [where the apartment was]. And I said, "What for?" He said, "I don't know; I was told you should come here." I went with one of my nieces and a few other people and asked what they wanted. And there was a gentleman with a rock. The gentleman said that the mayor wanted me to break the window of the house. I said, "No, because if I break it, they will arrest me." He said, "No, Mrs. Santos, look over there. The cranes are going to take the building down." The people had moved because they couldn't stand it there. It was torn down, but a new building later went up. One time John was kidding with me and told me he was going to report me to the police because I had broken that window. One day years later, I met with John and he told me that he wasn't the mayor anymore and offered to support our work. I said that we couldn't accept his money because our group didn't have a tax-exempt status. He still helped us by setting up an account at a bank in Milwaukee, and he made some deposits after that; we weren't charged for it.

The Kenosha Spanish Center closed around 2010. It was a blow to the community because people were still coming to our city, and they needed the same services from twenty to thirty years ago. The services were more about immigration than jobs. The people who are illegal in the United States are suffering, and we are doing the best we can with this new law. That is why I've been in contact with Congressman Paul Ryan, because he represents the Kenosha area. His staff helped us during the amnesty program and, at a personal level, he helped me with my brother who was seriously ill. I know that his position is that he wants to have the border guarded. People have lied about fieldworkers. Some got their green cards because they stole the letters from the real farmworkers who were here illegally, and that was not fair. The government has to protect these workers who have been here for many years. He sent me this letter explaining his position. We are watching Congressman Ryan, and other senators and congressmen, very closely. We need to let them know we vote and that we are watching them. I believe that if we all vote, politicians will help us with our needs.

I am now retired. I have my four sons, grandchildren, and even great-grandchildren. Being an older person, I am not as actively involved in community issues, but I will continue to help as I can.

Irene Santos, 2016. ELOISA GÓMEZ

NATALIA SIDON

Natalia Sidon was born in Zacatecas, Mexico, on September 9, 1976.
When she was just twelve years old, she immigrated to California to
live with her sister because her parents wanted her to receive a quality
education and have greater opportunities. At eighteen, she moved to
Green Bay, Wisconsin, to be closer to her brother. Eventually, she chose
to work for the Green Bay Police Department, becoming the city's first
Hispanic female in this civilian position.

Ethnic identity: Hispanic.

Do you consider yourself a community activist? No, I don't consider
myself a community activist. I see myself more as an advocate. What I do
is not for political reasons but more for humanitarian reasons.

**What is your definition of a community activist, even if you do not
consider yourself one?** One that is involved in political issues.

Area of advocacy and service: Most of what I have done is in relation to
human services. I've helped people with medical issues, landlord/tenant
issues, domestic violence issues, employment issues, parenting issues,
etc. I have made myself available as a general resource for members of the
Hispanic community who need direction and support.

Location of advocacy and service: Greater Green Bay area.

Years of advocacy and service: Since 1996 (shortly after my arrival in
Green Bay).

EMIGRATING TO CALIFORNIA

In 1989 [when I was twelve years old], I moved to California, where I started
middle school. I moved in with one of my sisters after my parents sent
me to the United States. They believed in the education system here. So
I was in California during my teen years. I came to a new country where
I didn't know anybody, and going to school with hundreds of kids was

really hard; back in my country there were only fifteen or twenty kids in my class. I remember feeling left out because I didn't understand what was taking place. The first year or two were hard. In this country, I saw a lot of people struggle without jobs, with kids getting into gangs; it was just very shocking to me. I didn't have a lot of resources at the time. It was a struggle, but I somehow managed to always find the right people that could help.

CREATING COMMUNITY IN GREEN BAY

I moved to Green Bay, Wisconsin, in the summer of 1995 when I was eighteen, and I've been here ever since. I didn't do any research before I moved here. My brother just said it was beautiful, and I believed him. Everything was green, and the summer weather was really nice, so it was a big shock for me during my first winter because I had no idea how cold it could get. But the first time I saw it snowing, I thought it was gorgeous. However, I didn't own a winter coat or boots, and I had never heard the term long underwear until then. It was quite a big change. I noticed that the Hispanic community was small, and I was not used to that. I had gotten used to being in California where everywhere you went you saw Hispanic people and most of them spoke Spanish. So I came to Green Bay, and it was new again. I needed to adjust and learn the culture and the people. I soon realized that others were also struggling with language barriers. It was kind of shocking, and it was hard to open doors at first.

The Latino community in Green Bay was small and concentrated, but there was a steady growth happening. There were few to no services for them, and there was very little understanding of Hispanic culture and little to no cultural sensitivity. In the neighborhood where I lived, I saw the need for helping people, whether it was translating or helping at the church I was attending. Little by little, I just started doing more things; it was just natural to me, and it needed to be done. I continued to do some of this work within the police department.

There was a Hispanic community advisory council to the mayor that advised him on issues facing the Hispanic people in Green Bay. I became involved in it before I began working for the Green Bay Police Department. The Mayor's Council was formed for community leaders to meet and help the Hispanic population better connect with community and with city resources. We advised the mayor on particular issues that were unique to the Hispanic community and recommended ways for city departments to better involve our community. In 1997 or 1998, a friend of mine who was very active and well-known in the community, Amparo Baudhuin, strongly encouraged me to join the council. I didn't know what to expect, but she felt I could contribute to their efforts, so I went and was invited to join. I made some good connections as well.

WORKING FOR COMMUNITY IN THE GREEN BAY POLICE DEPARTMENT

I joined the Green Bay Police Department in March of 2000. I'm not sure what drew me to this position. To be honest, I was more interested in the medical field. I first started working as a CNA [certified nursing assistant] in a nursing home and then went to work at a hospital. While there, a couple of detectives would come in from time to time with prisoners. They would say, "You need to come work for us at the police department." Then I started working as a part-time translator for the Green Bay municipal court, and this position opened up. I thought I would give it a try. I thought it would allow me to work more closely with the members of the community, and I think that's where it all happened. I realized I loved serving people, helping people. I was doing that at the hospital, but I felt like I needed to expand the help that I was giving, so I applied for this job.

I was hired as the Hispanic liaison officer and was the first Hispanic woman in this position. Just this last year, I had a title change. I am now the crime prevention coordinator, but continue to do much of what I have been doing for the last sixteen years. This is a civilian position. I work with all populations in this position. In my role, I help the public understand the laws and assist people in making connections to agencies and education programs. I go into the schools, churches, and other community places to explain rights and responsibilities under the law, how they can help each other and help the police.

In June 2000, I created a program called the Teen Police Academy. The program was five days long. It gave Hispanic students the opportunity to meet in small groups, have one-on-one time with officers, and talk about different topics or programs in the police department. It gave them insight into the workings of the police department and why they do things the way they do. A similar program was started for Hmong youth, and it morphed to include youth of other ethnic/racial groups. It is called Building Bridges. While the program became successful, I was getting overwhelmed trying to educate the community by myself. I was feeling like I was not reaching as many people as I thought should be reached, so I identified leaders in the community, and I got them together so they could expand the outreach into the community. I felt that if these leaders knew about the program, they would distribute the word to the rest of our community. So that was and continues to be a very successful program.

One of the biggest parts of my job with the Green Bay Police Department, in terms of helping the Latino community, has been reaching out to the victims of domestic violence and violent crimes, and helping with the education for new people who come into town. I advocate for people who are struggling to make a connection with city government, hospitals, or schools. It's community outreach for me.

When I began working with the police department, I was, first of all, entering into a man's world. I probably wasn't very well accepted by everyone at first. I was constantly questioned, and my abilities were challenged. Not only was I a female, but I was a Hispanic female, so there were some difficulties. I had to work extra hard to prove myself. The toughest thing about being a Hispanic female in my role was that I often felt that people thought I was ignorant; that I didn't know what I was talking about; or that I was too young and immature. I felt that I wasn't fully accepted.

I do what I do because it's rewarding to help people, especially during difficult times. It's hard to keep track of what I have done since coming to Green Bay. I always just put it in the back of my head, all of the things I have done, but I know much has been done in terms of reaching out to other agencies. I like to advocate for the Hispanic members that are struggling, whether it is with their kids, or single moms, victims of domestic violence, victims of sexual assault, you name it. I helped set up education programs such as parenting classes and how to understand the law. My job is never the same thing. I believe it is unique.

Providing Services to Women

When it comes to women, I like to help empower them: whether they're victims of domestic violence or whether they want to pursue an education. In the Hispanic community, we have some husbands who are controlling, or the women are so dedicated to the household that they forget who they are. I started a weekly multi-month program where I met

Natalia Sidon, 2014. NATALIA SIDON

with a small group of Hispanic women at various churches, to give them an opportunity to discuss women's issues. I like to help women strengthen their self-esteem, better understand who they are, and help them embrace and empower themselves. I think that as women, we need to be strong to care for ourselves and care for our family. To do that, we need to educate ourselves and our community. I started the program because often after each presentation, women wanted to talk with me. I chose church space because it seemed to be a safe space for women, acceptable to husbands, and churches were willing to help. I would bring in different speakers who could talk about services available to them and their families, if this was needed. These meetings gave them an opportunity to talk about what they were dealing with at home and to look for solutions. I'm not as involved with the groups [now]; I set the stage and some have taken over.

I am very involved with the community at large. I've been a part of many different committees, groups, and councils. I've worked with the Hmong community, and I work with the African American community. I serve on the board of directors of Casa Alba Melanie, the Hispanic Resource Center, and volunteer weekly in the YWCA Women's Empowerment Center, where I mentor and provide other support services to women from a variety of cultural/socioeconomic backgrounds.

I am working on my bachelor's degree in integrative leadership studies with an emphasis in human development at UW–Green Bay. In 2005, I received the Medal of Valor Award from the Green Bay Police Department for saving a neighbor's life.

RITA TENORIO

*Rita Tenorio was born on June 10, 1951, in Milwaukee, Wisconsin. She
began her career as an elementary school teacher who advocated for
strong educational programs for children, with an emphasis on multicultural, antiracist education. She was a founding member of Escuela
Fratney and the nationally circulated* Rethinking Schools *publication.*

Ethnic identity: Latina.

Do you consider yourself a community activist? Yes. As an educator, my
work affects children and families throughout the community. I encourage
them to be change makers for a better, more just future.

What is your definition of community activism? Engaging in work that
promotes social justice and encourages others to get involved in that work.

Areas of activism: Education: K–12, bilingual, social justice education.

Location of activism: Milwaukee, Wisconsin.

Years of activism: Since the early 1980s.

EARLY YEARS IN WISCONSIN

My mother is of German descent, and my father is first-generation Mexican American. He was born in Gary, Indiana, and moved to Wisconsin. So
I'm biracial and bicultural. When I was younger, I really didn't know much
about my Mexican heritage. I spent most of my time with my mother's
family and rarely with my dad's. It was in college and since then that I've
started to delve into that whole side of the family, and to improve my Spanish. My dad never spoke Spanish at home, and I don't think he spoke much
Spanish growing up. He was one of those kids whose family spoke to him
in Spanish, but he always responded in English. It was [through] becoming
a bilingual teacher and being more involved in education that my Spanish
got better. I identify myself as Latina. My identity is very important to me
at this point in my life, and it has been for a while.

Becoming an Educator

I grew up in a very middle-class environment and went to a Catholic elementary school and a public high school. Basically, I think I had a pretty traditional education for that time—growing up in a time when girls and women were second class in regards to expectations, standards, and encouragement. I never really liked school that much, but I feel like I did well. My dad had the expectation that we couldn't do anything but do well. His expectations were the primary reason for my academic success in high school. In my senior year, I went to see the guidance counselor to talk about what I would be doing when I graduated. He told me I had three choices: I could be a teacher, a nurse, or a social worker. He told me to pick one. You know, I was really taken aback because I thought I'd like to have a law degree, and I left his office feeling very disappointed. I knew I didn't want to be a teacher, and my mother was a nurse, so I did not want to do that. That left social work, so I started at the University of Wisconsin–Milwaukee (UWM) studying social work, but that changed pretty quickly when I did some fieldwork with children at Guadalupe Head Start. I am the oldest of six children, so it was an easy thing for me to work with younger children. I also had success as a camp counselor and taking care of others people's children. I realized that working with children could make a difference.

My experience in the School of Education at UWM was good. I had excellent professors and teachers who insisted on looking at the whole child, looking at multiculturalism, and holding firm to what was developmentally good for children. I learned that my role was to set an environment where children could learn, instead of teaching them by filling up their heads. Those were my guideposts, and they still are in a lot of ways.

I graduated from UWM in 1973. There were absolutely no jobs in education. I remember sending out resumes to school districts, probably twenty different ones, and never received one response. So I got out the Yellow Pages and started looking through the book. I began contacting Catholic and alternative schools. This is how I found my first job at Holy Angels Catholic School as a kindergarten teacher. It was almost 100 percent African American children. The whole school had such a strong mission to educate kids and to recognize their strengths, as opposed to thinking, "We have to fix these boys and girls." I learned how to teach at Holy Angels, and that experience was formative. My main goal as a new teacher was to help children learn. I was there for six years from 1974 to 1980, and I had a wonderful experience.

FROM CATHOLIC TO PUBLIC SCHOOLS

After Holy Angels, I helped to open the Spanish as a Second Language Program at Morgandale Public School here in Milwaukee in 1980, again as a kindergarten teacher. It was culture shock. After being in a place where children and parents were respected, it was really difficult for me because I witnessed two levels of student treatment by the teachers and staff, overall. Morgandale was a school on the South Side of Milwaukee in an all-white neighborhood. There were children, mostly African American, who came from the North Side on buses to get to the school as part of the desegregation effort. This had been going on for several years before I got there, but many of the teachers would describe the bused-in kids as "those kids." I felt that they were treated differently than the neighborhood children. Assumptions were made about the families and experience of those who were bused. Expectations for them were lower. It was hard to understand and harder to not speak up. That year there were only two of us in the new program, and we were hesitant to upset those who perceived that we, too, were intruding on their beautiful white school. Until the climate improved, I found it difficult to even go into the teachers' lounge because of the negative comments I would overhear about the bused students.

I had never felt in my life that I had been discriminated against so overtly as when I started in the public schools. The secretary, who was a sweet lady, said to me on one of my first days, "Oh, your English is so good." And I said, "Well, yes, I've been speaking it since I was a year old." She and others had assumptions like, "Oh, you grew up around Fifth and National, right?" (It was considered the heart of the Latino community.) And it was like, "No, I grew up out in West Allis." It was hard for many people there to not make assumptions about my experience because they defined me as a "bilingual" teacher. I personally felt the bias. It really woke me up.

This experience of how children were treated and my isolation from other teachers in the school pushed me to look for other colleagues with whom I could identify, who related to my Mexican culture, appreciated multiculturalism, and supported antiracism learning. In the 1980s, Milwaukee Public Schools had a human relations department that gave multicultural workshops to teachers on weekends. These workshops started after the schools were desegregated. There had been a lot of concern about teachers not being able to meet the needs of kids because they were of different cultures. And, as sad as it is, it is still like that today, where the majority of the teachers are not of the background of the students they teach. This is where I first met people who shared my concerns. Many of them have been important to my growth as an educator.

In the early 1980s, I began to network with other teachers who, like myself, wondered if they were the only teacher in their school who believed that being culturally competent was critical to good teaching. It was through these workshops, through other bilingual teachers' meetings, and with my colleagues in the teachers' union that I found others who had this same mindset. We felt a need for change, but didn't necessarily know what to do, or even how to name what was wrong with the school. This cohort and [my colleague] Bob Peterson, in particular, helped me to begin to think in different ways. The bilingual program at Morgandale grew and was successful with children and parents. But as I worked with my cohort of colleagues outside of the school, I developed a more critical perspective on teaching and, little by little, I began to realize that some of what I was doing wasn't enough. It wasn't enough in addressing antiracism and promoting multiculturalism. I was also concerned that these ideas were not being addressed throughout the district. So that's when I started to get more involved with others in what we called the "radical caucus" in our union.

UNION ACTIVISM

Milwaukee Teachers' Education Association (MTEA) is the union for the Milwaukee Public Schools. The MTEA focused on issues of wages, hours, and working conditions. The quality of education and issues related to school desegregation, multiculturalism, and curricula in general were given little if any attention. Some of us began to raise questions about the lack of equity in the district, the role of our union to give support to strategies that promote multiculturalism, and the need to give support to the educational part of the union's mission. We felt that it was important for the teachers' union to take stands on the quality of education, and not just the "bread and butter" issues for teachers. Changes like these that we proposed were like blasphemy in the minds of some of the teachers and MTEA leadership.

Our caucus of about ten, at that point, felt the union could be a vehicle for influencing teachers on issues of multiculturalism, learning more about teaching in diverse communities. The union was, as a whole, very white, and the staff and leadership were committed to maintaining the status quo. We spoke out at meetings, proposed amendments to the union constitution to strengthen the role of the membership in making decisions, and some of us ran for office. I was elected to the executive board of the union in about 1984. As I think back, I don't think there were any other Latinos or Latinas who were elected prior to me. I was definitely a fish out of water, and before I was on the board, few of the leadership or staff knew of my views and politics, but I found teachers who were open-minded to the notion of making change.

What the radical caucus and I more fully understood was how entrenched the staff of MTEA was in keeping the status quo. They, not the membership, really controlled the union. Just the fact that even executive board members required staff permission to get beyond the lobby of the MTEA was symbolic of the power they wielded. Also, there was no release time for teachers who were board members. With the level of resistance from MTEA staff and the president, we were engaged in a power struggle as we tried to create change within the union. I gave ten years of my life to the MTEA executive board, four years as the vice president. I understand that when the union president heard that I was the new vice president, he said my election was "a crime," and then I was told that I didn't need to participate in any of the meetings! Of course I did. There was definite chauvinism involved, too. There was only one woman on staff, and I don't think there was an expectation that female board members would have much of a voice in decision making. More progressive teachers joined the board over time, such as Bob [Peterson], Donelle Johnson, Paulette Copeland, Dennis Oulahan, Mike Langyel, and other progressive teachers. We wanted to build a network of like-minded people in the community, and we saw that the union leadership could be an important vehicle.

One of the earliest and most important projects we developed was the

Dr. Martin Luther King Jr. Writing Contest. This was not as part of the union, nor the school district, but an effort to call attention to the words and work of Dr. King. We also saw it as an opportunity for teachers to bring multicultural teaching into their classrooms. This was in the mid-1980s, before there was a national holiday for Dr. King. We chose a quote from Dr. King, and children K–12 wrote about the quote and how it applies to today. Even without specific sponsors, our attitude was, "We're just going to do this." It involved a lot of organizing, of getting information out to all the schools, encouraging teachers to submit essays from their children, figuring out the judging process, and inviting people from the community to judge what was submitted. I also helped to organize the awards ceremony, and boy, I learned a lot about organizing. I helped lead the effort for several years, and actually, the contest still goes on. A significant by-product of the contest was that it helped us to build a network throughout MPS, because we had people in all the schools who became our contacts.

Establishing *Rethinking Schools*

Beyond our ties to the union, we were also very involved in trying to bring issues related to multicultural curricula and progressive change to the school board. One of the things that many people in our cohort found frustrating was to go to school board meetings, to speak to the board, or to be in other places where your voice was shared, but as soon as you left, it was like your voice went out into the wilderness; it had no staying power. So another group of people, including Bob Peterson, myself, Tony Baez, and others formed a group to address this issue. Early on, Aurora Weier, director of El Centro de Enriquecimiento [the Enrichment Center], which she founded in 1984 on the Northeast Side, had joined our group. We were a real multicultural group of people involved in thinking about what we could do, like developing a newsletter or something where these issues could be written about and presented in a way that wouldn't disappear after the words were spoken.

First, we began as a study group. We read books and discussed critical pedagogy, like Paulo Freire's *Pedagogy of the Oppressed*. Through these conversations, we felt that we had to do something concrete. At first, we visualized something like a two-page flyer to promote a multicultural curriculum, but soon it was clear that to do a decent job with the ideas, it would need to be more. It took another year of planning where we tried to think through how we would create and use a newsletter. Our purpose was to provide another perspective on what was going on in the schools. The school board's perspective and union's perspective were clear, but the voices of classroom teachers, those who were closest to the teaching process, weren't being presented or heard very often. That was our goal and our mission: to try and offer not only critique and criticism on what was happening, but also offer thoughts and ideas about what can change and how to do it.

This was the foundation for *Rethinking Schools*, the name of our newspaper. It took those two years for the first issue of *Rethinking Schools* to come out—with many revisions and lots of meetings. There's always been, and still is, a high standard for articles that are accepted for publication. People wrote articles that were totally trashed sometimes. People in the group would say, "No, no, no, we cannot use this, this isn't right. Go back and try again." I think it was in 1986 that the first issue came out. The newspaper was published quarterly and continues now as a magazine.

We were a very small group of people who were bringing it together in a very small space. This was just kitchen table stuff with rub-on letters. We used an Apple 2E computer to type the articles into column format. Then it was all cut, pasted, and glued onto sheets. It was such an ancient technique by today's standards, and so it makes it even more amazing that we were able to get them printed. In the early years, I was a contributor, an editor, paper-bundler, and delivery driver—whatever it took. That was pretty amazing!

When the paper first came out, it caused quite a reaction. It was like, "Oh my God! Who are these people?" There was this notion that we were folks who were trying to undermine the district. There were folks in the union who accused us of trying to break up the union. They thought we had plans to join the AFT [American Federation of Teachers]. MTEA was affiliated with, or more aligned, with the National Education Association, as opposed to the AFT, which is the other big rival of union organizations nationally. That level of politics was not our focus, but our union and the school board began to hear the organized voices of those who had been dismissed. The newsletter opened the debate on what students really needed.

Rethinking Schools

P.O. Box 93371, Milwaukee, WI 53202 -- Nov./Dec. 1986 -- Vol. 1, No. 1

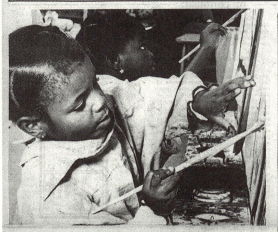

introducing
Rethinking Schools

The crisis in education continues. Young people find themselves confronting an educational system ill-suited to prepare them for life. Teachers find their creativity buried under increasing paperwork and administrative interference. Parents often experience schools as intimidating and unresponsive. Schools are marked by boredom, overcrowded classrooms, increasing violence, and a growing incapacity to help students acquire the basic knowledge and critical thinking skills they need. Several years of desegregation and compensatory programs have failed to close the profound gap between the achievement levels of white and non-white students.

Rethinking Schools is dedicated to helping parents, teachers, and students solve these problems. As teachers and community members, we want to promote thoughtful discussion and debate on educational issues and help unite the many groups currently working to make schools better. Discussion of educational issues is often dominated by administrators and educational consultants. We hope that Rethinking Schools will give teachers, parents, and students an effective voice in determining the future of our schools.

Rethinking Schools will be broad in scope, but will also focus on certain concerns. In upcoming issues we plan to consider the following questions:

1) How can parents, teachers, and students gain more powerful roles in determining school policies and practices?

2) What must be done to overcome the significant racial, gender, and class inequities which prevent many students from receiving an equal and effective education?

3) What specific approaches can teachers use to empower students within the classroom and the community? How can we make meaningful, community based work experience an integral part of each child's education?

4) What can we do to insure that multicultural and anti-racist education takes place?

5) What creative and peaceful methods can we use to resolve conflicts among students, and conflicts between students and teachers?

6) What specific teaching techniques and materials have proven successful in our efforts to motivate students?

Rethinking Schools will take up these and other issues with two goals in mind. First, we want to provide a forum which encourages debate and dialogue. Second, we want to act as an advocate for educational policies we believe to be sound and necessary.

As we balance advocacy with debate, we will also need to balance the theoretical with the practical. We will complement reasoned critiques with positive examples of ways in which teachers and parents are overcoming problems. We will strive to provide both informed analysis of controversial issues and specific ideas that teachers and parents can use to help young people learn more effectively.

Our new journal will need your help. Rethinking Schools can only succeed if it has your suggestions, letters, articles, and financial support. Please join us in this effort to enliven and improve education in the Milwaukee area.

Confessions of a Kindergarten Teacher
Surviving Scott, Foresman

by Rita Tenorio

As a kindergarten teacher, some of my most satisfying moments have come from working with children in the beginning stages of their literacy. I feel privileged to share their joy and excited sense of achievement when they realize for the first time they are actually reading.

Recently, though, I've also been feeling mounting anger and frustration over the policies and directives that come to us from the MPS Central Administration about how to teach reading. I believe the way we are asked to teach reading is ineffective at best and potentially detrimental to the cognitive development of the young child.

Early Childhood educators have long held that children learn best through concrete, socially relevant experiences. For years, successful kindergarten teachers have limited their use of workbooks and other mechanical "paper and pencil" tasks, focusing instead on such activities as art projects, stories, games and songs to develop pre-reading skills. We know that a strong oral language base, along with an understanding of the larger world based on concrete experiences, will help children become better readers.

Recently, the nation's most renowned experts on linguistic development and the study of reading have not only reaffirmed the value of experience-based learning, but have argued that mechanistic approaches to reading are a major cause of many students' lack of success in school. (See Peter Murrell's review of Becoming a Nation of Readers in this issue.)

Yet the administrators in MPS (and many school systems across the country) are responding to pressures to improve our schools by pushing these flawed, mechanistic methods even more! Thus they are extending the questionable basal reading program downward to the kindergarten. Apparently, their theory is that the earlier we begin the workbooks, the earlier the students will read, and the earlier they will be "on level."

continued on p. 6

On the Inside
This Issue's Focus: Reading

The first issue of *Rethinking Schools*. **SOMOS LATINAS PROJECT ORAL HISTORIES AND COLLECTED PAPERS**

The articles were thoughtful and thought provoking, about curricula and policies. It definitely caused a stir.

The first issues were newspapers as opposed to the current magazine format. We distributed them for free for many years, and the delivery of each issue was a large task. The papers were delivered early on to Bob Peterson's house, later to the Peace Action Center, and we had a group of people get together with lists of contacts from the schools. The network developed with the Dr. King Writing Contest, which connected us to teachers who would take them to their schools. They told us how many teachers were in their schools. We counted out the newspapers per school, bundled them, and then the volunteers delivered them. I had ten schools I had to deliver to, oh man! No staff and no money. Little by little, we expanded the number of people who got the newspaper because we shared with the broader community, too. In the beginning, we borrowed money just for the paper to be published. We collected the subscription money in this little shoe box. The subscriptions grew over time, and it raised attention not only in Milwaukee, but also beyond. Once this growth occurred, we began to hire some staff.

Besides the newspaper, we published other resources for teachers. One of the first was *Rethinking Columbus* in 1991 on the five hundredth anniversary of Columbus's arrival. The publication sold over 200,000 copies and helped our newspaper grow, but one of the repercussions of this work was that the union would not let us distribute the newspaper in the school buildings where the monthly union meetings were held. We had to put the bundles of papers in a spot outside of the school where the meeting was held, and then designated teachers would pick up the bundles from that spot. It might have been during the cold winter months that they started to feel sorry for us, and they let us conduct the drop-offs in the lobby. Then, after the MTEA elections in 1990, when our caucus won the presidency and more seats on the executive board, every building representative was encouraged to pick up the bundle for their school.

With [the newspaper's] growing popularity, it became clear that if we were going to have an impact beyond Milwaukee, that it needed to further evolve. We started getting subscriptions from all over the country, and even international subscribers. The discussion of keeping it a newspaper or to make it a magazine took a lot of time and discussion. It's now a magazine, and we have people all over the country who are editors. The managing editor lives in Berkeley, California. Writers and other staff live all over the country. We had a lot of conference calls, and two meetings a year where people got together and talked about the big picture of *Rethinking Schools*. I was on the editorial board for many years. Once I became the principal at Fratney, it became too hard. I just didn't have time. But one of my goals is to get back to being more involved in *Rethinking Schools* if I have more time.

The magazine also publishes other kinds of resources, books and pamphlets, to help support teachers in their classrooms. We have hosted several kinds of writing retreats and helped sponsor conferences, but the primary focus is publishing the magazine. The quarterly publication alone doesn't pay the bills, so the sale of books helps to make ends meet.

A Special Article on Race and Respect

I've written several articles for *Rethinking Schools*. One that I wrote was to help teachers who work with young children think in a multicultural, anti-racist way. It's called "Race and Respect among Young Children." I think it's a really good article. It's been used in various ways, and I think it is still current. My master's degree was on this topic. People have said that young kids don't understand racism, and that they're color-blind, but it isn't true. When you're in a kindergarten classroom, you say, "Come and sit down in the circle." I've watched kids who come to the circle and sit down, but when a kid of a different culture or different skin color sits next to them, some will get up and move to a different place. When they are in the house-keeping corner, the *casita*, role-playing can be very revealing. I overheard a conversation when a child said, "I'm gonna be the princess." And an African American child said, "Well, I want to be a princess, too." Some light-skinned kids then said, "Black people can't be princesses." One experience was that a kid was mad at another kid, and he called her "brownie." It may not have been the N-word, but for a five-year-old, it was very much an indicator that he recognized her racial background. We spent a lot of time in my classroom and our first grade unit working really hard to help the kids explore such issues in a safe and supportive environment. A social justice teacher doesn't wake up one day and say, "Oh, now I get it." We need the tools to get there. My article supports this learning.

Understanding how I taught about Thanksgiving Day with historically inaccurate and culturally biased curricula was another eye-opener. When I first started teaching, it had never occurred to me that there were other perspectives on Thanksgiving or Columbus Day. That was a long, hard road because you have to get past the notion of "but I have always done it this way," or feeling guilty and thinking, "How many lives have I ruined by talking about the Pilgrims and the Indians?" I don't think I ever went that far. The approach I began to use was to let the children talk about what they know about Thanksgiving and Columbus Days. I invite them to explore about how other people celebrate these days. I sent students home with an assignment to ask their parents about the holiday and to help them write about it. The next day, some would share that Columbus "sailed the ocean blue" while others said he founded the slave trade on this continent, or that he made the Indians sick. This becomes the opening for teachers to talk about information not found in our textbooks but that is historical and true.

Alma Flor Ada is definitely one of my role models. So is Louise Derman-Sparks. They have both written important resources for early childhood teachers to use in an antibias curriculum. Alma came to Fratney during our first year to work with teachers. I've also had the privilege of being and working with Louise. I was very pleased when she asked me to write an article for the second edition of the antibias curriculum. These things, little by little by little, help teachers to understand, "You might not be there, but you don't want to stay where you are." For example, once you hear the story of Thanksgiving Day from a Native American perspective, you learn that the commonly told story is really a myth. You won't forget about it once your consciousness has been raised.

FOUNDING ESCUELA FRATNEY

As many things have happened in my life, starting a school was not something I went looking for. There had been discussion among several of us, that if we had the best environment for children, what would it be? Through our activism, we looked for examples in other places around the country. In 1986, Bob Peterson and I ran a summer program with a couple other people. It was called Amazing Place. It was a wonderful experience that allowed us to teach kids in the way we believed they should be taught—as intelligent human beings, deserving respect and providing a supportive learning environment. We joked about someday having our own school and promoting this kind of education.

In November or December of 1987, we learned that the Fratney Street School building was going to be emptied of children and staff. The school community was going to a brand-new building. There were all kinds of ideas from the district administration about what should happen with the Fratney building. At that same time, there was a group of school board members that encouraged other proposals. We thought, "This is our chance." So Bob said, "We have to write a proposal." We had a week to write the proposal, but you know what? We did it. We turned it over to the school board and, unbelievably, they actually encouraged us to go further with it. The following February, the school board held a public hearing on the proposals for the use of the Fratney space. That night, there was a terrible storm outside, but seventy-five people came to the meeting to advocate for our proposal! Parents, community members, and teachers—all kinds of people—gave us support to do this. The proposal was approved, but then it was like, "Now we have to do this, and how are we going to do it?" And that was the beginning.

Over the next months and through the summer we worked hard to design Escuela Fratney [Fratney School]. We knew that we wanted parents and teachers to run the school, but it was way too radical for them, and the administration insisted on giving us a principal. Escuela Fratney would be a dual-language school—the first one in Wisconsin. We based literacy instruction on the "whole language approach" with a multicultural, antiracist curriculum as its core. Parents and teachers would be part of a shared governance council. We had the audacity to put all of these things forward and really work at it. There are multiple stories of resistance from the administrators. People did not give us the support we needed, with some exceptions like Olga Valcourt-Schwartz.

Today when you talk about a new school proposal, teachers are given support to develop the curriculum, and a principal is assigned from the get-go. We didn't get the principal assigned to our school until August, a few weeks before school opened. They had assigned someone newly hired to be the principal, from the Milwaukee suburbs. She didn't speak

Spanish. She spoke German, as well as English, and had never taught in Milwaukee Public Schools. So we had to tell her, "You can't be our principal." There was another strong, supportive group of people who came to a school board meeting, and their testimony convinced the board to table the assignment of the principal. Another bilingual Spanish/English principal was assigned. It was really hard on everyone, and we had no clue whether we'd even be around for a year. The struggle continued for the next weeks, but Escuela Fratney opened its doors on the first day of school in September of 1988.

Our initial groups of students came from all over the city and were referred by people who didn't understand what we wanted to accomplish. It was hard. But we had an amazing, amazingly strong group of people who were very dedicated to this idea. I don't think we knew at all what we were getting ourselves into. It has been a struggle since day one. We've had different issues. We were the first school in Milwaukee that negotiated a change to the school contract in order to hire teachers for our school and not to base teacher assignments solely on seniority. At that time it was a radical step, because the teacher contract required transfers and new hires to be assigned by seniority. Today, every school in Milwaukee hires their own teachers this way.

Teachers and parents were in equal numbers on the school governance councils. Being able to do some things outside of the contracts, or doing it inside the contract but with a contract waiver, was really a very unique thing. As a result of being trailblazers, I felt like there were some moments in time where the activism happened, not only at Fratney, but in the union and in the district as a whole. Those things took as much time or more time than my teaching, and that was hard because then I felt like, well, am I giving the children as much time as I should? But at the same time, those were the things that were going to make a long-term difference.

Staff know when they come to Fratney that they have to work hard, and we've had wonderful staff. Budget cuts, though, have taken their toll. At one point we had thirteen teaching assistants; now we have one, and there are several others but they are specifically for the children with special needs. We don't have music or physical education teachers, and our art teacher is half-time. We have battled to keep our school librarian because our library is so very important. But those have been battles as long as I can remember every year at budget time. This is a good fight. So far we have been able to hang on.

There is a lot of respect for Fratney. The primary things that people say to us when they come to visit have to do with the bilingual program, the dual-language program. The other thing is the atmosphere, the climate in our school. Visitors consistently say, "My goodness, people are really respectful, everything is calm and positive," and that is absolutely connected to the mission and vision we've held from the first day of opening the school. Parents and students are respected and valued. All staff are expected to be supportive of the families. There is a principal's office, but it's there to welcome people and not to restrict people. I am amazed when I hear about principals who rarely come out of their offices. I can't imagine that. Just being out and about is important, whether it is to go get a screaming four-year-old out of the classroom because they don't want to share, to counsel troubled students, to enjoy their writing celebrations with them, or to dump trays in the cafeteria. In my mind, all of those jobs are part of the principal's job.

I'd been at Fratney for eighteen years when I became the administrator at the school. I never wanted to be an administrator, but we needed a new principal who understood and would continue Fratney's vision. There was a real need for that kind of leadership. The school was already my second home as a teacher, so I agreed to take it on. I learned so much from the experience. The best thing about being a principal was that no two days were ever the same—from involvement with others in curriculum development, to managing the building. In this day and age, principals have to be everything. I had no other support; there was no assistant principal. So when something happened, I had to be there. I helped with recess and lunch duty because there wasn't enough staff. It was a really good thing in so many ways. But it was hard. So much harder than I ever anticipated it would ever be.

LIFE AFTER ESCUELA FRATNEY

I retired in 2012. The new principal is a dear friend, and I am always ready to give her support when she needs it, like just letting her know that she's doing a good job. As a principal it is hard not to get discouraged because you are trying to manipulate the mandates of the district for the integrity of your school and get through the district bureaucracy. I know that when she goes to board meetings, she may feel very alone because other people don't think like her. Even though there is lots of change, people still look at you like, "What are you talking about, antiracist?" It's hard. It's hard because you then feel like, "Oh God, I gotta say this again." They talk about some initiative that's going to take place and you say, "All right, but what about bilingual schools?" They say, "Oh, we haven't thought about the bilingual schools."

Rita Tenorio, 2014. ELOISA GÓMEZ

In retirement I'd like to think that I will spend some time at Fratney and love the children. How wonderful to go into a place and get a hundred hugs. But I am in need of time to restore my health and evaluate what is truly important to me. You know, Walgreens jobs sometimes look good to me, with no pressure or stress, but not really. I want to do things that are meaningful and promote social justice. I think about teaching at the university and working with young teachers, but I really don't know yet. I'll still be active. My husband, Mike, retired, and I'd like to spend time with him and our son. I am doing more gardening.

I'll mention two of the awards I received: in 1990, I received the Wisconsin State Teacher of the Year Award from the Department of Public Instruction, and in 2004, I received the Governor's Task Force on Excellence [SAGE] Award.

Ramona Villarreal

Ramona Villarreal Guerrero was born on July 31, 1954, in Laredo, Texas. Former migrant workers, she and her family settled in Wautoma, Wisconsin, in 1968. They were active in the labor organization Obereros Unidos, and Ramona became a Brown Beret in the 1970s. She worked as a schoolteacher in the River Valley School District, and she is a migrant and immigrant rights advocate.

Ethnic identity: I am Mexican American (Chicana).

Do you consider yourself a community activist? Yes, I always promoted the Mexican heritage. I am involved in fighting for equality and justice for people's rights. I was also the first and only Brown Beret in Madison, Wisconsin.

How do you define community activism? A person who is actively involved in efforts to promote changes for equality and justice for people.

Areas of activism: Migrant workers and immigrants' rights; women's and teachers' rights.

Location of activism: Weslaco, Texas; Madison, Bancroft, Wautoma, and Milwaukee, Wisconsin.

Years of activism: Starting in my childhood, in the 1960s, through today.

Family Life as Migrant Workers

We were migrants from Laredo, Texas, and traveled to Minnesota and Wisconsin in the 1960s. We worked on different farms and stayed in migrant camps. Some of the farms raised sugar beets and cucumbers. We traveled to the small Wisconsin towns like Wautoma, Bancroft, and Hancock. My dad, Perfecto Villarreal, found a job with the Wisconsin Gas Company, and we settled in Wautoma around 1968. My mother worked in different places over the years. She wasn't involved in the demonstrations, but she would bring us our food, like tacos, to eat while we were on the picket lines. She had fifteen kids, and eventually she returned to Texas, along with six of my brothers and sisters.

One recollection I won't forget was from back in the 1960s when we were migrants in Minnesota, and I was about nine. My dad and I went to the grocery store. He was going to buy me one of those Sno Balls, like a Twinkie, but it was white with coconut. We were about to go in, and they closed the doors on us because we were Mexicans. At that time, I didn't quite understand why they were doing that, and my dad said, "Well, as you get older, I will explain, but right now you cannot have your Sno Ball." And that's when I realized they weren't going to open the doors, although they let others go in and buy stuff. I just couldn't understand why we were treated different.

Around 1968, my dad and others worked in Bancroft at a potato processing factory. One day, my dad told Jesus Salas that Latino workers at the factory were going to stage a walkout and picket the factory because they were not paying them the same wages as the white workers. My dad was already a member of Obreros Unidos [United Workers], the farmworkers' union that Jesus and others formed two years earlier. Jesus's response was, "Let's do it." Since the Latino workers were more of the manpower, my dad thought the company would have a problem with processing the potatoes before they spoiled, so they walked out. The company finally agreed to increase their wages because they were unable to find enough replacement workers.

While we lived in Wautoma, my dad realized that when the migrant people left after the growing season, the prices at the grocery stores would go down, but as soon as the summer came, the prices would go up. We knew it was a real injustice for them to do that to us, and I didn't feel comfortable with the way we were being treated. I was young, but one time I asked the owner, "Why are you doing that? You can't do that." And he looked at me like, "Why are you, a little girl, telling me this?" It was as if my age was more the problem than the injustice.

INVOLVEMENT WITH THE UNITED FARM WORKERS AND OBREROS UNIDOS

We lived in Wautoma about the time of the grape and the lettuce boycotts led by César Chávez of the United Farm Workers (UFW). The UFW sent four people from California to Wisconsin because they sold a lot of wine here in Wisconsin. Certain liquor stores were targeted, and we formed picket lines to encourage others to boycott grapes, and that's how we had people following us. The grape boycott was successful with all the help of all of us, not only Wisconsin, but all the other states that helped. I started young.

It was also a time when other migrant activists like Jesus Salas and others formed a union in Wisconsin called Obreros Unidos (OU) in the 1960s to address the poor conditions of migrant workers in Wisconsin. We picketed with OU because the farmers were not paying us enough money for our work. I was selling the newspaper *La Voz Mexicana* [*The Mexican Voice*] to get the word out about OU. I worked with others, including David Giffey, who was a photographer/photojournalist and active with OU.

Through these organizing efforts and my own experiences, I understood that we had the right to better treatment in pay and housing. We fought for what we believed in. So the marches that we were involved in played a big role in getting better housing. I'll give you an example. When the migrant people came, the farmers put them in any kind of housing. They didn't even have hot water. The toilet was an outhouse. They had all kinds of equipment out, and the kids would cut their hands or feet. Tractors and other equipment could be very hazardous. When we marched from Wautoma to Madison in 1966, I was about twelve. I was right with my dad when we went into the capitol. I was right there when Jesus Salas recognized people who marched. We were right on the steps, listening to the speakers. Our roles were to have the signs and to continue marching and show them that we were strong activists. These demonstrations helped change laws. Farmers had to allow inspectors on their farms to see if it met some minimum standards for migrant families to stay, if it provided hot and running water, and a bathroom, and [had no] potential safety hazards.

I was around in the 1960s and 1970s when the national and local efforts came together. Local and national activists, like César Chávez, Jesus Salas, Ernesto Chacón, Salvador Sánchez, Corky González, and José Ángel Gutiérrez worked together, depending on the opportunities. As a result, I consider myself a strong Chicana because at that time we had political strength.

I began to get involved in the causes of the Latin American Union for Civil Rights and United Migrant Opportunity Services in the 1970s in Milwaukee. The leadership of these two organizations were also involved in

OU. By the time I went to college, I [had] traveled all over Iowa and different places for the many causes I believed in. I visited Corky González's school in Denver because I wanted to learn more about the Chicano movement. The Chicano movement was about justice, and the Brown Berets developed out of the movement. I always said this: Yes, César Chávez moved a little bit of the water, and then all the waters were moved around the United States. The waters were all the movements that continued. It included the fight for justice by Chicano activists Corky González and José Ángel Gutiérrez.

In 1971, some of my family moved to Madison, Wisconsin, and my sister Maria and I went to East High School.

From East High School to UW–Madison

Wilma Stump was a very strong activist who I had so much respect for because she was the first one who was hired by the University of Wisconsin–Madison to recruit Chicanos to the campus. She came to my school, Madison East High School, to recruit. I didn't think I was ready for college because I didn't have the money or the education that other people had, but she believed in students like me, so I enrolled.

In my freshman year, 1972, we started the student organization La Raza Unida [LRU, the student affiliate group of La Raza Unida Party] at the UW–Madison. It was Wilma who said, "Let's go and visit other schools; let's go to Denver, Colorado, and see Corky González's school, how he runs it, and how he's teaching our children." We hopped in one of the university vans and visited the school. At that time, the boyfriend of Corky's daughter had just been killed by the police. We felt that it was because of racial profiling. We went into the school and the teachers were Chicanos. It was a school with all grades, so it was quite impressive the way he was running the school; I was impressed that the kids had their own song. I don't quite remember the whole thing but it was something like, "Yo soy Chicano, tengo color Americano pero con honor, cuando me dicen que hay revolución defiendo mi raza con mucho valor [I am Chicano, I have the American color, but I feel honor when they say there's a revolution; I defend my people with valor]." That's what the kids would sing in the morning after the Pledge of Allegiance. So it was quite impressive.

In my sophomore year, I wanted to take a Spanish course. They didn't want me to do it. They told me, "You can't take Spanish; that's an easy credit and you don't need that." I said, "Well, just because I know Spanish, that doesn't mean I know how to read and write it. Let me take Spanish." This decision, [the administration's resistance to] our efforts to get a Chicano Studies program, and other incidents sent a message of disregard toward Latino students. We rallied together and staged a walkout. For one of these marches, we had about five hundred students and community members calling on campus administration to work with us.

A number of students received their degrees because Wilma Stump pushed them to continue. She didn't give up, even though we weren't prepared. She once said, "A doctor doesn't become a doctor from one night to another; he's got to work at it, and so you guys have to work at it, too. If they can do it, you guys can do it." She later moved back to Alamosa, Colorado. After I graduated in 1984, I went to look for her but learned that she passed.

There were a number of other Chicano or Latino students at UW–Madison. Students like Ely Marquez, Grace Leal, and Mary Godoy. There were other fellows, about four from San Antonio—Daniel, Leonard, Emit, David, and Gilbert, I believe (I don't remember their last names). The following year, there were even more Latino students. From our efforts, a Chicano Studies program was eventually established, and the administration hired Próspero Saíz as a professor in comparative literature, and Ernesto Monge, who was hired in the financial aid office and very active on the Madison campus.

RESPONDING TO SEXISM AND SEXUAL MISCONDUCT

My roommate was Grace Leal, and she knew another Latina student named Mary Godoy, who was very young. I think she was about seventeen, but we were all young. We would all get together sometimes for parties, and we would go to other students' houses, but what we were experiencing from the men was not very good. They were trying to see who they could take to bed or something else disrespectful. At one point, I slapped a fellow because I didn't like his comment to another male student when he said, "Well, I think you should try to take Ramona to bed." There were other parties that I went to where they tried to put something in our drinks. But I was one that was always sharp. I would not leave my drink anywhere.

One time, there was a Latina student whose name I cannot remember. She was with our group when we went to a party. About a half hour later, the girl became drowsy and she couldn't even walk, but she hardly had anything to drink. I just could not believe it when they said she was drunk. So they put her in a bathtub to calm her down. I said, "Take her out of the bathtub; just let her go to sleep or something." I think they were scared because, first of all, if she was drunk, how could they take her home, and how could they leave her by herself? So they laid her down in a bedroom.

I felt like a policeman because I tried to keep an eye on the women, and I was worried about the student upstairs. So I went and checked on her, when I saw this fellow was on top of her. I caught him as he tried to pull her underwear down. He already had pulled her pants down to her knees. I caught him, and I just grabbed and punched him as I threw him off the bed. I knew that he had a black belt in karate. I said, "You go ahead!" But he didn't do anything. I said, "How dare you be so disrespectful? You said we are like brothers and sisters, but this is the way you treat your sister?" He just got up and left. I don't think she even remembered what happened to her because she was completely out, but I won't forget that.

There were other incidents, and so I kept an eye on the women students. Some of us wanted nothing to do with these men. We stopped going to LRU meetings. Even before that, the men wanted to be in charge all the time; it was hard for us to have any real input because they wanted to run the show. We had good ideas that made sense, but they would not listen to them or would take the credit for something one of us women did. Other women can tell you how they saw things, but this is the way I saw it.

BECOMING A BROWN BERET MEMBER

I went to Milwaukee very often while I was at UW–Madison to help with the movement. People who I knew while I was a migrant worker also lived or moved to Milwaukee. I marched with Ernesto Chacón and Salvador Sánchez, Jesse [Jesus] Salas, Lalo Valdez, and others to protest the mistreatment of our people by the police department. Obreros Unidos did organizing there, too. A chapter of the Brown Berets started in 1968 in Wisconsin. I became Madison's first and only Brown Beret. I don't know if it was Ernesto or Lalo who gave me the patch; both thought I proved myself to be strong and determined. I was given the patch because I was there all the time, and I walked as much as they did. I was a part of the group that walked from Milwaukee to Madison. They may not have given the women enough credit, but I want to tell you they did respect me. As a Brown Beret, one of our roles was to protect the people who demonstrated. I helped with the march from Milwaukee to Madison. There were very few women on it. Marchers would walk for two or three hours and then stop and rest. We'd look for places where we could rest and return to the same spot to start back again. At night, we'd sleep in a church or outside. Not everyone walked the entire way. Some came and went. I stayed the whole time until I got to Madison.

There is a photo of me at the state capitol building at one of the marches wearing my brown beret hat alongside another woman. Her name is Amelia Ramirez. She's now an attorney who lives in Madison. She was from Texas but had moved to Wautoma. Blanca and Angela Ramirez were her sisters. [Amelia] didn't work in the fields, but I told [her and her sisters] that they needed to go to the march and help. We had just come in from Milwaukee. I saw her there, so we went to the army supply store, got ourselves some army jackets, and we put the words *La Causa* on them and we started putting all kinds of stuff on our jackets. People were looking at our clothing, and I got some of them to walk the picket line.

Ramona Villarreal and Amelia Ramirez posing before the Wisconsin State Capitol. SOMOS LATINAS PROJECT ORAL HISTORIES AND COLLECTED PAPERS, PHOTO BY LALO VASQUEZ

Another role that I had was to help the UFW staff that came to Madison; they came with very few things. I helped them find a place at St. Martin House on Beld Street, and they stayed there for $25 a month. So my role was to continue helping anybody who needed it. As a Brown Beret, I was the only one in Madison, so I felt like I had to try to do the best I could to educate others to help to fight the cause. I had some interesting experiences trying to recruit other Chicanas. Some didn't consider themselves Chicanas. One said to me, "Well, I don't speak Spanish." I said, "Well, do you understand your mom in Spanish?" She goes, "Yeah." Those kinds of comments didn't slow me down.

PROFESSIONAL CAREER

I applied for a job with the Madison [Metropolitan] School District in 1985. At that time, they didn't have a lot of Latinos in the school district. I had teaching experience, and I had the degree in education, but they didn't hire me, not even as a sub. It's why I decided to sue the school district. I didn't sue for the money. All I wanted was for the school district to hire

Latinos. I eventually won the lawsuit eight years later. Because of this effort, I believe there are a lot of Latinos working for the school district, which is great.

When I won the case, it made the Madison newspapers and my current boss saw it and asked me, "Is this you they are talking about in this article?" to which I responded, "Yes, that is me." Then he broke out into a big smile and said, "Wow, good for you!" This was quite a relief, to say the least!

I knew I had the opportunity to work for the Madison school district once the lawsuit was settled, but I wanted to stay where I was.

I am still actively involved at

Ramona Villarreal, 2014. ELOISA GÓMEZ

sixty-two years of age. I still participate in triathlons and marathons, and the Ironman, and I continue training for long-distance races. On September 7, 2014, I qualified for the World's Half Ironman.

Some of the recognitions that I have received include: Special Recognition from Senator Russ Feingold in 2002, United Migrant Opportunity Service's Hispanic Family of the Year in 2002, an award from the UW Chican@ and Latin@ Studies Program in 2012, and an award from the River Valley School District for twenty-three years of service.

Bertha Zamudio

Bertha Zamudio Navarro was born on April 10, 1950, in Michoacán, Mexico, and moved to Milwaukee in the early 1970s. She quickly became active in civil rights and education issues through her work with nonprofit organizations, including the Latin American Union for Civil Rights. Bertha has remained active in multicultural, antibias education for more than twenty-five years.

Ethnic identity: Mexican (Purépecha Indian), Latina.

Do you consider yourself an activist? Yes.

How do you define community activism? Someone who wants to make changes and works for social justice because she, or he, sees the economic and educational and political disparities. A community activist joins with others who agree that inequalities exist in society.

Areas of activism: Education (equal access to quality education, bilingual and multicultural), civil rights, and social and economic justice.

Location of activism: Milwaukee, Wisconsin.

Years of activism: Since 1972.

Transitioning from Mexico to the US

My father was a mechanic. He had a shop in Mexico but due to economic conditions, he migrated to the United States as a bracero [part of a contractual program between Mexico and the United States for short-term agricultural labor] around 1953. My parents had sixteen children. I was the fifth. Eight were born in Morelia, Michoacán, and eight were born in Chicago. My father came to the United States first, and then my mom joined a couple of years after he migrated to California. They later settled in Chicago. My mother came with the desire to work outside the home, but my father said it was better to take care of the children, so that's pretty much what my mom did.

At first, all the eight children stayed in Morelia with my grandmother. My sister and I were sent to Mexico City to live with aunts on my father's side. I lived with my Aunt Guadalupe, who didn't have children. They really took care of us like we were their own children. My other aunt was named Petra, and she was a teacher who taught sign language. Some days, she would tell me to come with her so I could see what she did. She was very dedicated to her job, and it was very gratifying for her.

When I lived in Mexico, I saw different kinds of inequalities among people. There were families of wealth and privilege who were educated, and then families, like ours, who had to struggle, who needed good education, adequate housing, and food. In Mexico, there was a level of discrimination based on skin color. If you were darker skinned, you would more likely experience the discrimination; if you were *India*, or lighter brown, you fared better; but if you were white-skinned, you did better overall. I had some difficulty with some of my classmates while in Mexico City. Some would say, "You're an orphan!" because my auntie was very green-eyed and very light skinned. She talked to the principal about the teasing, but no one did anything about it. I lived with my aunt for about ten years before I returned to Morelia and started high school.

I came to the United States in 1968. This was the same year that the Olympics were in Mexico City, and I was really excited. But I knew Mexico was spending a lot of money on the Olympics, and I was concerned because I knew there were not a lot of economic opportunities for the population, and ours was not such a rich country. So why was the government spending all this money? And then, of course, there was the massacre of the university students who were against the idea of having the Olympics in Mexico City. I was aware but wasn't involved.

I had to emigrate before I reached eighteen because I would be able to get residency status in the United States easier as a minor. My father made sure I arrived in the spring, a month before I turned eighteen. They were living in Chicago at the time. When I came here, it was culture shock. My family lived in one of the most notorious public housing projects in US history, called Cabrini–Green. It was very difficult for me to adjust to the poverty and violence of the projects, and I had to learn the English language at the same time. Given my age, my mom and my dad sat down with me and asked me what I wanted to do. My mom wanted me to stay home and help her with all the children, but I had the desire to continue my education. I graduated from St. Michael's Central High in Chicago in 1969.

During this time, I met a woman who became an inspiration for learning more about society. Her name was Maria Armendariz, and she was originally from Nicaragua. She was a widow, and she had a girls' club that was called The Place. She hired me as a youth worker. She wanted me to teach the kids Spanish, and arts and crafts. I knew how to knit, and I always liked the arts. After school, I would go home and knit and then go back to work. Later on, she told me about a program that might benefit me, and she enrolled me in Upward Bound, a college prep program for low-income students. I took Saturday classes that were very intensive. From the morning until after two o'clock, I would go to the classes to prepare for going to college. I took the SAT and ACT college entrance exams and all of the other requirements for college. I also worked as a nurse's aide in one of the hospitals.

I came to Wisconsin around 1971. I came to Milwaukee to find a summer job, after going to Dominican College in Racine for two years. To my surprise there was a large Hispanic community—and not just Mexicans, but Puerto Ricans—and they were getting along and doing things to change the conditions, like finding jobs for the youth. One community agency, Centro Nuestro [Our Center], hired me as a youth coordinator. They were originally located on Sixteenth Street, which is now Cesar Chavez Drive. I was able to teach youth workers how to respond to phone calls. Many of the calls were about needing child care and other services dealing with issues they had.

A good friend, Tony Baez, called and said he was working for the University of Wisconsin–Milwaukee (UWM) on a program dealing with incarcerated youth. I asked my parents about moving to Milwaukee [permanently], even though I was already an adult. My mom and dad were hesitant, but I came back to Milwaukee with the reason that I was working while going to UWM. I was at an alternative school, El Centro Cultural Chicano-Boricua [Chicano–Puerto Rican Cultural Center], with high school kids that couldn't really function in public schools, so I taught them social studies in Spanish.

Early Involvement in Activism

I took time off, about a year and a half, to join an underground cell of the Young Lords of Chicago [an organization that originated in Chicago in the late 1960s as a street gang, the Young Lords became a political force that addressed police brutality, housing discrimination, and other civil rights issues[1]]. While it had its origins in a gang I wanted to understand their ideology and to be a part of creating change. I returned to Milwaukee because I did not feel we were accomplishing much, but I learned organizing skills in the process.

Back in Milwaukee, I participated in some of the protest marches. I helped with the Milwaukee rally in support of Puerto Rican activist Lolita Lebrón, who was fighting for the island's independence from the United States. The rally was before her arrest in Washington, DC. I was also involved in the campaign to support James Ray Mendoza, a Milwaukee resident who was accused of murdering a police officer after leaving a bar on Milwaukee's South Side. He had been confronted by two off-shift police officers in 1974. He claimed he shot in self-defense. The police had been harassing Latino and black communities, and the Latin American Union for Civil Rights (LAUCR) was active in this and other civil rights issues. The police department chief, Harold Breier, was actually very racist and heavily harassed a lot of us. I later worked for LAUCR because Centro Cultural Chicano-Boricua closed. My main job was to help with their after-school program, but I also helped with some of the community organizing to raise funds for Mendoza's defense.

I helped at *La Guardia*, LAUCR's bilingual community newspaper, for several years in the 1970s. LAUCR staff, Charlie Quesada [the editor], and volunteers like me kept the newspaper going. We wanted to document everything that was going on in the community. We wanted to make sure that people knew what was going on in Mexico and here locally. I translated many articles for the paper and later learned how to do layout, proofread, and rewrite. So when I worked there, it was many hours because

---

[1] Martha M. Arguello, "Sisters, Brothers, Young Lords," *ReVista: Harvard Review of Latin America* (Winter 2009), https://revista.drclas.harvard.edu/book/sisters-brothers-young-lords.

we had deadlines and not enough volunteers. I'm glad that *La Guardia* is now in the archives of UWM. There was some good analysis of what was going on in the community, analysis that would not be found in the local newspapers. We got some money from ads, but it was mostly from donations and contributions from people who knew that we were doing a good job documenting community news. I thought it was really important to document what the larger media did not cover.

Many of the women who worked or volunteered at LAUCR were very active in the progressive movement. We formed a good network of women who were not just Hispanic—like Jean David, who was white. I got to know her for many years, but unfortunately, she passed away. She was always very active in the Latino community. Our network of women was very respectful of our differences, and we knew that there were a lot of issues in the community that we had to confront. We did have to deal with chauvinism among the community activists. Most of us felt that our Latino men did not recognize the contributions of women's efforts.

Another area I was involved in was the fight for bilingual education in Milwaukee Public Schools (MPS). In the early 1970s, we were concerned that MPS did not offer bilingual education. This was critical, but I think less visible was the deeper fight around acceptance of the growing multiculturalism of the students. I don't think the school system or the teachers knew how to handle this change, and it impacted our youth, especially those with limited means. I could see that many felt alienated, and that impacted their learning and their graduation rates. The services did not keep up with their needs. Some special women fought for bilingual education in the public schools, like Freya Neumann. Freya was one of my role models. She helped to make sure that there was bilingual education. I was proud of how very persistent she was with MPS. Through a community effort that also included Amparo Jiménez, Mercedes Rivas, and others, we were able to convince MPS that they needed to provide bilingual education because it was not right to only offer these services after school. A number of us were also involved in the issues facing migrant workers. They did not have adequate housing, and we participated in marches to Madison to ask for better living conditions for the families. We fought for better wages, education and day care services for the children, and improved sanitary conditions.

Formal and Informal Support Systems

I also met friends like Patricia Goodson and her mother, Mrs. Anderson. The family was active in community issues. Patricia was very close to me, and she said, "Mom, I have a sister that is new here to town," and they embraced me like I was part of the family. Mrs. Anderson invited me to "Come and eat whenever you want to," and I was like, "Okay, I'll be coming every day," because I missed eating tacos de frijoles. I yearned for the food I grew up with. Both women were active in civil rights issues at the time in the Latino community. They were a part of the sit-in at UW–Milwaukee to get an office for Latino students in August of 1970. I was proud of their efforts. Another woman who inspired me in Milwaukee was Clementina Castro. She was a single mother of seven children. She started Centro del Niño [Center for the Child], her own day care business, and I helped her with the children. She was able to be an entrepreneur and showed that women could run a business taking care of children. Centro later became La Causa, a very successful nonprofit agency in the Latino community.

The woman that I would have to say I really looked up to as a role model was la Señora Mercedes Rivas. She worked so hard to put bilingual education in MPS, and she fought for workers' rights and against police brutality. Most of all, the woman that was very conscious of the social issues was Mary Ann Onorato; she's my *comadre*, the godmother to my eldest daughter. Mary Ann was active in the civil and migrant rights issues, too. She volunteered with *La Guardia* and other social justice causes. In the Riverwest neighborhood where I decided to live, an informal child care co-op group started because we needed one and we trusted each other. Mary Ann was involved in our group, too. We gave points for caretaking, measured in time for our labor, and exchanged them when we needed them. No money was exchanged. There were also women that lived in housing co-ops. They would exchange their hours for taking care of the lawn, or taking care of paying the bills. I was a part of their group, but I owned a home, even though it needed a lot of fixing.

We would go to community meetings, and I think I really liked Riverwest because it was very multicultural. I could count with my fingers the Mexican families that lived over here, and I became good friends with them. We would see each other at St. Francis of Assisi Church on Fourth and Brown Streets. My children were baptized and confirmed there. That's also how I developed my spirituality. I had once renounced religion, and when I had my oldest daughter, I came back to Catholicism and became more involved in the church.

I need to also mention a wonderful friend and Riverwest leader. Her name was Aurora Weier, and she wanted to make life better for the youth of the area. She started El Centro de Enriquecimiento [the Enrichment Center], a small nonprofit organization in the 1980s. Her staff and volunteers would have neighborhood cultural events and celebrations for the many Latin American holidays. She was a Panamanian who was married to a Caucasian man and had two young sons. She wanted to make sure there was bilingual education and cultural activities for the youth because we were plagued with gangs. She found funds to employ neighborhood youth, and she started a high school with bilingual services as a way to ensure they received good education and could avoid their involvement with drugs. In 1985, she was murdered by someone who wanted to be the recognized Latino leader for Riverwest. This person was incarcerated for shooting her with a rifle as she walked toward the community center. I knew him personally, and I cannot understand why he killed her. Her death remains such a loss to our community. Her life was her work.

Focusing on Education

In 1998, I worked at Highland Community School, a parent-led Montessori school on Milwaukee's near West Side, where I worked as a VISTA volunteer. In my role, I developed a Spanish curriculum. My children Amada and Bernardo were able to start their education there. The school only accepted children from the neighborhood, but because I worked there, they opened up a seat for them.

I went to work at Fratney School, a dual-language charter school in the Riverwest community. I started working when the school opened in 1988, and I retired from the school in 2016—twenty-seven years! When I first started there, I enrolled my daughter after asking her what she thought. She liked Highland Community School, but I had limited transportation, and we knew many of the people who started Fratney School. It's a child-centered school and very nurturing, so I thought it would be a very good school for her. Then I heard there was an opening for a parent coordinator. I thought I could do the work and get more parent participation, because Fratney considered parents very important. So I applied, and they hired me. I was proud of school leadership's effort to offer a curriculum that we found or created to be multicultural and anti-bias. In this process of learning, or relearning, from this type of curriculum, we have been very successful in having children who are really scholars because the stigma of race, as a limitation, was greatly reduced in our school.

Bertha Zamudio, 2016. BERTHA ZAMUDIO

The summer of 2015, I volunteered with the Milwaukee teachers' union and helped to canvas the South Side, going door to door, to let parents know that the School Choice Program may water down education because Choice and private schools don't have to take the state tests. I wanted them to also know that bilingual and multicultural education is very important for them to be able to compete with the larger population.

I retired in 2016 and am active with my children—Xochitl, Amada, and Bernardo—and grandchildren. They say that if you are committed to social change you never stop, and I stay involved in immigration and other community issues. I'm also involved in church activities, like volunteering at the food pantry. I belong to Our Lady of Divine Providence in Riverwest.

PART II

EXPLORING KEY THEMES

Part II of this book examines three key themes that will provide readers with additional ways of thinking about Latina community activism. We posed a set of common questions to the Somos women during two rounds of audio interviews and other communications conducted in 2015 and 2016. In addition, we asked each woman to complete a brief profile form, which reinforces themes contained in this book. The audio recordings and profile forms are archived at the Wisconsin Historical Society in the Somos Latinas Project Oral Histories and Collected Papers.

The three key themes explored in these interviews were: the influence of role models and support systems on the women, the motivations that compelled them to activism, and the risks they took in working toward their goals. At the end of our Phase II interviews, we also posed the question: "What reflections and hopes would you like to share with readers?"

After identifying the three themes, we conducted a literature search, hoping to learn more about how these themes relate to Latinas. Although we were able to find some gender- and ethnic-specific material on these subjects in academic literature, we found very little that was accessible to the public.

The final section of Part II includes our own reflections on what we have begun to learn from the Somos women. It is our hope that the findings in Part II will open up new opportunities for research on Latina activism. We encourage all readers to utilize the Wisconsin Historical Society's Somos Latinas Project Oral Histories and Collected Papers and the Chicana Por Mi Raza website for continued research in this important field of study. Both website addresses can be found in the appendices of this book.

Role Models and Support Systems

One key theme that emerged from the Somos women's interviews was the influence of role models and support systems in their lives. We utilized the definitions of role models and mentors from a 2004 study of six female Mexican American school leaders in West Texas, which examined how the women selected and were influenced by role models and mentors. The author, Sylvia Méndez-Morse, defines a role model as "someone whose characteristics or traits another person would want to emulate."[1] When asked about their role models, the Somos women could have named men and women in highly visible positions with national recognition. However, most of the women identified lesser-known role models who reflect their own backgrounds and who live, organize, strategize, and/or work in close proximity to them.

On the whole, the women named close family members and elder or more experienced local activists as their role models. This finding is in line with research that points to the family as the frequent reason for Latinx individuals striving for or achieving success.[2] Many Somos women identified female role models they knew as young children—either their mothers, close female relatives, or friends—rather than recent influences.

Since the Somos women's lives often involved full-time work and activism during "off hours," the encouragement and affirmation they received from their support systems appears to have played a crucial role in their lives. As the Somos women became more involved in their activism and began building alliances to further change, their support systems frequently expanded beyond family and/or neighborhoods to include Anglo women, other Latinos, and other men and women of color.

While many of the Somos women were involved in activism related

---

[1] Sylvia Méndez-Morse, "Constructing Mentors: Latina Educational Leaders' Role Models and Mentors," *Educational Administration Quarterly* 40, no. 4 (October 2004), 561–590. http://journals.sagepub.com/doi/abs/10.1177/0013161X04267112.

[2] Jeanett Castellanos and Alberta M. Gloria, "SOMOS Latina/os—Ganas, Comunidad, y El Espíritu: La Fuerza Que Llevamos Por Dentro," in *Positive Psychology in Racial and Ethnic Minority Groups: Theory, Research, and Practice*, ed. Edward C. Chang, et al., (Washington, DC: American Psychological Association, 2016), 61–82.

to women's issues—including women's reproductive rights and advocacy for sexual assault, domestic abuse, and child care programs—they rarely built alliances with traditional Anglo women's organizations. Many did, however, form both formal and informal Latina/x groups, such as the Latina Task Force, S.O.S. Mujer, Las Adelitas, and Latinas Unidas. Several of the Somos women also joined women of color organizations such as the Wisconsin Women of Color Network.

Finally, many of the Somos women have become role models and mentors for others, and for younger Latinas in particular. They have created events and programs, and have taken public stands on issues that have contributed to increased leadership opportunities for younger Latinas, and the Latinx community in general.

The following interview excerpts reflect some of the ways in which role models and support systems made a positive impact on the Somos women and encouraged them to become role models to the next generation.

LUPITA BÉJAR VERBETEN

After my mom died, my oldest brother took over, and then my sister. As each one married, the next sister took *las riendas de la familia* [the reins of the family]. My sisters are very, very good people. I learned from them and am a product of their efforts.

My father and two uncles inspired me greatly because they stood up for their religious beliefs. They were brave in the face of death. During the 1920s Cristero War in Mexico, my two uncles, Miguel and Jesus, were killed because they defended the Catholic Church during the government's repression of the church. My father was about to be shot before a firing squad for the same reason when the archbishop intervened. He had just cleaned himself up and was about to be sent before the firing squad when he was released. My mother was pregnant with twins at the time. The archbishop in Irapuato appealed to his government captors to release him, as he was the father of twins about ready to be born. Because of his intervention, my father's life was spared.

My support system has been family; friends; my husband, Bill, whom I have been married to for over twenty-three years; and the Catholic Church. My parish is Our Lady of Guadalupe. These are all important to me.

Marie Black

I would have to say my mother was my role model. She was a very hard-working individual, very caring, very fair; she taught me to be like that. In Mexico, [she] did a lot for the poor. My parents were at a dinner party with the bishop, and somebody came and asked the bishop if he would go and baptize a child who was dying, and he refused. So my mom got up, she left the room, she came back with the child, and had him bless him in front of everybody. So can you imagine the courage that took? And so that's another example of her letting me know that "This is what you do—you don't let things go! You take care of them!" I would say there were other women, pioneer women in the community, Hispanic women who had started businesses in the time when it was difficult.

Maria Dolores Cruz

My mother [Maria Eufrocina Rea Perez] was an important role model for me. She was a homemaker and worked outside the house at times; she was also really active in her community. She was one of the first women in our barrio to speak, read, and write in both languages, and she could drive a car. She was already in her thirties when I was born, and eleven years before that, in the 1930s, she had helped a lot of the women on our street, especially those in their childbearing years.

During World War II, she recruited women to work for the Red Cross, where they would package bandages. Her community service never stopped, and it included promoting self-reliance and community building. She encouraged the neighborhood women to buy sewing machines, and they all learned how to sew by going to classes. During World War II, my mother helped to organize weekly rosary sessions at our house or at other women's homes, even though she wasn't Catholic; she would read her Bible while the others prayed the rosary. My grandfather, Santiago Rea, was very important in my life. My grandparents and their daughters, including my mother, lived during the 1910 Mexican Revolution. He taught me Mexican *poesía* [poetry], Mexican history, and culture, and politicized me about *los Mexicanos* coming to the States. When I was about twelve years old, my grandfather called me over to him the night before he died. He said to me, "Mi'ja, yo creo que este va ser la última mano en este juego [Child, I believe that this is going to be my last hand in this card game]." Because he used to play solitaire. He wanted me to understand that he would not be around any longer.

He also said, "La mujer educada vale más que un hombre [The educated woman is more valuable than a man]." I wondered about his message all these years. I think that because he knew he was going to die, and would not be there to guide me, he understood that at some point, a woman needed to take care of herself.

Yolanda Garza

My mother [Angelina (Helen) Garza] was very active on the South Side of Chicago. Attending community meetings with my mother, and watching her and some of the other women neighbors and those from the school/church addressing issues when I was young, filled me with pride and confidence. My mother and other Latinas stood up for injustices whether they won or not. I took it upon myself to try and do the same early on. Dr. Vernon Lattin was a role model for me early in my career. I came from a blue-collar, working-class family. He was the first Latino faculty member I ever met, and he was my supervisor when I was a graduate student in Illinois. He helped me believe in myself as a professional in the new environment of academia, where few Latinos worked. Dr. Lattin didn't know he was my role model, but I watched him and learned. He led me into higher education because my background was elementary education, but he must have noted my administrative skills.

Another role model was Roger Howard, who was the associate dean of students at UW–Madison and my boss. He believed in me, too. He gave me the space to develop my interests and skills as an assistant dean, and funded my many professional development requests. When I was working toward my bachelor's and master's degrees, there was only one Latino faculty [member] and no administrators at that time. This has begun to change, and it is our turn to mentor others in higher education institutions. I hopefully have done this for undergraduate and graduate students, and other staff, informally or through the Latino Academic Staff Association, which I helped create at UW–Madison. It helps [staff] build professional relationships to navigate the politics of work life, and is a great community of people to talk to—someone you can trust.

I also helped create the Mujer Latina Annual Conference in 1993, which draws university and community members statewide. The conference focuses on Latina education, health, safety, and policy. We have been able to bring in national, regional, and local Latina presenters each year. I believe this increases the number of role models that our younger Latinas can look to as they move into professional roles themselves.

Lucía Nuñez

I've found a group of women—women of color and white women—and we problem solve and help each other in our work for the city of Madison and the Latino community. I have watched people of color pull each other down. So I have finally found a group of support people who are not driven by their ego or self-esteem. As a support group, we are so comfortable that we are okay about being or feeling vulnerable in front of each other. That is a huge gift, because in a small city like Madison, there are no real secrets.

I also looked beyond Madison's borders to identify support systems and friends from other communities. Recently, the city of Madison has been involved in the Government Alliance on Racial Equity. I have found directors of civil rights offices in other cities and stayed connected. It is wonderful to be able to converse with these women of color, and they really understand what I am going through here in Madison, and can advise and support me.

Nelia Olivencia

My mother was *una jibarita del campo* [an endearing term for a rural woman; poor but having wisdom and dignity], as she always referred to herself. Later in life, I became an admirer of Sor Juana Inés de la Cruz, Julia de Burgos, Dolores Huerta, Angela Davis, and Lolita Lebrón. I met and kept in touch with two women's rights activists for a short while; I deeply admired Robin Morgan and Audre Lord. They provided me with hope, warmth, and love in moments in my life when I needed it. I maintained a running correspondence with both for a short time. I will never forget their kindness and understanding.

Leonor Rosas

Abuelita Maria Ester was a beautiful woman inside, although she was also a victim of domestic violence. I didn't want to go there, but I will, I have to, because that's perseverance, and it shows what the family went through. I talked about our family being middle-class. My grandfather's family used to own a trucking firm, and he was well-known and respected in the community, but he was an abuser, and he brutally abused my grandmother. My mother would always come in between them and got her fair share of abuse that included getting her nose broken. They never went to doctors or anything because this was something you kept at home. But they survived it, but not unscarred. My mother became afraid of physical contact and less emotionally attached to people, including her family, so my *abuelita* was our mother. She loved us, nourished, and hugged us all the time.

I spent much time with my *abuelita*. I remember going to the market with her each day. On the way back, at least two or three times a week, we would stop at somebody's home, just for a few minutes, and check on the kids. I would play with the kids, but I noticed my grandmother was helping the women cook or clean the house. I later talked to my mother to understand why we stopped at all these different houses. She said that these women had had some trauma in their lives, and my *abuelita* would stop to check in on them and make sure the kids were okay, that they were fed. You know, we never talked about that, but it was a lesson on compassion, and she just did it because it's the right thing to do.

When I worked for the Spanish Center in those early years, I realized how complicated life could be for some of the families who came to us. Their lives were very fragile. I started realizing we had gone through a lot of those things ourselves. The difference was that my mom had an education, and we had my *abuelita*. That helped us to see that we could have a way out. I guess I started to think, "I've got to help people see a way out, help them through the maze, through the criminal justice system and poor education and domestic abuse and drug abuse and alcoholism and discrimination and lack of education. Life [can become] real complex for anyone, [especially] someone who doesn't have a strong social network or a role model to follow.

MOTIVATIONS

Another key theme explored during our audio interviews and follow-up phone conversations with the Somos women was their motivations. We learned that the women were, by-and-large, not externally motivated by things like praise, awards, power, or money, but internally motivated by their desire to improve the lives of others.

In *Women Building Communities: Behind the Scenes in Milwaukee*, a 1997 book that documents interviews with fifteen Latina activists, editors Brooker and Scheible write, "The women we interviewed spoke with a great deal of humility about their work as community activists. They said they were doing the same things they had seen their mothers, aunts and grandmothers do. Despite the differences in their experiences, the impact of their past activism served as an example and motivation for these women. They hoped to pass on to other individuals in the community a commitment to activism and involvement."[1] This study reinforces a key motivation for the Somos women: the actions of their loved ones.

On the whole, the Somos women saw community engagement as a responsibility and an honor, and they enjoyed their work in the Latinx community. Some of the women were motivated by their early struggles with societal expectations and norms relating to gender, race, and/or class. Many were influenced by poverty, sexism, racism, and cultural ignorance that they either witnessed or experienced firsthand. In particular, the Somos women were motivated to improve access to quality education for members of the Latinx community and to increase services for Latinas.

The following excerpts provide a sampling of the motivations that spurred the Somos women's activism; we like to think of these motivations as seeds that took root and grew into action.

---

[1] Russell Gott Brooker and Linda Frances Lockett Scheible, eds. *Women Building Communities: Behind the Scenes in Milwaukee.* (Milwaukee, WI: Alverno College, 1997), 89.

Nedda Avila

My experience has been that race and the color of your skin matter. I'll share my experiences with prejudice, ignorance, and cultural differences even among Latinos. There are many, so I'll start with Indiana. By the time I arrived, my dad was already there. He came in the 1940s, and once he started working at the steel mills, he sent for us. We had lived in New York first, so we took a bus from Brooklyn, New York. When we got there, we had to live in a crowded place because it was hard for Latinos to find a place to rent. The whites didn't like us, nor did the blacks or Mexicans. My dad never owned a home in Indiana. He would rent big apartments, so he could take them and divide the rooms and rent to men or couples who came from Puerto Rico to work. My mom did the cooking, and I helped to cook and clean for the renters starting at age eight. Once they started working and could find a place that would rent to them, they would move.

An experience I'll never forget was the treatment I received in the fourth grade from a school friend's mother while my family lived in Indiana. The girl wanted to be helpful and offered to give me her comic books so I could start reading in English. I went to her house to pick them up, but her mother wouldn't let me go inside their home because she didn't want someone of my race in it. I could not go beyond the sidewalk.

Something else that influenced me was my domestic violence background. My mother was a batterer. She would hit us, my dad, and my neighbor's kids, anybody that came and didn't listen to her. Later, I became a battered wife at the age of fifteen or sixteen. I was married twenty-three years. When I decided to open my eyes, and said to myself that I couldn't do this anymore, I changed my life. When I had the opportunities, I've tried to increase services in outreach, prevention, and intervention services. Seeing the development of the Latina Resource Center makes me very proud; I fought for it, and I am one of its best advocates.

Patricia Castañeda Tucker

My dad had an expression: "If you can't do anybody any good, then you don't do them any harm." I understood it as helping people out if you can and always being a part of something that you believe in. He was always the kind of person that stood up for what was right. My father started as a journeyman and became a machinist, a skilled tradesman. He got a job with American Motors, which was later bought out by Chrysler, and retired from there. He took a leave of absence to start his own machine shop business through a business revitalization grant to strengthen businesses on the south side of Racine. He had this business for about five years, but then went back to American Motors. They weren't going to honor his seniority, but he fought them in a real quiet way. We all kind of knew about it, but he didn't sit there and discuss it with us. He stuck to his guns, and he fought it and won. Whenever anything happened to one of us at school, or we were out in public and people were rude to us, in the form of discrimination, he would take care of it, and always in a diplomatic way. He was always very correct in how he defended himself and us. So that has a lasting influence, and not just on me; I know it was the same for my siblings. I've always respected that aspect of my father. In a way, you know, I grew up with understanding what was good and what was wrong.

GABRIELA GAMBOA

My motivation to volunteer was because of people like Sandy, Connie, and Dawn, who gave me their time and talents. They didn't know me, but they gave me the best gift ever—to learn English! I felt I needed to give back because of what I received. Volunteers, like these women, don't understand how much they give to people like me. They are giving us power. They made me strong. They don't fully get it, but that's okay. These volunteers don't need much in return, so my purpose became, just like the movie, to "pay it forward!" I started doing volunteering professionally since 2007, and I know I will continue.

SYLVIA GARCIA

I learned that you don't just sit back if you see a problem; you do something about it. That was something ingrained in me by my own parents and grandparents, though I may not have realized it as a child. They were involved in helping Waukesha's Latino families. In 1943 or 1944, my grandmother and another woman started Las Guadalupanas [believers in La

Virgen de Guadalupe/Our Lady of Guadalupe] in Waukesha. Las Guada-lupanas was a religious organization that aided and comforted families who were going through turmoil and needed help. They provided spiritual support and, when able, made sure that people had some material things, such as clothing or other very basic survival stuff.

My father helped to start Los Caballeros [The Gentlemen], sponsored by St. Joseph's Catholic Church around 1956 or 1957. The club helped people from Mexico migrate to the United States by pooling money and other resources together in order to help families who wanted to come to Waukesha. My mother and father were involved in helping to support a group of nuns in Mexico. Their group was known as the Augustinians. Fund-raiser dances, called *tardeadas* [afternoon socials], were held at Mus-kego Beach in Waukesha on Sunday afternoons or early Sunday evenings. It would attract a lot of community members. One band, the Federales, became really famous. A lot of people, young women and young men, would come together to dance to Mexican music. The group charged an entrance fee and the net funds went to support this particular convent in Mexico. So even though I failed to recognize this as activism, I now realize that they worked really hard to help the nuns. I saw all their efforts and thought to myself that I'd like to get involved.

DEBORA GIL CASADO

I had to take on an adult role when I became a translator and interpreter for my mother at an early age. It made me bossy. At a young age, I had to support my mom, so I interfaced with many adults. I learned to make decisions in the role of interpreter to protect my mom from insensitive comments and advocate for her when necessary. I shouldn't have had to have this role, but perhaps it gave me some leadership skills early on in life.

CARMEN IRELAND

Early on, I was aware of class discrimination, starting in Mexico. There were those with money and those who had none or little of it. I saw education as the way out of poverty. I felt strongly that we all had a right to a good education, and I wanted equal access for all. I saw racial discrimination, too, and different treatment toward non-English-speaking Latino students. I felt that I needed to help as I could.

IRENE SANTOS

Because of the work that I do to help the poor, I have asked for donations from pastors of different faiths. We are sons and daughters of God. A pastor from another religion said, "But Ms. Santos, you are Catholic." And I said, "So what?" We are the same human family. If God had wished there to be only one church, one religion, he would have done that. A mother and father and all the children in one house, sons, daughters, great-grandchildren. I have worked with people of many faiths.

NATALIA SIDON

I think coming to the country, not speaking the language, and being without my parents had a lot to do with who I am today. Being away from my parents was hard. I knew that I had come to this country to get an education. I faced a lot of struggles growing up without them during my middle school and high school years. In a way, I had a lot of responsibilities then, and I saw a lot of people in my same shoes. I remember doing things at school with girls who were struggling, going through challenges. There was always something inside me to extend my hand to someone struggling and having the right words at the right time if people needed me.

I didn't feel like I belonged at schools. I was told by school staff that they didn't think I would graduate and that I was likely going to be pregnant before fifteen. I was around students who were getting pregnant and others who were joining gangs. I guess I associated with some of those people. You know, they would tend to compare you to those who you hang around with, but I had this desire in me to prove them wrong. It made me more determined to get an education. I think that I am in this position now because of all the struggles I had growing up. It made me want to become a better person.

Rita Tenorio

Being bilingual and bicultural, I think I have an advantage in being able to see things in different ways. Just like being bilingual gives you the chance to look through two different sets of eyes, it's the same kind of thing. You know how language helps you to see things in different ways, based on where that language is from. Same thing for me; I grew up in the culture of Germans, a white culture, and aware when people referred to minorities or Hispanic people without them realizing that I was part of another culture, too. Especially as I got older, starting in college and as I was beginning my career as a bilingual teacher. It gives you sort of an invisibility, sometimes, with each culture.

Bertha Zamudio

Faith has always played a very important part in my life because it was a big part of the lives of my grandma, Mercedes Romero, and my grand-father, José Navarro. Both were orphans and lived with the upheaval of the Mexican Revolution. She was still so young when her parents died, but she raised two sisters and a brother. She was very humble and made a small income from making and selling her tortillas at the train station. And that's where she met my grandfather, José. She would get up in the morning, go to the mill, and get the masa to make fresh tortillas—I still remember the smell of them!

My grandma was very spiritual; she would always attend Mass every morning, and during that time, I was in high school, she would say, "You can very easily go to church at seven o'clock and be at school at eight." And I said, "Oh, I don't think so." I felt bad, but she still encouraged me anyway. I had questioned religion for a while. I think now that I'm older, what great examples they were to me. Now the church and my faith are a big part of my life, too.

Also, I have been influenced by the racial and economic [environments I have lived in]. I saw this in Mexico and both exist here, too. Because of the cost of living, we now live in a situation worse than before because of the fact that most of the children attending our schools come from very low-income families.

Risk-Taking

The third key theme exlplored in our later conversations with the Somos women was risk-taking. Merriam-Webster's definition of risk-taking is, "the act or fact of doing something that involves danger or risk in order to achieve a goal."[1]

The Somos women have risked marriages, jobs, arrest, imprisonment, condemnation, personal safety, and more to advance community change on behalf of Latinx people. For some, risk-taking reduced their access to institutions of power, and it sometimes resulted in social isolation from friends, coworkers, employers, and other community members. Some of the women were labeled as troublemakers, white feminist wannabes, and man-haters, among other derogatory terms. In many cases, the women not only put themselves in physical danger, but endangered others who worked alongside them.

However, what became clear to us as we listened to the Somos women's stories was that they had all reached crossroads in their lives when risk-taking was required to create change. And each discovered in her own way that being a community activist necessitates overcoming fears, confronting challenges, and taking risks. What we heard over and over from the women was, "We just did it because we felt it needed to be done."

In addition to the risks already mentioned in Part I, the following excerpts provide examples of the various risks that the Somos women took during their years of activism.

Carmen De La Paz

Let me tell you about one specific racial incident that I'll never forget. It was Christmastime in the 1990s. My husband and I were at a shopping mall in Waukesha called Brookfield Square. And you know that being raised in

---

[1] "Risk-taking." Merriam-Webster.com. https://www.merriam-webster.com/dictionary/risk-taking.

Puerto Rico, I'm always going to have my accent. That will never, never go away! *¡La única manera en que yo pierdo mi acento, es que me corte la lengua!* [The only way I will lose my accent is if they cut my tongue!]

We were at J.C. Penney's, and I always liked to look at jewelry. The store was very crowded, and I was maybe talking with my broken English to the saleslady, who was behind the counter. Suddenly, I felt somebody pinch my arm. I turned and saw a white woman passing me. I'm not sure what came over me, but I acted *como era una emergencia* [as if it were an emergency]. I just went after her because I had seen the blouse she was wearing! Once I reached her, I could feel her flesh between my fingers, and then I pinched her hard! She turned around and said, "Why are you pinching me?" And I said, "Because you pinched me first!" And then she said, "Why don't you go and learn English!" "Lady! You know what? I consider myself lucky because I can talk to you in English, and I can also talk to you en Español," *le dijé* [I said], with a snappy attitude.

My husband was in a nearby area, and when he heard my loud voice he knew that I was in trouble. He said to himself, "Oh crap! Oh crap! Oh crap!" because he thought of the possibility of a front-page story in the *Waukesha Freeman* newspaper, headline saying, "Carmen De La Paz in a Fight at the Mall" because I was so well-known! Then my husband grabbed me, and he took me away. But, honest to God, the only thing I thought was, "If I had gotten into a fight, I would be on the front page of the *Freeman!*" You have to wonder why people have that level of reaction to people with an accent.

I remember going to the Kincaid Farms about six-thirty in the mornings; it was not my job to drive the van to the farms to bring the migrant workers' children to La Casa de Esperanza and take them back in the afternoon, but it was a pleasure for me to do it. I never, never complained that I had to get up early in the morning to get them. I remember when I visited a family at this farm, *el rancho,* I saw the poor conditions of those families. I saw how they had only the basic necessities, but they were very happy! The children didn't have any toys to play [with], but they played with the *piedras* [rocks] and other things they could find. You know that taught me, *me enseño mucho; me enseño a valorar la vida* [it taught me much, it taught me to value life]. It was an important lesson that you don't have to have much to appreciate and enjoy life.

Barbara Medina

Being one of the leaders in the redistricting effort was my biggest risk taken. It was massive, extensive, and the turnaround time was incredibly short; I think the new boundaries had to be established within 120 days, so there was not much room for error. The potential downfall of not succeeding at getting a Latino district was of great concern, but I think we would have learned much about the process to be successful at the next opportunity; it would have prepared us for the next big challenge.

Maria Luisa Morales

I was at that rally [against proposition 187 in Waukegan, Illinois]. We had a hard time getting there because all the streets were blocked and the police were on every block. There must have been maybe a couple of thousand or more people and reporters and Jesse Jackson was there too. A few blocks down, there was a group of maybe twenty to twenty-five anti-immigrant protestors when the announcement was made that the bill passed. I was facing people and I turned around and I see a wall of police officers fully geared with the helmets, shields, sticks, rifles, dogs, and sharp-shooters on top of the buildings. The police had helicopters above us and I have never been as scared.

I have been to many protests, marches, and I have never been scared like I was at that time. Because you turn around and to see those police slowly moving towards you like a black wall. Some people started running, some started crying, some started to kneel down and they had babies on their shoulders. You have to remember, that was after they had had a rally in California where police beat Latino protestors. The fear was the police would beat us, so some of the protestors showed their children to the police in hopes that would stop any violence. But I thought, "I am not going to kneel down to anybody. I will leave, but I will not kneel."

Maria Rodríguez

Being Catholic and working for Planned Parenthood in the 1980s was difficult. I felt like I was at a crossroads. I realized that I was going against something that is part of my religious beliefs, but I also felt strongly that Latinas and all women needed reproductive health education and access to services, many of which were health screenings and prevention-related. I could use my position to talk to women about being aware of their own bodies and that they could make choices about having children. My parish is not that big, and some members knew that I worked for Planned Parenthood and did not approve. Once I debated a priest on the need for AIDS education on a TV show, so I was visible in my role and who I represented. That really went to my core. There were other challenging jobs in my career, but I think that went to my core.

Leonor Rosas

I was working as the assistant chief of staff in the County Executive's Office. We were asked by the nonprofit agency Esperanza Unida, around 1990, to allow them to create a mural on the Milwaukee Transit Building wall that faced the busy streets of South Kinnickinnic Avenue and Mitchell Street. They told us generally what it would entail and that it would involve South Side youth as a summer work project. When the mural was done, the director of economic development charged into my office and demanded that we require the agency to remove the mural because of some of the activist portraits on it that included: Father James Groppi, Aurora Weier, Jose Martí, Lolita Lebrón, Shaka Zulu, Vang Pao, Chief Joseph, and other internationally known activists.

His demand was largely based on his own political views. I felt that the youth had put much work into the project and did not view the mural as a negative political issue. I refused to support his request, and his response was that he'd take this matter further. My response was, "Okay, well, bring it on!" The mural remains up today, I believe it's entitled *Peacemakers*, and it continues to get the community discussing these historical international leaders. I'm proud of this mural and my role in keeping it alive.

Ramona Villarreal

As a strong activist, I can tell you that after applying for a teaching job in Madison Public Schools and not being hired, I had to get a job outside of town, so I taught twenty-three years in Spring Green, Wisconsin. Madison District would not hire me, even as a substitute teacher, and I had three licenses. They hired people right out of college, including a nephew of a district administrator, and he did not have any teaching experience. I had teaching experience and I had the degree in education, and they didn't hire me, and so that was the reason I decided to file a lawsuit against the school district.

I was a bit worried that my current school district might find out about the legal case against Madison and label me a troublemaker, and it was a little stressful for me. That legal case took eight years, but I fought them and I beat them on this issue. I was never interested in any money settlement for being discriminated against. I wanted our kids to have Latino teachers because we can relate better. As a result, Madison School District had to actually use their affirmative action hiring targets for Latinos! It means they hire Latinos now, and that's all I wanted from the district!

REFLECTIONS AND HOPES

Out of respect for the Somos women's generosity of time and spirit, we thought a considerate way to end our final phone interviews was to ask them to share any overall reflections, and any hopes they have for the current and future generations. This section features their answers to these questions. What began as a sign of respect turned into precious gifts of wise counsel and inspiring messages.

The women encouraged younger Latinx people to never undervalue the importance of *cultura* (culture), know their histories, maintain the Spanish language, be proud of their Latinx heritage, and be resilient. Some specific advice to women and girls was for them to believe in themselves and not let anyone make them think they have less value because they are female.

The women also shared strategies on how to be an effective community activist, including identifying the right alliances for specific issues, being open to people of all racial and ethnic backgrounds when building coalitions, and making an effort to understand the challenges all people endure. More generally, the Somos women urged others to confront injustices in the many ways they exist, and to be conscious of those in power who further injustice.

Unsurprisingly, many of the women reflected on the value of persistence. From years of activism, they learned that change does not occur overnight and is not easily won. In order to navigate the inevitable twists, turns, and roadblocks, the Somos women stress the importance of offering and accepting love and support for the long journey.

GLADIS BENAVIDES

My concern is: How do we translate ourselves to the young women who are getting lost by living the corporate life and are disconnected from our community? I don't see some of these young Latinas coming back to the community. We have a Centro Hispano here in Madison, and it's a wonderful center. The director is doing a fantastic job of reaching people to come in and volunteer, but still I see a lot of the professional Latinos, Latinas especially, being disconnected from the community.

I hope that the professional Latina, on her own or through Latina organizations, seeks opportunities to volunteer in the mid- to lower-income communities. They should experience what we experienced, being actively involved with those in the community who need services, those going to school with great difficulty, those who are not a part of a system for which services are available. I don't want them to lose themselves in this kind of "professional environment." They would learn that they gain even more than what they give. We don't need to be in the streets yelling and using the power sign. On the other hand, we do have to be actively involved in our own communities. If Latinos become silent because we have achieved individually, or we are in a place where we have to watch what we say, or we feel the pressure to be mainstream American, then our community doesn't grow stronger. I think we can watch what we say by still saying it in the right way, and we change how "American" is defined. Don't accept something that doesn't feel right. I recall a woman who said to me, "I don't see color." And I said, "Well, I don't see your right arm." I explained that color is connected to culture and ethnicity, and if you disregard that, you don't see the total person. Diversity is a strength. Sometimes it's misunderstood and we need to defend it. There are many ways to do so.

Patricia Castañeda Tucker

There's this renewed sense of bigotry and racial hatred that is on the rise in this country, and I know where it comes from; it comes from the conservative politics of our government [officials] who are defending the banks and big business owners who don't want to share their wealth with the people who made their wealth possible. It also comes from the ignorance that prevails among many in our nation and the failure to educate ourselves with the truth. I feel like this is happening because, as it has always happened in the past whenever we have problems within our economy and there are conflicts between different groups, the governing bodies and their institutions tell us that it's our fault for overpopulating our country with immigrants.

I got involved because I really believed in what I was doing and believed that something had to be done. I really do believe strongly that we need socialism; I don't know how that's going to happen. I became a teacher because, as I was getting older, I thought education would be an avenue for change, and I am very dedicated to it. I love teaching and want to continue to do that. In terms of developing my curriculum, I'm always thinking about what readings I want students to analyze critically. I want them to be challenged intellectually about ideas of difference, justice, and humanity.

DAISY CUBIAS

I want to share two quick stories to help younger Latinos to remember to never give people permission to put you down. If somebody insults you, find a way to deal with the situation without insulting them.

In the 1980s, when I was an immigrant services specialist for state government, I was traveling to northern Wisconsin in a state car to outreach to migrant workers. I stopped at a restaurant in a small town to eat, and people were looking at me probably because migrants didn't stop to eat there. Well, someone called the police, and the police officer came in and asked me what I was doing there. They thought I stole the state car. I had to show all kinds of identification to prove it. I did not get upset. I just told the officer to call Governor Thompson, and when I left, he followed me for a couple miles.

Another time, a school principal walked into a room while I was talking to high school students, and said I was talking too fast. I said, "No, you listen too slow." The kids were clapping. She tried to put me down, but no one has the right to insult you. You can tell me in any other way to slow down, but she did it in a disrespectful way. So nobody should put you down, and it's great to see Latinos going to the universities and becoming doctors, writers, and lawyers. I think twenty years from now, people will be different.

GABRIELA GAMBOA

I believe you can impact whomever you need to; for me, it's something that I learned. To be a good leader, you have to be the impact you want to see. I know that I am capable of creating change.

I'm a more recent immigrant, and I want to share a message with other immigrants. I am the one who decided to come to this country. I am the one who wanted to stay here for a lot of reasons. The only thing that I want people to know is that each of us has to be an example for others. Get involved, and don't stay in the shadows. You just have to make the decision to get your needs met. I don't like to think about it being a fight; just do it.

There are Latinos I try to recruit into our organizations. I tell them that it is very important to volunteer and why they should do it. I'm so grateful when I am helping somebody; I spend a lot of my time volunteering. At the end of the day, it's a good feeling. Some days I get upset, but at the same time, if you put everything on a scale, it's just amazing.

The situations that your life gives you can be very difficult. Some people say, "Oh God, help me!" Well, God sends you tools, and people don't always see them. For me, this interview is part of my tool kit because I want people to know that God is giving you miracles and tools every day, every moment; use it, people! Don't look for something surreal. By helping each other, we are the angels, one of the miracles.

Debora Gil Casado

Get the skills you need to make change. If you don't have the skills, figure out what you need; there are people who are willing to help and give you advice. It's hard, but try and maintain balance in your life; it's really important. When I talk to my students now, I always try to say it is their job not just to lift themselves up, but to think about who else they are going to lift up. We need to give back, but this can be tougher for women. Even today, women who are activists do double duty in terms of taking care of home, and then taking on community organizing, so it can be very, very hard. I think this is a big reason why women get burned out; it's easy to get very overwhelmed quickly.

I think, for a long time, we haven't seen an upsurge of activism from young people in general and in the Latino community, so I have high hopes in seeing many of these young people step forward, not just in becoming lawyers and doctors, but becoming activists. I hope they are going to build that infrastructure, create the change, and ensure that we maintain our language, because English is absolutely necessary, but speaking two languages is always better than one.

I think that one of the most profound lessons I learned from my work with Nuestro Mundo was learning how to create change within the system, because it's really easy to be critical from the outside.

Carmen Ireland

One thing that brought tears to my eyes was a speech I heard by Dr. Antonia Novello, who was the US Surgeon General in the 1990s. Her opening remarks affected me profoundly. She said that for many years she was laughed at because of her accent. Her honesty struck a chord with me. It was my own experience in this country. It brought to mind one experience in particular. I was the president of a club and I pronounced something and they could not understand, and they asked me when I was going to learn English; that really hurt me and I answered back, "the day you can learn Spanish." This doctor, somebody with an expertise and holding a national position, went through the same kind of experiences I had.

I liked the way she started her speech. She said, "My accent doesn't represent my knowledge; what's in my brain is not my accent," and I began to cry because I faced the same challenge. And so I thought, if she can do it, I can. Sometimes I would be asked, what beautiful accent was mine? French? German? When I responded that it was Spanish because I'm Mexican, all of a sudden it was not that cute an accent. The cute seemed to become unappealing. The difference was the race, so I think accents don't have anything to do with smarts; that's the most important thing.

Because racism still exists, we have to keep on fighting for what we want, and we need many other women activists. Dr. Novello's message is still important: you are just like me; don't worry about your accent or any other difference, just keep on learning and fight for what you think is correct. That's what I have done. I fought on behalf of, and with, the students to support their dignity, especially through these struggles, and to succeed academically.

When I left UW–Parkside, I made sure there was a bilingual young lady in the admissions office and another from the multicultural office. I told them this: "If you think about the students' needs, don't worry about the rest. You don't have to worry about what so-and-so is thinking, or the names they might call you." I had a nickname; it was Here Comes Trouble, but it didn't bother me because I knew where I was going and what I wanted to get done for my students. If others do that, they are going to be advocates for the students.

I think there's a lot of things to be done. The things we had in place in Wisconsin, like the implementation and expansion of bilingual education, the migrant education services, the Affirmative Action program annual reporting requirement to the UW System on how many students we recruited into the thirteen universities, were very good because they demanded that UW staff do the right thing—to help all the students, not just certain ones. These requirements are not in place anymore and that can put our Latino students at risk, so we need more women activists that will accept responsibilities to help build a better future for others.

BARBARA MEDINA

The Latino leaders that I was mostly involved with in the 1970s through the early 2000s are all getting older, and the torch is being passed on. It's up to our newer and emerging Latino leaders to try and impact their environment, their community. They're young, they have a whole lifetime, so they have the time to invest and actualize change. I think we've set the foundation and showed that it can be done. I think they can certainly start from what we started. So I think they need to take and review what has been done to help define the future.

We are now reaching the point where the Latino population is becoming the majority. Now we just need to translate that into exercising our vote to be able to make sure that when we define what we need, we do the work, do the coalition building, are able to reach across the aisle, talk to people, and are able to see another side of the story. So I think that they have an excellent base from which to start, and they can pretty much define it in their own image, into their own priorities.

My advice for today's young activists is to keep your mind open. What you will hear at some point might not seem like a good idea, or might just not gel with you, but always keep it as an option, because you never know in what situation you will find yourself, where that piece of advice that you heard at some other point might be the appropriate thing to do. So keep yourself open. Don't be afraid to ask for feedback, not so much from your contemporaries, but also from people who are not of your circle;

they can tell you things that people close to you don't see. If you have an issue, make sure that you see it from different angles, not just from yours, because you'll need to be prepared to argue all the points involved with your issue. You'll need to see something from beginning to end, and then be able to identify the key parties to support you, and don't be afraid to try something different.

Maria Luisa Morales

Just be part of everybody's life, and let them be part of yours. Don't separate them; don't think you are better than them. That goes for your neighbors in every aspect, not just the area where you live, but in your work, in your church. We are all humans, one big race, there is no white race, black race, yellow race. We all make up the human race. With my kids, I told them the Golden Rule: do unto others as you would like them to do to you. I always tell my kids, no matter how bad a person is, you can find a little good in them; don't write them off.

Nelia Olivencia

Don't take anything for granted; don't think that because people got services funded that those services are going to be here in the future. Now we are seeing many of these programs being dismantled, so don't be complacent. Things didn't get there by just you sitting on your behind; they got there because people made sacrifices. Now it's up to you to make sure that they're available to other people. You have a role to play as a human being in this society; play it. First, become knowledgeable; that's what college is all about. The point is for you to educate your mind. Become knowledgeable so that when you speak, you make sense. Know your history, facts, how to debate, how to write, and know how to communicate in all these different ways.

The longer I've lived, the more my views have become international in perspective. We need to respect and to learn about the history of all racial groups and cultures. Students need to learn about Black Studies. I got to see Malcolm X speak earlier in life, a few months before he was killed. I saw Dr. Martin Luther King Jr. speak; I saw some of the Black Panthers speak, like Huey Newton and Bobby Seale. We need to be exposed to other groups within the United States and internationally. We can better learn from each other, recognize more of what we have in common, and become more unified.

Maria Rodríguez

One of the things Latinas struggle with is that word *feminism*. They struggle with that word because it seems so selfish, and we are so family oriented. So we struggled with that, but we want to help women find their potential. And whether it is a good word or a bad word for someone, I think in some way we are [feminists]. I have grandchildren, and I have six granddaughters, and I think I struggle every day with what's going to be out there for them. There's a challenge every step of the way for young people. I'm hopeful for them, but I still think it's going to be hard, and I worry about them.

Natalia Sidon

The road hasn't been easy. There've been a lot of struggles. I mean, I've knocked on doors that have been hard to open because they questioned my ability, but I continued to knock until they listened to what I had to say. I sought chances to tell others where I was coming from, where some of my people are coming from. I often tell people to put themselves in the shoes of others to better understand their life experiences, to see what they're going through. So that's kind of what I mean by knocking on doors.

I sacrificed family time. Not being home on time, or getting home and having people come to my home with their needs, even though it's my time to be with family. When I go to church or grocery shop, even at restaurants, people know who I am, and they often stop me with questions, so it feels like my job never ends.

The most important work I've done? It is hard to select one specific thing. I think it's probably education. Not too long ago, within the last six to eight months, I was giving a presentation at one of the churches. After the presentation, a lady came up to me and said, "I really want to thank you for all the support you gave me when I was struggling." I didn't remember this lady's name or what her situation was, but she said, "You really encouraged me and empowered me to get out of a relationship I was in. It was a domestic violence relationship." To know that was very rewarding. I can't change everyone's life, but if I'm able to help one out of a hundred, then I think I've done my job.

Green Bay's Hispanic community has grown significantly, and we have more leaders who are stepping up and contributing, young adults who have educated themselves and are now taking on the role of community leaders.

Bertha Zamudio

For the upcoming generations, the future is up to them. They are the ones who have to lead the future, and they have to be consistent and persistent; it's important that they don't give up the rights that we have fought for and continue to advocate for better economic and social conditions— educational, too. Because education is the answer to a lot of the problems. Youth have to make sure that they are educated and make sure that they are part of society, and to recognize that we live in a democracy, not just for the Latinos but for everybody.

It's not easy; you can't do it alone. You need to develop a network of people who think like you and have the same goals. Immigration is something that they should continue to work on. There should be no *fronteras*, no borders, because we came to the United States to contribute to society; we've been contributing to society for many generations. People come here not to commit crime, but to enrich the country. They come here to work hard and to be able to take care of their families; many US citizens forget that this country was built by immigrants. The newcomers should not be discriminated against for doing the same thing.

Summary

"We Are the Leaders We've Been Waiting For!"

In a 2007 television interview, Bill Moyers asked venerable civil rights activist Grace Lee Boggs how she would respond to the question, "How can I make a difference?" Her clarion response was: "Do something local, do something real, however small." She further stated, "We have to appropriate, embrace the idea that we are the leaders we've been waiting for."[1]

As authors of this book, we would be hard-pressed to say that this notion—this identification as a leader—was embraced by all of the Somos women. When asked if they were willing to be interviewed about their activism, many responded: "Why me? I just did what had to be done." Despite countless acts of sacrifice to improve their communities, and their success in those endeavors, many of the interviewees did not see themselves as special or worthy of any type of documentation.

Yet the profound question posed by Ms. Boggs and asked throughout the centuries—"How can I make a difference?"—was answered by each of the Somos women at some point in their lives, whether in response to one significant experience or over a longer period of time, and whether forcefully or so subtly as to almost go unnoticed.

We are so fortunate that these women, mostly ranging in age from their fifties to their seventies, shared their stories with us. Younger generations may not be familiar with the historical, geographic, or cultural details included in the women's stories. Some lived under Jim Crow laws that separated people by race and ethnicity. Most were raised in Latinx communities much smaller in size than those that exist in Wisconsin today, and during a time when the needs of these populations were less known or understood by non-Latinx communities. All lived in a time when fewer affirmative action or equal employment opportunity laws existed or were

---

[1] Bill Moyers, Interview of Grace Lee Boggs, in *Bill Moyers Journal*, June 15, 2007. http://www.pbs.org/moyers/journal/06152007/transcript3.html.

enforced to serve US minority populations, women, or girls. The Somos women all came up in an era when Latinas—and Wisconsin women, in general, regardless of color—held few private and public leadership roles. But gradually, Wisconsin Latinas sought to use their voices, talents, and sheer determinism to create new pathways for Latinx communities.

In hearing these stories, we have learned that, as in other Latinx communities throughout the United States, Wisconsin Latinas were involved in supporting the development of their communities. We have also learned that, historically, due to cultural norms or societal gender roles, Latino men often did not see women as full partners capable of sharing leadership roles for change. The Somos women's experiences prove that Latinas began to successfully jump these real but invisible barriers to leadership starting in the 1970s. Having secured leadership roles, these women largely utilized networks and relied upon collaboration and cooperation with individuals and institutions to create change, rather than relying on the confrontational approaches used by their male counterparts. They built and navigated viable alliances—a method that stands in sharp contrast to the traditional, hierarchical, and authoritative leadership approach. They also identified themselves in various terms, such as community activists, advocates, educators, and humanitarians.

Regardless of definition, all of the Somos women worked (and many continue to work) in their own ways toward community improvement. In most cases, their activism did not come out of training or any particular expertise. A potent combination of role models, support systems, motivations, and risk-taking shaped them into the women they are today; and they developed self-confidence as they navigated uncharted waters of community change.

It is also important to note how many of the Somos women expanded the focus of their energies over time. Many began working in their respective geographic and/or ethnic communities, and eventually became involved in broader electoral politics. Several of the women spoke about how the desire to help their communities led them to meet with politicians, applying pressure from outside the system to make public institutions more responsive. Other activists, however, worked within systems, such as school and criminal justice systems, to create change.

What of the other Latina community activists in Wisconsin who ought to be in this book? One of the questions we, as authors, feel certain we will face as people learn about this book is: "Is my *madre/tia/hermana/colega* (mother/aunt/sister/colleague) in this book?" Unfortunately, the answer is more likely to be no than yes. Phase I, our basis for this book, could not possibly include all the Latina activists in Wisconsin who should be included. Time, energy, labor, and funding restrictions did not permit this opportunity. When we think of younger community activists such as Christine Neumann Ortiz, State Representative JoCasta Zamarripa, Teresa Tellez Giron, Eileen Figueroa de Lopez, and the many other passionate advocates for Latinx families and communities, we know that enough stories exist to fill many more books.

What does the journey look like for our newer generation of Latina community activists? Certainly many of their experiences will be different from those of the women in this book. Several of the Somos women worry about the relentless forces of racism, sexism, and classism in our society. Will it impede or galvanize younger Latinas to pick up the torch of activism?

And what will life be like for those who have begun to pass the torch? Many of the Somos women are now retired, and some are no longer the activists they had once been. A number have significant health issues, and some now spend their time engaging in hobbies they only dreamed of doing while they worked, although we have found some at social protest events. In tribute to their decades of community involvement, we celebrate their journeys by sharing their stories and highlighting some of the results of their generous spirits and multiple talents.

Latinas have a rich history of being agents of change and community builders in Wisconsin and across this country, but there is very little *recorded* history about them. So now we start and build upon this book and the few that already exist, as there will always be Latina activists, advocates, and humanitarians working toward building strong, equitable communities in this country.

We encourage you, our readers, to create history by being activists in your communities. Archive your efforts, find creative ways to share your work with family and the public, and make us all proud! Here's the torch . . . *¡Hacia adelante!* (Onward!)

We'd like to close with a collectively written poem by high school–age Latinas participating in Tess's Latina Poetry Group at Centro Hispano in 2012. The poem was written as a companion piece to the iconic 1960s Chicano movement poem "Yo Soy Joaquin" by Rodolfo "Corky" Gonzáles.

Yo Soy Eva

I am a sister
A mother
An aunt
A grandmother
A daughter
And never forget
The giver of life

I am Mother Nature.

Yo soy Eva.

I am the cheetah
cunning
clever
crafty
Protector of La Tierra as far as your eyes can see
Which I toil, sow, and harvest
Our crops
Our love
Our power
And
Our courage.

Yo soy Eva.

Yo soy la curandera
Que cura tus males
Con mis herbas

Candles
Prayers
Chants
And spirits

I am the healer AND the cure

So Evas of *el mundo*, join hands!
Evas of *el mundo*, rejoice!
Together we are amazing!
Who is Eva?
I am Eva!
Who is Eva?
We are Eva!

This art was inspired by the poem "Yo Soy Eva." It was designed
by UW–Madison student/mentee Jessica Alanis and created for the
Somos Latinas History Project's community fund-raisers. JESSICA ALANIS

Appendix A
Impact Chart

There are several reasons for the Impact Chart below. First, the Chican@ and Latin@ Studies Somos Latinas student teams often asked, "Did her activism make a difference?" and "Was she successful?" We wanted the students to see the impact of the activists' efforts, and to feel empowered to become community activists themselves.

Secondly, at a panel presentation that was part of the Civil Rights in Black and Brown Oral History Project conference in San Antonio in March 2017, women activists from La Raza Unida Party spoke about their activism being documented in journal articles and books. These *veteranas* (veterans) stated: "There is a lot about how we got started and the organizing strategies we used, but very little about our impact." These Tejana activists confirm that documenting their impact is critical to legitimizing and validating their efforts.

Finally, listing the impacts of the Somos women's community activism removes any doubt that they have made significant contributions in their quest for justice, peace, and equity.

A few caveats about the list:

First, the list does not represent every impact of the Somos women's work. We created this list based on the women's responses to our interview question: "What are you most proud of?" and the impacts/accomplishments mentioned by the women in other parts of their interviews. Secondly, while some of the positive impacts of the Somos women's activism are the result of their solitary efforts, others are the result of collaborations.

Rather than attach names to these accomplishments—an idea that runs counter to the Somos women's humility and spirit of solidarity—we have divided the items into categories of impact. We hope that this macro-level perspective will cause readers to appreciate the wide array of positive impacts achieved by the Somos women.

Latina Advocacy

- Implemented domestic abuse and sexual assault programs

- Founded the Latinas en Acción Fund in conjunction with the Women's Fund of Greater Milwaukee

- Founded S.O.S. Mujer, a Latina support group in Milwaukee

- Founded the Latina Task Force, a statewide Latina advocacy organization focused on education, health, and employment

- Created Latinas Unidas Inc., Sheboygan, which provided legal and employment advocacy and skill-building services

- Advocated for the Latina Resource Center, a program of United Migrant Opportunity Services, Milwaukee

- Co-founded the Wisconsin Women's Network, Madison, a multiracial women's professional and advocacy organization

- Established La Mujer Latina Conference at UW–Madison

- Brought the Rape Crisis Center onto UW–Madison

- Obtained funds for, organized, and implemented the Sí Se Puede Latina Training Program in the 1980s through the Latina Task Force

Migrant Worker, Civil, Human, and Immigrant Rights Advocacy, and Support Services to Low-Income Communities and Spanish-Speaking Populations

- Taught antiracism, human rights, and diversity skills to municipal governments and businesses

- Supported organizations to provide relief to El Salvador and Nicaragua, and raised $5 million for relief funds

- Collected thousands of toys for low-income children for Christmas with La Casa De Esperanza, Waukesha

- Provided court interpretation and translation services when no formal services existed for Spanish-speaking defendants

- Provided cultural training to Waukesha police serving Latinx communities

- Used radio program to inform Latinx community of services, rights, etc.

- Supported the transportation network from Green Bay to Milwaukee to Mexican Consulate

- Created the Latino Outreach Program for the American Cancer Society in Madison

- Created the nonprofit Latino Health Council, Madison

- Organized the first Immigration Summit, St. Patrick's Church, Racine

- Created the Santos Fund, a charity program for Latinx residents in need, Racine

Use of the Creative Arts for Change and Cultural Pride

- Participated in statewide cultural and educational events/performances

- Increased visibility of civil rights and labor struggles, and increased services to reduce poverty, through music

- Depicted Latinx identity, racism, and other issues in literature and art

- Contributed to the creation of Chicano mural, Memorial Union, UW–Madison

- Coauthored children's books related to peace

- Created Three Kings Day Celebration, Waukesha

- Advanced Latinx issues through weekly newspaper column in Sheboygan

Educational Empowerment

- Cofounded a bilingual immersion school, Escuela Fratney, in the Milwaukee Public Schools

- Cofounded a bilingual immersion school, Nuestro Mundo, in the Madison Metropolitan School District, which led to the creation of more immersion schools in Madison

- Created college scholarships for Latinx people in Milwaukee

- Created scholarships for Latinas in Green Bay

- Supported the creation of the Chicano Studies program, UW–Madison

- Assisted the development of Waukesha Public Library's Spanish/bilingual section

- Created a bilingual curriculum and eased the transition of hundreds of Spanish-speaking children to English Escuela Preschool, La Casa de Esperanza, Waukesha

- Motivated and mentored K–12 Latinx youth

- Created the Childcare Center on UW–Madison Campus

- Co-founded the WI Council on Hispanics in Higher Education

- Created a Latino Parent Group, Racine

- Co-founded Rethinking Schools Inc., a national antiracism and multicultural PK–12 publication and alternative curriculum used nationwide, Milwaukee

- Engaged in many forms of activism to support the Dreamers

Electoral Politics and Public Policy

- Ran for state senate in Wisconsin in the 1980s as first Latina candidate

- Helped to solidify Latinx voter block in Milwaukee in the 1990s through redistricting coalition, which led to the creation of new aldermanic district in Milwaukee

- Provided advocacy and input to Green Bay mayor's office through Hispanic Community Council of North East Wisconsin

- Served as first Latina on the Police and Fire Commission in the city of Madison

- Served as first Latina on the Police and Fire Commission in the city of Racine

- Helped to hire the first Latina fire chief and African American police chief in the city of Madison

- Increased voter registration throughout the state

- Contributed to numerous local and statewide races of non-Latinx candidates who supported key Latinx community issues since the 1980s

- Contributed to the identification and support of Latinx people running for public office and leading campaign efforts, Milwaukee

Employment and Economic Rights

- Collaborated with nonprofit to target EEO/AA violations

- Helped to increase worker pay and other benefits at Farrah Co.

- Co-Founded the Latino Academic Staff Association, UW–Madison

- Helped manage a credit union founded and organized by Latinx people in Milwaukee

- Organized and led union rallies and protests through the promotion and use of multiracial, multiethnic coalition-building strategies

- Challenged the city of Racine's hiring practices that excluded Latinx people in the 1980s

- Won a lawsuit against the Madison Metropolitan School District to hire Latinx educators

Empowerment through Awareness of Latino Culture and History

- Created *Hispanic Chronicle* newspaper in Racine

- Co-founded Hispanic Business Council, Racine

- Helped to organize Fiesta Mexicana (now called Mexican Fiesta), Milwaukee, to promote ethnic pride, cultural awareness, and educational scholarships

- Created historical tribute in Humboldt, Kansas, to Mexican cement factory workers and wrote book, *Life Among the Smokestacks*

Contribution through Religious Affiliations

- Raised funds for services to Latinx and/or low-income communities in Waukesha, Green Bay, Racine, and Milwaukee

- Initiated and led Spanish-speaking Catholic marriage encounters for couples in Wisconsin and the Midwest

APPENDIX B
THE SOMOS LATINAS COLLECTION

The Somos Latinas Project Oral Histories and Collected Papers continues to accept submissions of historical archives and other relevant information about Wisconsin Latina activists from the public. Submissions can be made by faculty, university students, and community members. If you have a family member or friend who you believe could be included in the Somos Latinas collection, please contact Jonathan Nelson in the archives at the Wisconsin Historical Society to discuss this before you bring anything to the Society.

The current Somos Latinas collection is just a starting point, and the addition of other activists is an important aspect of retrofitting Latinas into the Latinx historical narrative. Someone must fit the following criteria in order to be eligible for inclusion in Somos Latinas:

- Latina over the age of fifty or deceased

- Worked on issues in a Latinx community in Wisconsin

- Is/was a reputational leader/activist in the community

- Emphasis on low income, former migrant, and working class women

Note: being the "first" Latina is not a qualifying criterion, because it is the activism that qualifies for inclusion in Somos. For example, a woman who was the first Latina principal of an elementary school would not qualify. However, if that woman was active in the Latino community organizing parent workshops in her "free time," she would qualify. Being the "first" may be an important accomplishment, but by itself is not considered activism.

What are archives? In this case, archives are historically important materials that document the life of a Somos woman such as birth and baptismal records; report cards; correspondence; speeches, presentations, and other writings; photos with an emphasis on career and activism activities; some family photos; political buttons; posters; etc. Original materials are preferred, but scans are accepted. Newspaper clippings are not generally accepted if the article appeared in a mainstream publication that the Wisconsin Historical Society already has in the library, but articles from small Latinx presses may be accepted. Award plaques and large items are not accepted due to space limitations. Profiles for deceased women should have been completed by the woman herself or a friend or family member with intimate knowledge of the woman's life and activities. If submitting archives and a profile for a deceased Latina activist, resumes can be helpful for tracing the areas of activism. The final selection of archives for a woman will be determined by the Wisconsin Historical Society.

BIBLIOGRAPHY

Acuña, Rodolfo. *Anything but Mexican: Chicanos in Contemporary Los Angeles*. New York: Verso, 1995.

———. *Occupied America: A History of Chicanos*. New York: Harper and Row, 1988.

Anzaldua, Gloria. *Borderlands: The New Mestiza*. San Francisco: Aunt Lute Books, 2007.

———, ed. *Making Face, Making Soul/Haciendo Caras: Creative and Critical Perspectives by Feminists of Color*. San Francisco: Aunt Lute Books, 1990.

Arenas, Andrea-Teresa. *Yo Soy Eva*. Madison, WI: Latina Poetry Project, 2011.

Arguello, Martha M. "Sisters, Brothers, Young Lords." *ReVista: Harvard Review of Latin America* (Winter 2009). https://revista.drclas.harvard.edu/book/sisters-brothers-young-lords.

Blackwell, Maylei. *¡Chicana Power!: Contested Histories of Feminism in the Chicano Movement*. Austin: University of Texas Press, 2011.

Bonilla, Christopher M. "Racial Counternarratives and Latina Epistemologies in Relational Organizing." *Anthropology and Education Quarterly* 45, no. 4 (2014): 391–408.

Bowers, Jill R., David M. Rosch, and Daniel A. Collier. "Examining the Relationship Between Role Models and Leadership Growth during the Transition to Adulthood." *Journal of Adolescent Research* 31, no. 1 (2016): 96–118.

Brooker, Russell Gott, and Linda Frances Lockett Scheible, eds. *Women Building Communities: Behind the Scenes in Milwaukee*. Milwaukee, WI: Alverno College, 1997.

Buss, Fran Leeper, and Daisy Cubias. *Journey of the Sparrows*. New York: Lodestar Books, 1991.

Cardenas, Gilberto. *La Causa: Civil Rights, Social Justice and the Struggle for Equality in the Midwest*. Houston: Arte Público Press, 2004.

Castellanos, Jeanett, and Alberta M. Gloria. "SOMOS Latina/os—Ganas, Comunidad, y El Espíritu: La Fuerza Que Llevamos Por Dentro (Latina/os—Drive, Community, and Spirituality: The Strength Within)." In *Positive Psychology in Racial and Ethnic Minority Groups: Theory,*

Research, and Practice, edited by Edward C. Chang, et al., 61–82. Washington, DC: American Psychological Association, 2016.

Chang, Edward C., Christina A. Downey, Jameson K. Hirsch, and Natalie J. Lin. "Positive Psychology in Racial and Ethnic Groups: A Second Call to Action!" In *Positive Psychology in Racial and Ethnic Minority Groups: Theory, Research, and Practice*, edited by Edward C. Chang, et al., 3–12. Washington, DC: American Psychological Association, 2016.

Cotera, Martha. *The Chicana Feminist*. Austin: Information Systems Development, 1977.

Delgadillo, Theresa. *Latina Lives in Milwaukee*. Champaign: University of Illinois Press, 2015.

Delgado Votaw, Carmen. *Puerto Rican Women/Mujeres Puertorriqueñas*. Washington, DC: National Conference of Puerto Rican Women, 1995.

Foucault, Michel. *Discipline and Punish: The Birth of the Prison*. New York: Vintage Books, 1995.

———. *Power/Knowledge: Selected Interviews and Other Writings, 1972–1977*. New York: Pantheon Books, 1980.

Freirie, Paulo. *Pedagogy of the Oppressed: 30th Anniversary Edition*. New York: Bloomsbury Academic, 2014.

Geenen, Paul H. *Civil Rights Movement in Milwaukee*. Charleston, SC: The History Press, 2014.

Giffey, David. *Struggle for Justice: The Migrant Farm Worker Labor Movement in Wisconsin*. Milwaukee: Wisconsin Labor History Society, 1998.

Gittell, Ross, and Kathe Newman, eds. *Activist Scholar: Selected Works of Marilyn Gittell*. Los Angeles: SAGE Publications, Inc., 2011.

González, Sergio. *Mexicans in Wisconsin*. Madison: Wisconsin Historical Society Press, 2017.

Gramsci, Antonio. *Prison Notebooks, Volume 2*. Edited and translated by Joseph A. Buttigieg. New York: Columbia University Press, 1996.

Gupta, Vipin, Sylvia Maxfield, and Mary Shapiro. "Risk Aversion among Women: Reality or Simply 'Doing Gender'?" In *Handbook of Gendered Careers in Management: Getting In, Getting On, Getting Out*, edited by Adelina M. Broadbridge and Samuel Fieldson, 208–222. Cheltenham, UK: Edward Elgar, 2015.

Harding, Sandra, ed. *The Feminist Standpoint Theory Reader: Intellectual and Political Controversies*. New York: Routledge, 2003.

Kummerow, Jean M. "Step 11™ Facets of Community Leaders: Comparison to the National Sample and Comparisons between Community Leaders of Different Ethnicities, Genders and Ages." *Journal of Psychology* 7, no. 4 (2011): 26–45.

Kuperminc, Gabriel P., Natalie J. Wilkins, Cathy Roche, and Anabel Alvarez-Jimenez. "Risk, Resilience, and Positive Development among Latino Youth." In *Handbook of US Latino Psychology: Developmental and Community-Based Perspectives*, edited by Francisco A. Villarruel, et al., 213–233. Los Angeles: SAGE Publications, Inc., 2009.

Martínez, Elizabeth Sutherland. *500 Years of Chicana Women's History/500 Años de Historia de las Chicanas*. New Brunswick, NJ: Rutgers University Press, 2008.

Melero, Pilar. *La Casa de Esperanza: A History*. Waukesha, WI: La Casa de Esperanza and National Council of La Raza, 2011.

Méndez-Morse, Sylvia. "Constructing Mentors: Latina Educational Leaders' Role Models and Mentors." *Educational Administration Quarterly* 40, no. 4 (October 2004), 561–590. http://journals.sagepub.com/doi/abs/10.1177/0013161X04267112.

Merriam-Webster.com. "Risk-taking." https://www.merriam-webster.com/dictionary/risk-taking.

Mireles, Oscar. *I Didn't Know There Were Latinos in Wisconsin*. Madison, WI: Focus Communications, 1989.

Montevirgen, Alexis S. "Consciousness, Resistance, and Praxis: Counter-Narratives of Transformative Leaders of Color." PhD diss., San Francisco State University, 2011.

Moyers, Bill. *Bill Moyers Journal*. Interview of Grace Lee Boggs. June 15, 2007. http://www.pbs.org/moyers/journal/06152007/transcript3.html.

Naples, Nancy A. "Women's Leadership, Social Capital, and Social Change." In *Activist Scholar: Selected Works of Marilyn Gittell* edited by Ross Gittell and Kathe Newman, 265–266. Los Angeles: SAGE Publications, Inc., 2011.

Navarro, Armando. *La Raza Unida Party, a Chicano Challenge to the U.S. Two-Party Dictatorship*. Philadelphia: Temple University Press, 2000.

Pardo, Mary. "Mexican American Women Grassroots County Activists 'Mothers of East Los Angeles.'" *Frontiers: A Journal of Women Studies* 11, no. 1 (1990): 1–7.

Pew Research Center. Demographic Profile of Hispanics in Wisconsin. http://www.pewhispanic.org/states/state/wi/.

Ramirez, Leonard G., et al. *Chicanas of 18th Street: Narratives of a Movement from Latino Chicago*. Chicago: University of Illinois Press, 2011.

Rodewald, Adam. "Changing Face: Minorities to Triple In Coming Decades." USA Today Network-Wisconsin. October 22, 2014. https://www.usatoday.com/story/news/local/2014/10/22/changing-faces-minorities-triple-coming-decades/17689341/.

Richards, Erin. "Wisconsin Posts Largest White-Black Graduation Gap." *Milwaukee Journal Sentinel*. October 17, 2016. http://www.jsonline.com/story/news/education/2016/10/17/wisconsin-posts-largest-white-black-graduation-gap/92306710/.

Rodriguez, Joseph A., and Walter Sava. *Latinos in Milwaukee*. Charleston, SC: Arcadia, 2006.

Rodriguez, Marc S. *The Tejano Diaspora: Mexican Americanism and Ethnic Politics in Texas and Wisconsin*. Chapel Hill: University of North Carolina Press, 2011.

Rodriguez, Maria Ana. "Latino Family Involvement: An Exploratory Study of Latina Mother-Daughter Relationships and their Effects on Educational Attainment and Resiliency." PhD diss., University of Denver, 2012.

Ruíz, Vicki, and Virginia Sánchez Korrol. *Latinas in the United States: A Historical Encyclopedia*. Bloomington: Indiana University Press, 2006.

Salas, Jesús, and David Giffey. *Lucha por la Justicia: Movimiento de los Trabajadores Migrantesen Wisconsin = Struggle for Justice: The Migrant Farm Worker Labor Movement in Wisconsin*. Milwaukee: Wisconsin Labor History Society, 1998.

Sava, Walter, and Anselmo Villarreal. *Latinos in Waukesha*. Charleston, SC: Arcadia, 2007.

Stall, Susan, and Randy Stoecker. "Alinsky Meets Feminism." Presented at the Midwest Sociological Society Annual Meetings, 1994.

———. "Community Organizing or Organizing Community? Gender and the Crafts of Empowerment." Paper presented at the American Sociological Association Annual Meetings, 1994.

Sundheim, Doug. "Do Women Take as Many Risks as Men?" *Harvard Business Review*, February 27, 2013. https://hbr.org/2013/02/do-women-take-as-many-risks-as.

United States Census Bureau. "Wisconsin QuickFacts." http://www.census.gov/quickfacts/table/RHI725215/55.

Villarruel, Francisco, Gustavo Carlo, Josefina M. Grau, Margarita Azmitia, Natasha J. Cabrera, and T. Jaime Chahin, eds. *Handbook of US Latino Psychology: Developmental and Community-Based Perspectives*. Los Angeles: SAGE Publications, Inc., 2009.

Zambrana, Ruth E. "Toward Understanding the Educational Trajectory and Socialization of Latina Women." In *UCLA School of South Welfare Education Feminism, Classic and Continued Readings*, edited by Barbara J. Bacon, Lynda Stone, and Catherine M. Sprecher, 75–86. Albany: University of New York Press, 2013.

Zinn, Howard. *A People's History of the United States*. New York: HarperCollins, 2010.

Acknowledgments

In Phase I, Somos received outstanding support from UW–Madison's College of Letters and Science. Senior Associate Dean Nancy Westphal-Johnson provided Tess with support for over four years, as did Mehdi Rezai, Cathy Conley, John Varda, and Allen Geibhart, who managed multiple funding sources.

The student staff of the Office of Service Learning and Community-Based Research provided much-needed infrastructure support: Hector Salazar, Santalucia Hernandez, Edith Flores, Nicole Cancel, Jessica Alanis, Beda Martinez, Yesenia Saavedra, and all the others who were affiliated with the office.

The faculty directors of UW–Madison's Chican@ and Latin@ Studies (CLS) department, Alberta Gloria and Ben Marquez, supported the concept of embedding Somos in four CLS courses without hesitation. CLS student advisors referred students for independent study to work on Somos. Sylvia Garcia, program assistant and Somos interviewee, willingly provided Somos with ideas, names, and other critical resources throughout.

A special thanks to Troy Reeves, oral historian at UW–Madison, for his guidance and support throughout the project. Troy provided readings on oral history methodology, tips for the Institutional Review Board proposals, and moral support as the authors moved into Phase II telephone interviews.

The Wisconsin Historical Society has been a partner since the inception of Somos in 2012, and archivist Jonathan Nelson has been an invaluable researcher, teacher, historian, and collaborator for the entirety. A consummate listener and trainer, Nelson provided archival research and archive collecting strategies at the Society each semester with a terrific attitude and demeanor. Other Society staff provided tours and orientation to the archives so CLS students could later navigate the historical records.

Thanks to the Chicana Por Mi Raza Digital Memory Collective—a hybrid archive, museum, and digital curriculum organized around capturing important Chicana and Latina voices from the Civil Rights Era. Chicana

Por Mi Raza is an oral history project with over 150 oral histories and over 5,000 digitized supporting archival records. Visit their website at http://chicanapormiraza.org/.

Thanks to the students in Tess's CLS classes who contributed to this project: Gabriela Adame-Barcenas, Lisette Aguila, Jocelyn Alday, Lala Andrea Bolander, Ashley Butalla, Nicole Cancel, Hervin Centeno, Alberto Cuevas, Eduardo De La Torre, Arturo Diaz, Jessica Diaz-Hurtado, Maegan Rae Evans, Edith Flores, Catherine Garcia, Alex Gemeinhardt, Amanda Goetsch, Aidee Guzman, Yodanna Katiuska Guzman, Colleen Hamilton, Marcelo Heredia, Santalucia Hernandez, Joaquin Herrera, Maria Huerta, Ricardo Lopez, Heidi S. Luft, Rachel Margolies, Jeanette Martin, Johnathan Martinez, Joseph Ramon Mendoza, Ricardo Mora, Carolina Ortega, Steve Pereira, LaTreal Kenneth Peterson, Alexandria Rauchle, Chinar Raul, Casey Resendez, Sasha Reyes, Sergio Rodriguez, Edgar Roman-Alvarez, Hector Salazar, Marlon Salgado, Isaac Salomon Solano, Nurys Uceta, Stephanie Ugalde, Amanda Villanueva, Andrea Walker-Cousins, and Hanna Watson.

Special thanks to the following students who consistently volunteered on the UW–Madison Community-Based Research Project: Jessica Alanis, Nicole Cancel, Alberto Cuevas, Edith Flores, Amanda Goetsch, Aidee Guzman, Santalucia Hernandez, Marcelo "Richie" Heredia, Ketzholly Lopez, Sasha Reyes, Sergio Rodriguez, Amanda Rosales, Hector Salazar, Candice Tescher, and Amanda Villanueva.

Phase II thanks go to special individuals who donated their time to transcribe the interviews, including Hector Salazar, Richie Heredia, Edith Flores, Amanda Rosales, and Amanda Villanueva.

A variety of support came from Juan Carlos and Miguel Gómez Bartkowski, Olivia Arenas Shanahan, Victoria Arenas Shanahan, Tony Marquez, and Joanna Dupuis.

Dr. Michael Gordon, UW–Milwaukee professor emeritus in the history department and labor history activist, provided much-needed counsel and support.

We thank Liz Wyckoff, our developmental editor, for her steadfast support and editorial guidance from beginning to end.

Dr. Yolanda Garza deserves acknowledgment for the years of support she has provided to both authors through friendship and professional counsel on the book's framework and much more. *¡Un million de gracias, hermana!* (A thousand thank yous, sister!) Finally, we thank all the women in Phases I and II for the generosity of their time, sharing their memories, and opening up their hearts to us: Nedda Avila, Rosa Aguilu, Yolanda Ayubi, Lupita Béjar Verbeten, Gladis Benavides, Marie Black, Patricia Castañeda Tucker, Maria Dolores Cruz, Daisy Cubias, Carmen De La Paz, Alejandra Elenes, Elvira Erdman, Gabriela Gamboa, Sylvia Garcia, Yolanda Garza, Debora Gil Casado, Mary Godoy, Eloisa Gómez, Anita Herrera, Karen Herrera, Carmen Ireland, Eva Jackson, Sister Melanie Maczka, Sandy Magana, Barbara Medina, Maria Luisa Morales, Ramona Natera, Teresita Neris, Christina Nosek, Lucía Nuñez, Nelia Olivencia, Maria Rodríguez, Judith Rosario, Leonor Rosas, Yolanda Salazar, Irene Santos, Romilia Schlueter, Natalia Sidon, Rita Tenorio, Ramona Villarreal, Patricia Villarreal, Maria Elena White, Rebecca Yepez, Bertha Zamudio, and Dora Zuniga. Without you, this book would not be possible. *¡Gracias, compañeras!* (Thank you, companions!)

Phase I Financial Sponsors and In-Kind Support

Wisconsin Historical Society and Helmut Knies, Collection Development Coordinator, Emeritus

Chicana Por Mi Raza: Linda Garcia Merchant, University of Nebraska, and Maria Cotera, University of Michigan

Chican@ and Latin@ Studies, UW–Madison

College of Letters and Science, UW–Madison

Office of Equity, Diversity and Educational Achievement, UW–Madison

Pathways Program, UW–Madison

Morgridge Center for Public Service

Somos Fund-Raising Committee Cochairs, Milwaukee: Eloisa Gómez and Yesenia Saavedra

Somos Fund-Raising Committee, Madison: Yolanda Garza, Sylvia Garcia, Janice Rice, Jessica Alanis, Santalucia Hernandez, Nicole Cancel, and Mariah Barger

Index

Page numbers in **bold** indicate illustrations.

ABOUT THE AUTHORS

Andrea-Teresa "Tess" Arenas, PhD, recently retired from her positions at UW–Madison as a Chican@ and Latin@ Studies faculty affiliate and the director of the Office of Service Learning and Community-Based Research in the College of Letters & Science. In the mid-1980s, she was a founding member of the Latina Task Force and the Wisconsin Hispanic Council on Higher Education, and she has been active in the UW Women's and Gender Studies Consortium for many years. She is currently the director of the Somos Latinas Digital History Project.

Eloisa Gómez is the director of the Milwaukee County UW–Extension Office. She was a founding member of the Latina Task Force and the Wisconsin Hispanic Council on Higher Education in the mid-1980s, and she served on the Wisconsin Women's Council in 1984. In 1988, she was the first Latina to serve in the mayor's office for the city of Milwaukee. From 2008 to 2012, she was the vice president of the Latino Historical Society of Wisconsin, and she served on the Somos Latinas Advisory Committee from 2012 to 2015.

Tess Arenas (left) and Eloisa Gómez, ca. 1983. SOMOS LATINAS PROJECT ORAL HISTORIES AND COLLECTED PAPERS

Tess and Eloisa, 2017. PHOTO BY EMILY BUCK

The authors have donated their time and energy in the creation of this book and are donating the book proceeds to the Wisconsin Historical Society's Latina/x Research Fund and the UW–Madison Chican@ and Latin@ Studies Program. For more information on tax-deductible contributions, visit their websites.
https://support.wisconsinhistory.org/donate
https://chicla.wisc.edu/giving